How to Master
Psychometric Tests

Expert advice on test preparation with
practice questions from leading test
providers

Revised 4th edition

Mark Parkinson

KoganPage

LONDON PHILADELPHIA NEW DELHI

Whilst the author has made every effort to ensure that the content of this book is accurate, please note that occasional errors can occur in books of this kind. If you suspect that an error has been made in any of the tests included in this book, please inform the publishers at the address printed below so that it can be corrected at the next reprint.

Publisher's note

Every possible effort has been made to ensure that the information contained in this book is accurate at the time of going to press, and the publishers and author cannot accept responsibility for any errors or omissions, however caused. No responsibility for loss or damage occasioned to any person acting, or refraining from action, as a result of the material in this publication can be accepted by the editor, the publisher or the author.

First published in 1997
Second edition 2000
Third edition 2004
Fourth edition 2008
Revised fourth edition 2010

120 Pentonville Road	525 South 4th Street, #241	4737/23 Ansari Road
London N1 9JN	Philadelphia PA 19147	Daryaganj
United Kingdom	USA	New Delhi 110002
www.koganpage.com		India

ISBN   978 0 7494 6128 7
E-ISBN   978 0 7494 6129 4

British Library Cataloguing-in-Publication Data

A CIP record for this book is available from the British Library.

Library of Congress Cataloging-in-Publication Data

Parkinson, Mark.
  How to master psychometric tests : expert advice on test preparation with practice questions from leading test providers / Mark Parkinson. – Rev. 4th ed.
       p. cm.
  ISBN 978-0-7494-6128-7 — ISBN 978-0-7494-6129-4 (ebook)   1. Employment tests.
2. Psychological tests.   3. Psychological tests–Problems, exercises, etc.
4. Psychometrics.   5. Employee selection.   I. Title.
  HF5549.5.E5P37 2008
  153.9′465–dc22

                                                                                    2010010497

Typeset by Graphicraft Limited, Hong Kong
Printed and bound in India by Replika Press Pvt Ltd

Contents

To the reader

Psychometric tests of ability and personality are used by many organizations throughout the world for selecting people for jobs. They are also used within companies to help with development and promotion.

This book is about preparing you for the main types of tests and increasing your chances of getting to the next stage, the job interview. This is a vital step in the selection process when you consider that 50 per cent or more people fail the tests they take.

All of the tests described in this book are commonly used for recruitment purposes. My job has been to explain what they measure, what they look like, who they are used to assess and how to approach the questions. The focus is on developing an effective test-making strategy or a personal approach that you can apply to any new test you might encounter.

I also concentrate on the psychological preparation for tests, and how to put yourself in a positive and winning frame of mind. This is just as important to test performance as understanding how the actual questions work.

This is the revised fourth edition of this book and it now includes practice material from three leading UK test publishers. There is also an example of the type of test used to help select students for popular degree courses. In addition there is an interesting section on the 'dark side' of personality and a specially written Leadership Style Questionnaire. Finally, this latest revision includes a unique list of the top 100 practice test websites, giving access to thousands of extra practice questions.

Introduction

If you were a personnel manager how would you select new staff?

Probably you would place a job advert and ask people to send a curriculum vitae (CV), or to complete an application form. Then you might look at the forms and invite, depending on how many people applied, between 6 and 12 people to come for an interview. After the interviews, or maybe at the same time, you would follow up references on the best candidates. If this is all you would do, you would be ignoring a technique that has become an essential part of the modern selection process – the psychometric test.

Application forms or CVs are an exercise in seeing how well an applicant, or frequently an agency, can fill in a form or design a work history. Interviews are an example of how prepared a candidate is for a number of standard questions, and of appearing to be interested and motivated for a short period of time. The reference, *at worst*, damns with faint praise, even if the subject has previously been an entirely unsatisfactory employee. In contrast, psychometric tests can identify objectively where the abilities lie, and what sort of personality you have. So as long as the appropriate tests are used, they can provide a fair and accurate way of helping to pick the best person for the job.

Tests are also desirable because not everyone is a good interview candidate, but many may still be ideal candidates for the job; and application forms are sometimes so badly designed that it is difficult to present yourself in a positive light. Conversely, skilled CV authors or interviewees may be quite hopeless when they actually secure a position. What this means is that in most circumstances it is to the applicant's *and* employer's advantage that tests are used.

To cut a long story short, what employers want to know is whether you can do a particular job and if you will fit into an existing workplace. This has more to do with your potential abilities and personality than the number of examination passes you have, or whether you liked going to school or college. Since tests are probably the most efficient way of assessing these factors, it should come as no surprise to discover that most medium- to large-sized organizations now use this method of selection.

So, in reality, when you apply for a job, whether this is through a job agency, cold canvassing, an advert in a newspaper or via details held on a website (recruitment information on the world wide web), the next step for the 'successful' candidate is frequently a series of psychometric tests.

Which tests are used?

In the UK, USA and many European countries the most popular tests are those of general intelligence, verbal and numerical ability, and personality. General intelligence tests are concerned with how well you can solve problems from first principles; verbal and numerical tests with aspects of verbal and numerical comprehension, and problem solving; and personality questionnaires with attributes like how outgoing you are, your degree of anxiety or emotionality, mental toughness and personal organization.

In the UK, if you are invited to attend a test session you will find yourself taking the sort of tests just described. This will be true of virtually all the major retail, manufacturing and service companies, as well as government and some educational and non-profit making organizations. Indeed, over 70 per cent of the *Times Top 1000* companies use tests of this nature. The picture is similar if you apply for jobs in many European Union countries, although some supplement testing with other techniques. For example, in France about 60 per cent of the top companies use tests, but 80 per cent also use graphology or handwriting analysis! The same is true in Germany, where, while around 60 per cent of firms use 'assessment centres', which include tests, interviews and other exercises, great weight is still placed on application forms and reference checks.

Make no mistake, tests are here to stay, so it makes sense to prepare yourself thoroughly for what has become a routine part of the job application process.

About this book

The first chapter of this book looks at the concept of psychometric testing. It explores the different types of tests, and the ways in which they measure both maximum and typical performance. The idea of 'intelligence' is introduced, as well as the differences between tests that measure knowledge (attainment) and potential (aptitude). An explanation of what makes a 'good' test is given, and also how we know that tests actually work. The chapter concludes with details on what employers do with test results, and the different ways in which they can be used to select candidates for jobs.

The next chapter explains the testing process and takes you through a typical selection scenario. This includes the basics of test preparation, and includes what you need to consider before a test session. The problems of test-taking anxiety ('examination nerves') are explained, and a number of methods of reducing anxiety are provided. Additional advice is given on preparing physically and emotionally for tests; and what to do if you have eyesight, hearing or other problems.

Chapter 3 covers, in separate sections, tests of abstract (logical), verbal, numerical, perceptual (diagrammatic), spatial and mechanical ability. The nature and purpose of each type of test is explained, and a number of examples are provided. An explanation of how to approach and to solve each example question is given. Each section also includes information on the sort of candidates who would face each test, eg if you are a graduate the sort of tests you would be asked to complete. Some practical hints are included for each type of test. The chapter concludes with 10 additional ways to improve test performance.

Chapter 4 contains an extensive collection of practice material from Saville & Holdsworth Ltd (SHL®). SHL is the leading UK test publisher and supplies assessment materials to most of the FTSE Top 100 companies as well as many smaller organizations. The practice tests are just like their full-length cousins and are arranged in three levels of difficulty. Readers will be comforted to know that the answers are provided at the end of the book!

Chapter 5 includes additional practice questions from one of the most innovative publishers in the marketplace, Team Focus Ltd. The example questions provided are typical of those that are now used for paper-and-pencil and internet based testing. In the second part of this chapter there is a discussion of a relatively new development in testing in the UK, the university admissions test. To illustrate what these tests are like, a section of a genuine practice test, the Thinking Skills Assessment (TSA), is included. This has been supplied by Cambridge Assessment, which is the business name of the University of Cambridge Local Examinations Syndicate (UCLES). Answers to all the practice questions are provided at the end of the book.

Chapter 6 concentrates on the ideas behind personality assessment, and describes the two main models that underpin personality questionnaires. These are the 'type' approach, which emphasises preferences for different sorts of behaviour; and the 'trait' school, which concentrates on direction and 'quantity' of personality. Extensive details on the format of 'self-report' questionnaires are included, as well as information on how different questionnaires are used. A list of hints for improving performance is provided, such as how to decide what an employer is looking for, and how to assume the correct test-taking attitude. Finally, other self-report questionnaires, such as those measuring values, motivation, integrity and interests, are explained.

Chapter 7 provides a list of the top 100 practice test websites. These sites provide an important resource for anyone preparing for a test session, be this either for a job, or when applying for popular university courses.

The appendix contains useful information on 'competencies', or the work attributes that tests are designed to measure; plus an example of the sort of exercise used by employers simultaneously to assess a group of job applicants.

In conclusion, this book is about helping you to understand the sort of psychometric tests that you may be asked to complete. It also includes details on how to prepare for tests and what to do if you are nervous about the testing process. The main sections deal with the most popular ability tests and personality questionnaires, and provide up-to-date information on:

- what different types of test measure;

- when they are used in selection;

- what the questions look like;

- how to answer typical questions;

- successful strategies and approaches.

The idea is to give you a set of practical tools, which will boost your chances of achieving test and career success. In this way *How to Master Psychometric Tests* will appeal to all those seeking employment with organizations that use tests. It will also be valuable to those who are tested while working within an organization for development or promotional purposes; and to employers, personnel and human resource professionals unfamiliar with psychometric tests, but who want to know more about what they are and how they can be used.

Note: Masculine pronouns are used in this book to avoid awkward grammatical constructions. In most cases, feminine pronouns can be used interchangeably.

CHAPTER 1

What are psychometric tests?

A psychometric test is a standard way of measuring an aspect of mental performance. Practically this means that tests assess things like verbal ability, such as how good you are at understanding the meaning of words, or comprehending the information in a written passage. They are also used to explore personal attributes like personality or temperament, careers or employment interests, values, attitudes and motivation.

The fact that tests are *standard* methods of assessment is extremely important, and is what makes them different from the 'Personality' and 'Check your own Intelligence' quizzes found in magazines. Psychometric tests are different because everyone is presented with the same questions and instructions for completing them. Crucially, tests are also administered under carefully controlled and timed conditions by a trained individual, who additionally follows precise instructions for scoring and interpreting the results. In this way there is no room for subjectivity, and everyone is treated in exactly the same way. Furthermore, the results a person achieves are compared with a representative sample of people (the normative group) who have completed the test before. This allows a psychologist or personnel professional to decide accurately how well a person has done compared to everyone else. Is the person above or below average? How much is the person above or below?

These features of psychometric tests are also what distinguish them from most forms of examinations. It's true that examinations are timed and that everyone attempts the same paper, but there are usually a variety of questions to choose from. In an essay-based exam it is also the case that there are a number of possible answers to the questions. Clearly some answers will be better than others, and so there are a range of marks on offer. The marking system obviously has to reflect these differences, and so cannot but fail to reflect some of the personal preferences of the examiner. All of this makes most examinations rather less objective than a well-constructed psychometric test.

Personality questionnaires differ in a number of ways from ability tests simply because there are no 'right' or 'wrong' answers. After all there is no such thing as a 'good' or 'bad' personality, just a variety of personal characteristics, which may be more or less useful depending on what you are trying to do. However, despite the nature of what is being measured, personality questionnaires still contain questions that everyone must answer; and are administered, scored and interpreted in a standard way.

Different types of tests

For most purposes psychologists distinguish between two broad types of tests. The first type is concerned with measuring maximum performance, or how well you can do something. This means that they measure what you know, or what your potential might be, when you are trying to do as well as you can.

The second type of test measures typical performance. In consequence these are concerned with finding out what you are like in normal, day-to-day situations. For instance, are you outgoing and sociable, or do you prefer your own company? Personality questionnaires are an example of this second sort of test, and are particularly useful in those situations where job performance is dependent on how you present yourself to other people, eg all forms of selling activity.

Returning to tests of maximum performance, we find that practically all the ability tests you will be asked to complete as part of a selection process fall into this category. To be even more precise they can also be classified as follows:

- general intelligence tests;

- attainment tests; and

- aptitude tests.

General intelligence tests

Some tests are formulated so that they measure your overall ability to succeed in a particular activity. These are known as general intelligence tests and are designed to produce a single indication of your ability. This is similar to the concept of the intelligence quotient or IQ. Although in the case of IQ tests the results are expressed in terms of the ratio of your mental age (as measured by a test) to your chronological age, with the resultant multiplied by 100. Thus, if your mental and chronological age are the same you end up with the average IQ of 100. All tests of this sort operate on the principle that your 'general intelligence' affects all of your individual abilities. So, for example, it's your overall intelligence that makes you good or bad at things like verbal or numerical problem solving.

Attainment tests

Attainment tests measure your ability to use the knowledge or skills you already possess. So, if you like, they are designed to assess what you know at the time of the test. For example, can you understand a simple electrical circuit, or do you know the name of the second-highest mountain in the world? However, you could ask yourself whether this really is 'typical' performance in the sense of the ability you will bring to a job. Also, most attainment tests demand a knowledge of things that may not generalize to every aspect of a job.

Some attainment tests are described as mastery tests. These are based on specific tasks, which directly relate to a particular work activity. They are also characterized by the fact that there are only two outcomes; you either 'pass' or 'fail'. The driving test is an example, because you either pass and are permitted to drive a car on the road, or you fail and have to take the test again. Most professional examinations are also mastery tests. This is a sensible thing if you imagine the chaos that would ensue if there were different pass grades for something like medical or dental examinations. Would you go to a particular doctor or dentist if you knew he had only just managed to pass his exams?

Another sort of attainment test it's useful to know about is the work sample test. These are tests based on the things you actually do in a particular job. For instance, giving someone a typing test, which involves measuring their ability to type a dictated letter accurately, is a work sample test. Another example is the 'in-tray' or 'in-basket' exercise used in executive assessment centres. This involves presenting a candidate with a number of letters, faxes, e-mails, reports, computer printouts, invoices and other pieces of information, and asking for them to be put in order of priority and actioned accordingly. This is a highly stressful test, maybe, but one that does simulate the work required of many managers.

The most advanced form of work sample test is the aircraft simulator. This allows skills to be assessed, and training to take place, in a safe and cost-effective manner. In fact modern simulators are so realistic that most, if not all, basic training can take place without the pilot ever leaving the hangar. Indeed, legend has it that at least one airline has used pilots who have done all their advanced training on the ground!

Aptitude tests

Aptitude tests measure your 'natural' ability to do things. Unlike attainment tests they do not require specialist knowledge or skills.

Obviously some understanding is involved, if only to comprehend the instructions, but as far as possible the results are designed to reflect your potential to achieve in the future. This makes the aptitude tests a fairer assessment for anyone who lacks traditional school qualifications; or who just hasn't had the opportunity to acquire specific skills.

Aptitude tests are frequently used for careers counselling, and also form a useful tool for any employer who wishes to identify potential. Like work-related measures many aptitude tests are constructed so that they indicate whether a person is suitable for a particular job, eg computer programming. However, in contrast to the work sample approach, they do not assume that you have a range of existing skills. The argument is that if you have the potential you can be taught to write programs, calculate exchange rates, compose a technical report, or whatever. Naturally there is also a counter-argument, which suggests that aptitude tests do not relate to real job tasks and do not measure experience. This is an interesting point and one that highlights the essential difference between the attainment and aptitude approaches.

You might have noticed in the descriptions of attainment and aptitude tests that they seem to relate to specific abilities. That's because, in contrast to the general intelligence approach, they rely on the idea of different types of intelligence. In many ways this is a far more useful approach because it recognizes the fact that we all have different combinations of abilities. It also recognizes that one factor, general intelligence, does not dictate everything we can do.

As you might expect, some psychologists believe in the general intelligence approach, and others in the existence of many separate, specific abilities. However, in the real world of work it is usually your specific abilities, whether they be attainment or aptitude based, which are measured in a test session.

What is a 'good' test?

Whatever sort of test is used to assess someone for a job, it must fulfil a number of important requirements. From the employer's point of view it should obviously be cost-effective, relevant to the position in question, and fair on the people applying. Even more importantly, the test, or tests, must actually work. This depends on the standard administration and objective scoring mentioned earlier, but, even more crucially, on any tests being reliable and valid.

Reliability is all about getting consistent results over time. For example, if I tested you today, and then again in four weeks' time, I would expect to get more or less the same results. I wouldn't expect your abilities to have changed, unless you had learnt something in the interim; or, indeed, for something like your personality to have altered significantly. However, being reliable is not enough because it is possible to achieve consistent results and still not be measuring anything meaningful. A good example is the 'buttercup test' we used as children.

If you hold a buttercup under your chin on a sunny day it will cast a yellow shadow. This is supposed to indicate a liking for butter. However, as you will no doubt appreciate, if it's sunny you will always get a yellow spot on your chin. It's a very reliable test, but unfortunately there is no real link between yellow shadows and butter appreciation.

Clearly it's not enough for a test to be reliable, it must be valid as well. Indeed validity, or the extent to which a test measures what the designer says it's measuring, is the most fundamental attribute of any measure. However, validity is rather a complicated thing to establish, and to confuse things further there are a number of different types.

For example, face validity refers to the extent to which a test measures what it looks as if it's measuring. If a test is designed to assess numerical ability you would expect it to contain mathematical problems. You would not expect it to have a lot of highly verbal items, or ask you about how you prefer to socialize with other people.

While face validity is important it does not guarantee that a test works (think about the magazine 'tests' mentioned at the beginning of this chapter); so it's important to establish what is known as criterion-related validity. This is also sometimes called external validity and is the degree to which a test correlates with another measure of the same thing. For instance, you might expect a numerical test to correlate with mathematical ability, as measured by a formal examination. Yet, important as this might be, the ultimate sort of external validity is predictive validity. This sort of validity is when we can demonstrate that a test predicts a future measure of performance. Put simply, if I give you a particular test, can I say that if you achieve a certain score there is an increased chance of you being a more productive employee?

To summarize what we have learnt in this chapter so far, a 'good' test should be as follows.

- *Objective.* Each person who takes it should be treated in exactly the same way. The scoring and interpretation of the results should be conducted according to the directions laid down by the test designer.

- *Standardized.* The score a person gets on the test should be compared against a representative group of people who have taken the test in the past (the normative group). Any decisions should then only be made in comparison with this standard group.

- *Reliable.* The test must consistently measure the same thing, with no marked differences over time. The exception, of course, is where we use an attainment test and wish to measure what you have learnt over a period of time.

- *Predictive.* The test must be a valid measure of what it's supposed to measure. It is also important to establish that it's an accurate predictor of how someone will perform in the future.

- *Unbiased.* The test should only measure an aspect of maximum or typical performance. It should not discriminate in terms of race, culture, gender or any similar factor. Naturally there may be differences between different groups, but these must only be due to actual differences in ability or personality, and not just a product of the way a test is worded or constructed.

Considering these requirements, it should now be obvious that writing a test is a complex process, and perhaps not the 'armchair' exercise many people imagine it to be. Then again, the fact that 'good' tests conform to all these requirements should be a comfort to the potential test taker. After all, tests are used to assess people for one of life's most taxing environments – the workplace.

How are test results used?

There are a number of ways in which tests results can be used to assess people. However, the prime objective of all these methods is to identify at an early stage those job applicants who are unlikely to fill the requirements of the position on offer. They do this by providing a scientific benchmark against which all applicants can be assessed. In this way ability test results can be used to supply information on current knowledge or performance; and personality questionnaires the sort of insights that are difficult to achieve in a 45- or 60-minute interview.

A warning should be sounded at this point because, while what has just been said is correct, the usefulness of any testing process depends on knowing exactly what you are looking for in the first place. This depends on a comprehensive analysis of the job, or jobs, in question. It's only after the personnel professional or psychologist has established a specification for a job that meaningful comparisons can be made. Thus in the normal course of events information is gathered on the following.

- *Knowledge.* Is a specialist sort of knowledge required? For example, do you need an in-depth understanding of legal terms and procedures?

- *Skills.* Are particular skills crucial to good performance? For example, are certain computer or IT (information technology) skills essential?

- *Abilities.* Are particular underlying abilities considered necessary? For example, do you need an aptitude for verbal or numerical problem solving?

- *Experience.* Is a certain type or range of experience valuable? For example, is experience of doing business in different countries required?

Sometimes these different sorts of job requirements are combined into what are called competencies. These are 'clusters' of abilities, experience and knowledge, and are frequently the things asked for in job advertisements. For example, an advert may demand leadership skills, creativity, persuasiveness and planning ability. If you want to know more about competencies, a list, with definitions, is provided in the Appendix to this book.

After the job analysis and the testing, the first step is to compare the results against the appropriate normative group. The findings can then be expressed in a number of ways, but one of the commonest is to describe the overall results in terms of percentiles. For example, if you score at the 70th percentile it means that you have done better than 70 per cent of the population; or, to put it another way, you are in the top 30 per cent.

The next step involves taking one of three approaches. The first approach is called 'top-down' selection. As the name implies this means that you select the top scorers, from the highest downwards, until you have filled all your positions. However, there can be problems, for example what happens if all the test takers actually got relatively low scores? In reality none of them may be particularly good prospects. Also, if you only select from the top scores, you might recruit people who are too high powered for the job in question. This is a real danger and was a mistake made in the 1980s by a number of major UK banks. The end result was a rapid and expensive turnover of staff as a result of their boredom.

An alternative approach is to use a 'minimum cut-off' technique. This relies on setting a minimum level for a test, or tests, above which candidates have to score. The level is usually established by testing existing employees, and is set at the point that represents satisfactory performance. But, as with the top-down approach, there can be difficulties, especially if the job is a new one. How can you set a standard for a job no one else is doing? It also relies on existing personnel being willing to be tested, and clearly on them actually being good performers in the first place! However, all other things being equal, this is still a very popular approach.

The last way of dealing with test results is to concentrate on profiles. What this means is that if a number of tests have been taken it is possible to look at the 'shape' of the results. In this way the psychologist or personnel manager can see the relative strengths and weaknesses of an applicant. For example, many administrative jobs require greater verbal and numerical ability than they do perceptual ability (understanding diagrams). This difference is obvious if the relative levels of test results are compared. Once this initial assessment is made the minimum requirements on individual tests can then be considered.

Example: selecting civil aviation pilots

In the United Kingdom, after applicants for pilot training have been pre-selected on the basis of their qualifications, age and interest in flying (which may include having a Private Pilots Licence), the next step is to complete a battery of tests called the Morrisby Profile. This involves 12 different tests that measure a range of different aptitudes and work-based personality. The results for each candidate are then compared with the ideal profile for the job.

The assessors look for good general reasoning ability, which is related to the ability to plan well; strong numerical and diagrammatic aptitude, with a slightly lower level of verbal aptitude, characteristic of those with technical ability; and a practical problem-solving style. In terms of personality, the best candidates are flexible and able to cope with change, possess a high degree of motivation and confidence, and are good team players.

After the results for each candidate have been analysed, candidates are graded into one of three categories: Grade 'A' for those who meet all the requirements, 'B' for those who meet most of the requirements, and 'C' for those who have serious weaknesses or who just have the 'wrong' sort of profile. When this is done it is not unusual to find that only 12–15 per cent make it into the 'A' category.

Obviously this is a very rigorous form of assessment, as would be expected when the responsibilities of a pilot are considered. It should also be noted that in this case the profile approach implies that effective pilots have, for example, good numerical and diagrammatic ability, but a lower level of verbal ability. This does not mean that verbal ability is not important, but rather that the other two general abilities are of greater importance in this instance.

The different sorts of abilities and personality characteristics that can be measured are explained in more detail in Chapters 3 and 6.

The profile approach is the most complex, but probably also the fairest of them all. However, as it takes more time than straight 'top-down' or 'minimum cut-off' approaches, it tends to be used less.

What influences test performance?

There are many techniques you can use to improve your test results, and these are covered in the chapters that follow. However, there are some factors you cannot control and that will inevitably influence how you perform in a test situation. These include things like age, gender and health, and also your educational, ethnic and home background.

As we get older some of our mental faculties tend to decline. For example, if you measure general intelligence you find that the peak ages are from about 15 years old to the mid-20s. After that it's downhill all the way! But before you get too depressed, this does not apply to all abilities, and general knowledge and experience increase with age. Personality also tends to stabilize with age, and the older you get the better you are at coping with your own personality.

Your gender can also influence your test performance. It's a fact that women do less well, on average, on tests of mechanical and spatial ability. These are tests that measure how good you are at understanding basic mechanical principles, and at imagining objects in three dimensions. However, to even up the balance, women frequently do better than men on tests of speed and accuracy. On average, this time, they are quicker and more precise in what they do.

If you are unwell at the time you do a test it will affect your performance. For example, if you have a temperature or just feel generally below par, it's unlikely that you will be able to do your best. Other long-lasting conditions such as anything affecting the movement of your hands, wrists and arms will also tend to interfere with your test-taking ability, especially how quickly you can work. This is important because many of the tests you will encounter will have strict time limits.

Aspects of where you come from, the standard of your education, your ethnic origin and your home environment can also influence how you do. For example, if you didn't do very well at school, or just didn't like it, it's probable that your results on attainment tests will be lower than they could be. Conversely, if you come from a home environment where study and reading were encouraged, this will probably increase your chances of getting better results.

Another very important factor is your ability with the English language. This can make a real difference because if English is your second, or even your third, language, you will be at a disadvantage in most tests. The reason is that the vast majority of tests are only available in English, and if you have to think in your native language and then translate answers into English it will significantly slow your progress. The end result will be lower marks because tests operate within strict time limits.

In conclusion, what we are really talking about is opportunity, and if there are any factors that reduced your exposure to good education and learning, these will have an effect.

Key points

- A psychometric test is a standard and scientific way of assessing an aspect of human performance or behaviour.

- Tests measure things like general intelligence, attainment, aptitude and personality. They can also measure attitudes, interests, values and what motivates you.

- Tests are constructed so that they are objective, reliable, valid and unbiased. A great deal of effort is put into making them a fair way of assessing people.

- Tests results are used to assess people against the requirements for a job. Jobs are usually specified in terms of the knowledge, skills, abilities and the experience required to do them.

- Tests results are interpreted by comparing them against a standard group of people who have done the test in the past (the normative group).

- Decisions are made by applying one of a number of techniques. The most common approaches are 'top-down' and 'minimum cut-off' selection, or profiling.

- There are many factors that can influence your performance on a test. These include age, gender and health, and all aspects of your personal background.

CHAPTER 2

Preparing for psychometric tests

When you apply for a job your application form or CV is compared against the requirements for that job. If you fulfil the initial requirements, in terms of things like qualifications and experience, you may then be asked to attend a test session. This session is designed to fill in some of the gaps, to provide additional information on your abilities and, more often than not, your personality.

The test session is usually scheduled for about 7–10 days after all the applications have been processed, and is marked by a letter of invitation. In the letter you will be told about the time and place of the session, how to get there, and any other points that might be important. Some employers will also include a practice test, which will explain why the test, or tests, are being used; how you might benefit from the testing process; and what the questions will look like. Indeed most practice tests include a number of questions for you to attempt and, of course, the answers. The purpose of practice tests is to give everyone an equal chance and, importantly, to give some practice material to those who have not done tests before.

A typical letter of invitation looks like this:

Mr D Grayson
12 Oak Tree Avenue
Longton
East Middleshire
EM12 4TX

[Date]

Dear Mr Grayson

Administration Manager Position

Thank you for applying for the position of Administration Manager in our Holytown store. We have now assessed all the applications and would like to invite you to a psychometric testing session to be held at the Holytown store on 18 May at 9:30 am. You will find a map and details of car parking attached. If you are coming by train the nearest station is Holytown Riverside, on the Eastern Line.
The test session will last for two hours with a short break in the middle. You will be asked to complete two tests of ability, and a personality questionnaire. To give you an idea of what to expect we have enclosed a practice paper. If you read the instructions and answer the questions it will help you understand what the tests are measuring, and what the real test questions will look like.
You do not need to bring any pens, writing materials, or a pocket calculator to the test session, as everything will be provided. However, if you normally wear reading glasses make sure you bring them with you. Also, if you are going to find it difficult to go for two hours without anything to eat or drink, remember that there will be a break in the middle when refreshments will be provided.
Please let me know as soon as possible if you can attend this session. If you have any questions contact my assistant, John Blake, on Holytown 339978. I look forward to meeting you on 18 May.
Yours sincerely,

Jenny Munroe
Human Resources Manager
Triangle Stores Group

Coping with test anxiety

The prospect of being tested fills many people with anxiety. Indeed, even those who are used to formal tests and examinations are likely to suffer from at least some degree of nervousness. This is all perfectly natural and is a consequence of the importance of the situation, where a job may depend on your performance; and the unknown elements of the testing process. Practice tests, if they are used, are designed to help with the last point, but even so there is still room for the imagination to do its worst!

The first thing to appreciate is that a certain degree of anxiety actually improves performance. The trick is to manage it, and to make sure that it does not reach an unacceptable level. You will know if it's unacceptable because you will start to show some of the classic physical and behavioural signs of stress. These include the following.

Physical signs

● general fatigue;

● sleeplessness;

● headaches;

● back or shoulder ache;

● upset stomach.

Behavioural signs

● irritability;

● loss of concentration;

● depression;

● change in appetite (eating more *or* less than usual);

● drinking or smoking more;

● feelings of panic.

Before you get too worried, there are effective ways of controlling all of these stress symptoms. By far the best is to know what to expect, and this is what this chapter and the rest of the book is about. It's also important immediately to control unwanted and irrational thoughts, and to dismiss notions such as:

- Tests confuse me.

- My mind will go blank.

- I can never remember anything.

- I always go to pieces.

- I always run out of time.

- My memory will let me down.

- I'm stupid, I won't be able to do it…

As any counsellor or psychologist would point out, having these thoughts does not make them happen. They are just a reflection of the performance anxiety you feel before a test session. The key is to keep everything in proportion and not to start to believe what are frequently completely unrealistic personal 'predictions'. It's very unlikely to be a complete disaster, your family will not disown you; and if the worst comes to the worst, there are always other opportunities.

Practically, you need to get yourself into good mental and physical shape for a test session. This means getting enough sleep, eating and drinking properly, and making sure that you have taken enough exercise. If you're going to prepare for tests by working through practice questions or specialist books, do not stay up all night studying. Let's face it, it's very unlikely that you will do your best if you are tired, hungry and pumped full of caffeine!

You will also find it useful to build in periods of formal relaxation to your daily timetable. These may include any sort of activities that help you to unwind, and perhaps one of a number of special methods of stress reduction. Strategies such as these are important if you're presently unemployed and looking for a job, and also if you already have one and wish to move to a new position.

The two methods of stress reduction it is useful to know about are simple body relaxation and visualization. Both these approaches have proven ability to reduce anxiety levels and to make taking tests a less stressful process. They can be practised in the days leading up to the test session, and while waiting to go in to the test room itself.

Simple body relaxation

This is a technique that will help you to relax your muscles in sequence from your feet to your head, taking in your legs, thighs, chest, shoulders, arms, neck and head. It's a classic method and is very effective in calming the body and reducing feelings of stress and anxiety. Interestingly, it is also a technique that is taught to people who want to learn about self-hypnosis. However, in saying this, do not worry about putting yourself into a trance. If you are tired to start with the most that will happen is that you will fall asleep.

The sequence of instructions is easy to remember and you can practise relaxing yourself at any time when you have 10 minutes or so to spare. All you need is a quiet room, which is at a comfortable temperature, where you are unlikely to be disturbed. Prior to a test session you can achieve the same results by sitting quietly with your eyes closed, silently working through the instructions in your head.

To relax your body, work through the following steps. Concentrate on your:

- *toes* – tense the muscles in your toes, and then relax;
- *feet* – tense the muscles in both your feet, and then relax;
- *lower legs* – tense your lower leg muscles, and then relax;
- *thighs* – tense your thigh muscles, and then relax;
- *stomach and lower back* – tense the muscles, and then relax;
- *chest* – tense the muscles in your chest, and then relax;
- *shoulders* – tense your shoulder muscles, and then relax;

- *upper arms* – tense the muscles in your upper arms, and then relax;

- *lower arms and hands* – tense all the muscles and then relax;

- *neck* – tense your neck muscles and then relax;

- *head* – tense your head muscles (frown!), and then relax.

If you follow this sequence you should feel a warm wave of relaxation spreading up your body. It should help you to feel comfortable and less anxious. If you only have time to follow a shorter sequence just concentrate on your shoulders, neck and head. Systematically tensing and relaxing just these muscle groups will make quite a difference. Finally, remember that if you want to try this technique immediately before a test session you can always use the washroom.

Visualization

This technique, also known as 'mental picturing', is designed to put you in a positive frame of mind. It's routinely used by sports professionals as it also has the effect of focusing the attention on the task at hand.

The idea is to put yourself into a daydream state and to imagine success. In this case you imagine the successful and satisfactory completion of a test session. It works because it has been found that repeatedly picturing something, clearly and vividly, acts on the unconscious mind. In fact the mind begins to believe the 'dream', and starts to mobilize resources to make it a reality. At the same time, because your mind is focused on a successful outcome, you do not have time to worry.

In order to use visualization to help you prepare for a test session you need to do the following:

- Make yourself comfortable. You can do this by using the progressive body relaxation technique described earlier. Alternatively you can just settle yourself down in a warm, quiet room and empty your mind of extraneous thoughts – try focusing on something in front of you, maybe a plant or an object, and letting any thoughts you have drift away.

- Check that you feel relaxed. Mentally run round your body and make sure that no particular part is feeling tense. If it is, concentrate on that part and relax the muscles.

- Think about a time when you were successful at something. Remember the feeling of success, the euphoria at having achieved something worthwhile. Imagine doing the same thing again, and the pleasant feelings that went with it. Try and visualize yourself passing that examination; winning the sports competition; signing the big contract – whatever has made you feel proud and successful. Hold on to the positive and warm thoughts you are having…

- Now visualize yourself waiting outside the test room feeling confident. You are well prepared, *you know what to expect*. You enter the room and sit in your place. On the table in front of you are some test books and answer papers, *as you anticipated*. You look around the room at the other candidates. You feel confident and know that you are just as well, if not better, prepared, than anyone else there. The test administrator introduces the session and *tells you what to expect*. The session starts and you carefully read the instructions for the first test. You have prepared yourself for this sort of test, and so you can immediately start on the first question. After the appropriate amount of time has passed the administrator asks you to stop. As you were told how long the test would last you have *budgeted your time accordingly*. More instructions follow, and you *complete* all the remaining tests and questionnaires. At the end of the session you know that you *understood the instructions for all of the tests, and completed every one to the best of your ability*. Hold on to that thought.

- Practise and follow the same pattern of thoughts in the days before the test session, and especially if you start to feel any nervousness or anxiety.

Both body relaxation and visualization only work if you practise. So think of them as new skills, and make sure that you put some effort into developing your techniques. They really can help you relax, and will put you in a winning frame of mind.

The test session

If you were expected to make any particular preparations before the test session these will have been outlined in your letter of invitation. However, it's probably worth mentioning at this point that if you have any special requirements you *must* make sure that the testing organization knows about them in advance. For example, if you have mobility problems ensure that provision has been made for you to get to the test room. If you have stiff or arthritic hands or wrists, tell them. Remember that many tests are timed and so you will not be able to work as quickly as other people. Also, if you have restricted eyesight, or hearing problems, make sure this is known. Larger print tests are available, and it is possible to 'reserve' a seat in the front row.

A test session is a formal event and so you can always expect the test administrator to explain exactly what is required. The following description covers the main features of *any* selection test administration, and concentrates on those things you need to consider in order to do your best.

In the test room

Tests take place in rooms with desks or tables laid out in rows, and at most sessions you will find yourself being tested with up to 20 other candidates. It is very unlikely that you will be tested by yourself, unless the test(s) are administered by computer.

In most test sessions it does not matter where you sit. However, if you are unsure, always ASK.

The test materials

When you sit down you will typically find a number of test question books, answer sheets, two pencils and an eraser in front of you. You will only be supplied with other items, rough paper or an electronic calculator, for example, if they are essential for any of the tests.

Use the materials provided. Do not use any pens or pencils you may have brought with you. The reason is that many test papers are marked by optical scanning systems, and these work best with pencil marks.

If the test materials do not comprise separate question books and answer sheets they will be in one of the following three formats:

1 A combined question and answer book that allows you to write your answers by the questions.

2 A question book and a 'palmtop' computer. In this arrangement you read the questions in the book and enter your answers using the computer keyboard.

3 A 'palm-top' or personal computer. This time the questions appear on the computer screen and you enter your answers using the keyboard.

There are also an increasing number of tests and questionnaires available via the internet. This means that it is possible for employers to sit you at a computer and present you with online assessments, taken directly from a website, or indeed from their own intranet.

The session introduction

When everyone is settled the test administrator (a personnel assistant, human resources (HR) manager or psychologist) will introduce the session. A typical introduction follows:

> Good morning, I would first like to welcome you to The
> Triangles Stores Group – TSG. My name is Jenny Munroe

and I am the Human Resources Manager with TSG. I will be organizing your activities this morning, and for the rest of your time with us.

Second, can I just check that you all received the details that we sent to you, and you know what is going to happen to you this morning. You should have received a practice test, which covered the verbal and numerical tests you will be completing, and some details on the personality questionnaire. Did you receive the details?

[Any questions are answered]

We use the tests described in your letter because they give a fair and objective view of your abilities and personality. We have found that people who do well on these tests also tend to do well in the job. However, I would just like to assure you that we do take other information into account, in particular your application details.

Before I introduce the tests themselves I would just like to make sure that you are all comfortable and ready to begin. Also, if you would like to visit the washroom, now is a good time. It's out of the door, turn left, through the double doors, and straight ahead. Are there any questions before we begin?

[There is a short break for visits to the washroom and questions]

The test session will last for two hours with a short break in the middle. There will be two tests of ability, verbal and numerical, and a personality questionnaire. I will tell you when to start and stop each test, so please do not open any of the booklets in front of you until you are told to begin.

In order to do your best you need to keep the following points in mind:

- Please ask questions *before* the tests if you do not understand what to do. I can always explain what you need to do again.

- Read the instructions for each test carefully. Don't rush as it's very important you complete the tests in the correct way.

- Work as quickly and as accurately as you can. Remember that there is a time limit for the tests.

- Don't spend too long on any question. If you can't do one, make an informed guess and go on with the next.

- Overall, the more questions you do, the better your chances of getting a higher score.

Do you have any final questions before we begin?

The tests

The administrator will read out the instructions for each test in turn. These will include details on how to approach the questions and the time allowed. You will also have an opportunity to complete some practice questions and ask any questions yourself.

Make sure you understand the practice questions. If you find them difficult, or just don't know what to do, ASK.

During the test session the administrator watches the candidates and records any events that may affect performance, eg excessive noise or disturbance. The administrator will also make a note if you ask for assistance or, for example, mark your answers on the wrong answer sheet. These factors will be taken into account at the marking stage. For instance, if you do put your answers on the wrong sheet, they will be transferred to the correct form and marked accordingly. It will not put you at a disadvantage.

The end of the session

At the end of the session the administrator will collect all the answer sheets, making sure that none is missing, and that they all have the candidates' names and other details on them. You will be thanked for attending and the next stage of the selection process will be explained. This will normally involve the scoring of the tests and the selection of people for interview.

In many cases tests can be marked very quickly and so interviews can take place on the same day as the testing. While this is happening your time may well be spent on a tour of the site or premises, or having lunch. After this period the 'successful' candidates will be invited to stay for interview.

If you are unsuccessful always ask if you can have some feedback on your test results.

A knowledge of your results will be invaluable for any further applications you make. Most companies are happy to give feedback, although it may only be at a later date and over the telephone. However, it's still going to be useful information about your test performance in a real selection situation.

Testing on the internet

Basically everything that applies to a paper-and-pencil test session also relates to one conducted via the internet. So either you will go to an employer's premises and the test will be administered automatically by computer, or you will be sent a link and be able to do the tests at home. And like paper-and-pencil tests there will be full instructions, example questions, practice items, and the whole session will be strictly timed.

It is interesting to note that online testing provides employers with a rich source of additional information, quite apart from the scores that you might obtain. For instance, the employer can quickly receive a highly comprehensive report on your abilities, or personality, which includes data on response patterns and timings. The latter can provide clues as to whether you were guessing or trying to answer according to some system; or, when it comes to time, those questions you were finding it difficult to understand.

As for sitting at home doing the tests, care is taken to ensure that individuals are issued with codes and asked to supply identifying information. This is to help to protect against someone else completing the tests for you! Also, it is worth bearing in mind that if you pass any online assessments you will probably be reassessed at the next stage of the selection process. All this means is that it is better to play by the rules.

Countdown to test-day

In the lead-up to a test session, make sure you learn as much as you can about the sort of tests or questionnaires you may be asked to complete. If you are sent a practice test make sure that you try it; and read any other details very carefully. It's also useful to work out exactly where you are expected to go for your tests, how you are going to get there, the time it will take, and so forth. There's nothing more unnerving than getting lost on the way and arriving late. Indeed, if you arrive very late you will not be able to take part in the test session.

T-DAY minus 7: the seven days before the test session

- Read all the materials that are sent to you with great care.

- Complete any practice tests supplied and check the answers.

- Use this book, and any other books containing practice questions, to prepare.

- Familiarize yourself with different sorts of test formats and questions.

- If you suffer from pre-test nerves try one of the relaxation techniques recommended earlier.

- Make sure you know *exactly* where, and at what time, the test session is being held.

T-DAY minus 1: the day before the test session

- Keep calm. If you've prepared yourself properly you don't need to panic.

- Review what you know about the tests you will be asked to complete.

- Reduce any tension by using a relaxation technique. Exercise is also a good way of reducing stress – try a brisk 20-minute walk.

- Eat normally. Don't overeat, or be tempted to drink a lot of alcohol, tea or coffee.

- Get a good night's sleep. Don't stay up all night 'cramming', or go out on a date!

T-DAY: the day of the test session

- Eat normally. Even if you don't feel like it have a decent breakfast. This is especially important if you're diabetic and suffer from low blood sugar.

- If you wear reading glasses or a hearing aid make sure you take them with you.

- Take the letter of invitation and the directions.

- Arrive at the test venue in good time. This means at least 15 to 20 minutes before the billed start time.

- Visit the washroom and have a quiet think.

- Make sure you know where to sit in the test room.

During the session

Here are 24 key points for test success:

1 Keep as calm as you can. Remember that a certain amount of anxiety is perfectly normal.

2 Don't show any agitation and don't lose your temper. You need to appear confident because your general behaviour will be under scrutiny as well as your test performance.

3 Make yourself comfortable. Loosen your collar and tie (if appropriate), and kick off your shoes if you need to.

4 Listen carefully to the administrator's instructions.
Ask questions if you do not understand something.

5 If you can't see or hear things properly tell the administrator.

6 Read the test instructions carefully and do not assume that
you know what to do.

7 Put your answers in the correct place on the answer sheet.
If you miss a question out, because you intend to return to it,
make sure you do not get out of sequence. Of course with
computer or online testing the system will make sure that you
are answering the right question. Most will also allow you to go
back and change answers, within the time limits of the test.

8 Record your answers in the correct way. For example, do not
tick boxes if you're expected to strike through them with short
pencil lines.

9 Read the questions properly before you attempt to answer
them.

10 Don't agonize over a question you can't do, but move on to
the next one.

11 Don't waste time double-checking questions with easy or
obvious answers.

12 Don't waste time looking for 'trick' questions as there won't be
any.

13 If you can't work out an answer, make an informed guess.

14 Work as quickly as you can, but don't race or you will make
avoidable mistakes. For example, it's very easy to reverse
numbers and to imagine, say, that an answer is 145 rather
than 154.

15 Remember that the more questions you answer the greater
your chances of getting a higher mark.

16 Keep an eye on the time. If you have time left at the end of
a test go back and check your answers. Computer or online

tests will provide an on-screen clock. This will count down the time to the end of the test.

17 Don't stick slavishly to a certain amount of time for each question, eg 30 seconds for each question, if there are 60 to complete in half-an-hour. Many tests are designed so that the questions get harder, and so need progressively more time as you go on.

18 If you want any assistance during a test ask the administrator. The administrator won't give you further instructions once the test has started, but will be able to help you with any problems you might have concerning the 'mechanics' of the session, eg not knowing where to write your answers, a defective question book, blunt or broken pencils, no eraser...

19 Look around occasionally and relax: take some deep breaths, rest your eyes, stretch your legs. This will help to break the tension that will inevitably build up in your body.

20 Don't be put off if the questions seem difficult. They may well be just as difficult for everyone else, and you don't know the pass mark.

21 Don't be alarmed if your neighbours appear to be working much quicker than you. It's no guarantee that their answers are correct!

22 If for any reason you feel unwell tell the administrator. There are no prizes for suffering in silence. This applies to online tests as well. If something happens during the test session, or if you feel ill, contact the administrator by telephone after the session.

23 Don't be hard on yourself, you can only do your best.

24 Keep a cool head and, if you need help, ask for it.

CHAPTER 3

Ability tests

There are about 50 human abilities that can be measured using psychometric tests. These fall into four main categories covering the cognitive abilities such as numerical or verbal reasoning; psychomotor abilities like hand–eye co-ordination; physical abilities relating to stamina and strength; and sensory abilities concerning vision, hearing and speech.

In an assessment context the tests used may be selected from just one of these categories, or from a number. For example, some jobs require verbal and numerical ability; while others demand numerical and perceptual reasoning (understanding diagrams) *and* perfect colour vision. So the task of the personnel specialist can be very complicated because different jobs require different tests, and also because there is a vast range of tests to choose from. In fact there are between 4,000 and 5,000 tests on the market, with virtually all of them designed for use in English-speaking countries.

This makes the job of preparing for ability tests sound rather overwhelming, but in reality most selection procedures focus on the six main types of cognitive reasoning test:

● abstract;

● verbal;

- numerical;

- perceptual;

- spatial;

- mechanical.

There are other sorts of cognitive tests such as those that assess the ability to check information quickly and accurately. This is an important ability to measure in any job requiring the processing of large quantities of detailed information.

The next section deals with the six main types and provides information on what is being measured, the different sorts of question format, and hints on improving your performance. There is also some guidance on which type and format of test is used to assess which sort of job, along with the names of some of the most commonly used tests.

Abstract reasoning

Abstract reasoning tests measure general intellectual reasoning ability. This concerns how well you can solve a problem from first principles. It involves identifying the underlying logic of an 'argument' or question.

The questions in this sort of test are usually in the form of sequences of symbols arranged in rows or squares, and in order to solve them you must work through three distinct steps: your first task is to identify the different sorts of symbols, and decide what they have in common. For example, in most tests the differences will include some or all of the following:

- *shape*, eg circles, triangles, squares, rectangles, pentagons, hexagons;

- *size*, eg small, medium and large;

- *colour*, eg the three primary colours;

- *features*, eg the number of circles, lines or points on a star.

Having examined the symbols, and what they have in common, the next step is to identify the pattern. This involves seeing how the symbols are ordered or grouped. For example, are they in repeating patterns of two, three or more symbols? If they are in a square format, does the order go from left to right, right to left, top to bottom, bottom to top, or diagonally?

The last step is to predict the next part of the sequence from what you have learnt about the logic of the pattern.

Example 1: Abstract reasoning
What are the next two symbols in the sequence?

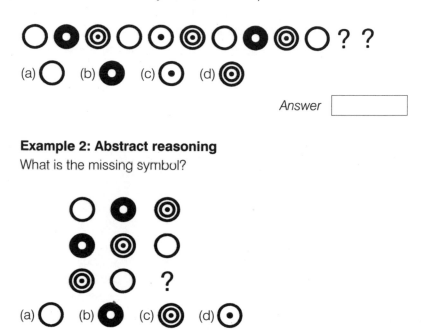

Answer _____

Example 2: Abstract reasoning
What is the missing symbol?

Answer _____

In Example 1 you will see that there are four different types of symbol, all of which are the same size. The (a) symbol always goes immediately after the (d) symbol, leaving the other two to alternate. Since there are two (b)s and only one (c), the next symbols in the sequence must be (c), followed by (d). Likewise in Example 2, it's a question of working out what is happening in each row or column.

This one is obviously easier because there are three symbols in use, and they appear in each complete row or column only once. Thus it is logical to assume that the missing symbol is (b). However, it's also interesting to note that there is a sequence, which runs (a)–(c)–(b). This is an important point to grasp because in questions presented as 'squares' there is often more than one way of reaching the correct answer.

Uses

Abstract reasoning tests provide the best single measure of general ability and so are used for all types of jobs at all levels. This means that there is a chance you will have to do this sort of test whatever the job for which you are applying. However, they are obviously of particular value for any job that focuses on the ability to deal with abstract ideas, concepts or theories. Thus they are generally a fixed feature of recruitment to scientific or technological jobs.

The most widely used tests of general intellectual ability are *Raven's Progressive Matrices*, published by Pearson. Another popular measure is the *Compound Series Test* from The Morrisby Organization.

Hints

Seek out abstract problems in newspapers, magazines and quiz books, and practise working through the three steps suggested. You may also find it useful to make up your own questions and try them on other people. The action of explaining the answers will help fix in your mind the different ways in which these questions can work. Finally, if you get stuck on a particular question in a test, always go back to first principles and identify the component parts of the symbols, and then the pattern. Sometimes it also helps to continue with the other questions and return to a problem question later with a fresh viewpoint. This will stop you becoming fixated on a particular solution.

Verbal reasoning

Verbal reasoning tests measure your ability to understand and use words. They are concerned with things like spelling, grammar, sentence completion, analogies and following verbal instructions. The more complex verbal tests look at how well you can understand and reason with passages of verbal information. The questions in verbal tests come in many different forms, but they all rely on understanding the meaning of words, and the structure and logic of language.

Example 3: Spelling
Which of the following words are *incorrectly* spelt?

A. Persistant   B. Separate   C. Success   D. Recieve

Answer [   ]

Example 4: Grammar
What, if anything, is grammatically *incorrect* with the following sentences?

A. The elephant was very enormous.

B. Its unlikely that we can catch the train.

C. She took the books and the rest of the money off of me.

D. They should have took the boxes with them.

Answer [   ]

Example 5: Sentence completion
Which word best completes the sentence?

1   The painting, originally .... to a Dutch artist, is now thought to be by John Constable.

A. prescribed   B. assigned   C. attributed
D. linked   E. designated

Answer [   ]

2 Our company's name is .... with quality and value for money.

A. connected   B. synonymous   C. aligned
D. concerned   E. equated

Answer [   ]

In Example 3 you need to know how to spell a series of everyday words, and (a) and (d) are incorrectly spelt. The trick with Example 4 is to understand some of the principles of English grammar, and to realize that there are errors in all of them! In (a) the word 'very' is not needed, as 'enormous' means 'very large'; in (b), 'Its' should be 'It's'; and in (c) the word 'of' is not required. Finally, in (d), the word 'took' should be 'taken'. In Example 5 the questions are known as 'cloze' tasks, and the idea in each case is to identify the best possible word. Therefore in question (1) the most correct answer is (c), because paintings are 'attributed' to artists; and in (2) the answer is (b), because 'synonymous' means 'closely associated'.

Example 6: Verbal analogies
Letter is to word as sentence is to:

A. verb   B. paragraph   C. phrase   D. book

Answer [   ]

Over is to under as below is to:

A. beneath   B. beside   C. above   D. submerged

Answer [   ]

Example 7: Word groups
Which *two* words do not belong with the other four?

1 A. stone   B. wood   C. plastic
D. coal   E. nylon   F. gas

Answer [   ]

2   A. trousers   B. hat   C. socks
        D. shirt   E. boots   F. shorts

                                    Answer [   ]

Example 8: Following instructions

Use the information below to answer the questions. For each question select the correct answer from the five options provided.

Surgery times

The surgery is now open from 8.30 am to 12.30 pm, and from 1.00 pm to 6.30 pm.

There is a late surgery on Tuesdays and Thursdays from 7.30 pm to 10.00 pm. If you have a minor surgery appointment please confirm at the beginning of the week, as all procedures are performed on Thursday afternoons. The 'Well Woman' clinic continues to take place on alternate Saturday mornings. The next meeting is scheduled for the 25th of this month, please see the practice nurse for details.

If you have a minor surgery appointment when must you attend?

A. Normal surgery hours.

B. Late surgery on Thursday.

C. The beginning of the week.

D. Monday or Wednesday morning.

E. Thursday afternoon.

                                    Answer [   ]

In Examples 6 and 7 you need to understand directly the meanings and relationships between words. Thus, in Example 6, the answer to the first analogy is B, because the progression is to bigger units; and in the other analogy the answer is C because the starting analogy was one of opposites. Readers should note that in this sort of question there may be *any* relationship between the words, eg:

- *synonyms*, ie words with the same meanings;

- *antonyms*, ie words with opposite meanings;

- *part to whole*, eg 'letter' is to 'word';

- *cause and effect*, eg 'exercise' is to 'fatigue';

- *sequence*, eg 'summer' is to 'autumn';

- *degree*, eg 'hot' is to 'warm';

- *object and action*, eg 'kick' is to 'football';

- *groups*, eg 'red' is to 'green' (other colours).

Indeed, Example 7 is a case of words falling into particular groups. So the answer to (1) is C and E because they are both man-made, while the other materials are natural; and to (2) it is B and D, because they are items of clothing worn above the waist, while the others are worn below. In Example 8 details are given of a doctor's surgery times and the question is designed to discover whether you can understand simple instructions. The answer is actually very straightforward and is E. However, these sorts of questions can be much more difficult, eg on what date was the last 'Well Woman' clinic?

The most complicated sorts of verbal assessments are called verbal critical reasoning tests. These present you with a short passage of written information followed by a number of statements. The task is to decide whether each statement is 'True' (follows logically from the information provided); 'False' (does not follow logically); or if you 'Cannot Tell', because there is insufficient information. All the information required to make the decision is contained in the passage. However, just to complicate the issue, the information given frequently relates to subjects about which you may already know, or have formed particular opinions about.

Example 9: Verbal critical reasoning
Read the passage and decide if the statements that follow are True, False or if you Cannot Tell.

'Smoking can cause problems in many work environments. In the office it can not only lead to heated arguments, but to health problems as well. Indeed the *New England Journal of Medicine* (NEJM) recently reported that passive smoking, or the involuntary inhalation of other people's smoke, can be a major health hazard. Like regular smokers, it puts passive smokers at an increased risk of developing chest and circulatory diseases.'

1   Smokers are more likely to have heart attacks.

   True   False   Cannot tell

                                    Answer [   ]

2   Passive smoking means inhaling someone else's smoke.

   True   False   Cannot tell

                                    Answer [   ]

3   Smoking can make offices calmer places in which to work.

   True   False   Cannot tell

                                    Answer [   ]

Some verbal critical reasoning tests have more than three answer options, and split the reasoning tasks into a number of types. So, for example, you have to decide if a statement is 'True', 'Probably True', 'False', 'Probably False' or if you 'Cannot Tell'. The questions are then based on different types of logical argument, eg:

● whether deductions (judgements based on general principles) are valid;

● whether inferences (conclusions based on given facts) are accurate;

● whether valid assumptions are being made;

● the strength of verbal arguments;

● whether conclusions based on factual interpretations are valid.

For example, deductions are sometimes based on pairs of logically consistent verbal arguments or 'syllogisms'.

Example 10: Verbal deductions

'Some animals are venomous. All venomous animals are dangerous to touch.'

Which of the following are valid deductions? Answer 'Yes' or 'No'.

1 All non-venomous animals are safe to touch.

Answer [   ]

2 Some animals are dangerous.

Answer [   ]

3 Some animals are safe to touch.

Answer [   ]

The answers to Example 9 are (1), 'Cannot Tell'; (2) 'True'; and (3) 'False'. If you made a mistake it's probably because you allowed your opinions or existing knowledge to cloud your judgement. Thus it is well known that smoking increases your chances of having a heart attack, but the necessary information is not provided in the passage. In a similar way in Example 10 you have to be careful what you assume. The answer to (1) is 'No', because we have no information on non-venomous animals, and some may be dangerous. The answer to (2) is 'Yes', because according to the statements the animals that are venomous are dangerous to touch. Finally, the answer to (3) is 'No' again, because although we know there are animals that are safe to touch, we have no given information on which to base that conclusion.

Uses

Verbal reasoning tests are probably the most widely used type of ability measure. They are popular with employers because every job requires the ability to assess and use verbal information, whether it be understanding instruction manuals or writing management reports.

In practice the formats illustrated by Examples 3 to 8 tend to be used in selection for semiskilled, general administrative, clerical and customer service positions, whereas the verbal critical reasoning tests (Examples 9 and 10) are generally used for managerial and graduate selection.

There are many verbal tests on the market including *Working with Words*, *Verbal Comprehension*, *Verbal Usage*, *Verbal Reasoning*, *Verbal Analysis* and *Verbal Critical Reasoning* from Saville & Holdsworth Ltd. Other examples include the verbal component of the *Graduate and Managerial Assessment* and *First Graduate Assessment*, published by PreVisor; and the *Watson Glaser Critical Thinking Appraisal* from Pearson.

Hints

A good way to prepare for verbal tests is to read and analyse complex verbal information. Try reading a quality newspaper and deciding if the assertions and assumptions made by the journalists are supported by the facts. You might also find it useful to read manuals and technical reports, and 'test' them for the logic of their arguments.

Other things to try are word games like Scrabble and the verbal logic puzzles you find in puzzle books available from newsagents. You must also attempt to expand your word power by reading more, and looking up any words you do not understand in a dictionary. A thesaurus, available from any good bookshop, will also be a useful addition to your library as it contains lists of synonyms and antonyms.

On a more technical note, when you are reading the questions in a verbal test it's worth remembering that if you read all the possible answers carefully, they will often give you clues as to the correct response. For example:

- the correct response is often shorter and more detailed;

- information given in the other answers may help to identify the correct response;

- the incorrect answers are often inconsistent or implausible;
- the use of absolutes (eg 'every', 'all') often appear in false statements.

Numerical reasoning

Numerical reasoning tests measure your ability to understand and use numbers. They are concerned with the four basic arithmetic operations (addition, subtraction, multiplication and division), number sequences, simple mathematics and the use of numerical data to solve problems. The latter is usually the case with numerical critical reasoning tests in which blocks of information are provided that require both interpretation and the application of the appropriate logic.

Example 11: Arithmetic
Solve *without* a calculator.

1 $24.7 \times 4 = ?$ A. 84.3   B. 89.8   C. 92.3
                          D. 96.7   E. 98.8
                                         Answer [   ]

2 $719 + ? = 866$ A. 156   B. 142   C. 177
                          D. 147   E. 158
                                         Answer [   ]

3 $? - 48 = 112$ A. 152   B. 162   C. 154
                          D. 160   E. 149
                                         Answer [   ]

4 $24.6 \div 5.3 = ?$ A. 3.7   B. 4.2   C. 4.6
                          D. 5.1   E. 5.4
                                         Answer [   ]

Example 12: Number sequences
What is the next number in the sequence?

1   1   4   7   10   13   16   ?

Answer [   ]

2   3   9   27   81   243   729   ?

Answer [   ]

3   1   4   9   16   25   36   ?

Answer [   ]

4   1   1   2   3   5   8   ?

Answer [   ]

Example 13: Mathematics
Solve *without* a calculator.

1   25% of 500 = ?   A. 120   B. 250   C. 125
                                D. 220   E. 175

Answer [   ]

2   3x + 12 = 18, x =   A. 2   B. 2.5   C. 3
                                D. 3.5   E. 4

Answer [   ]

3   (7 × 6) + ? = 70   A. 38   B. 32   C. 18
                                D. 42   E. 28

Answer [   ]

4   1/6 as a decimal   A. 0.155   B. 0.333   C. 0.225
                                D. 0.166   E. 0.175

Answer [   ]

The answers to Example 11 are E, D, D and C. Note that it's often a lot easier to work out the answer if you round the numbers, eg in question 1 if you look for the answer that is nearest to 25 × 4. In Example 12 the answer to 1 is 19, because the difference between each number and the preceding one is 3. Sequences like this, where you add or subtract a fixed number, are known as arithmetic progressions. In 2 the answer is 2187, because the next number is always found by multiplying the preceding number by 3. This is an example of a geometric progression. In 3 the answer is 49, because all the numbers are squares (1 × 1, 2 × 2, 3 × 3, 4 × 4, 5 × 5, 6 × 6, 7 × 7). In 4 the answer is 13, because the next number is the last two numbers added together. For the mathematically minded this is an example of what is known as the Fibonacci sequence. All these types of sequences are frequently used in numerical tests.

In Example 13 you need to go beyond simple arithmetic and understand how percentages work, simple algebra, the meaning of brackets and how to convert to decimal fractions. The answers are C, A, E and D. All these mathematical operations are based on the sort of things you learn in secondary education.

Numerical critical reasoning tests present you with a range of numerical information, usually in the form of tables of data, charts or graphs. The task is to understand the meaning of the questions, find and interpret the appropriate data, and then perform the necessary calculations. In most cases the calculations are not difficult and the emphasis is on developing the correct problem-solving strategy. In this way, although the problems can seem complicated, they do not usually require a calculator. Indeed in most tests of this nature candidates are not allowed to use calculators.

Example 14: Numerical critical reasoning

Use the information below to answer the questions.

STUDENT EXAMINATION PERFORMANCE

Qualifications by Level and Gender

College Qualifications by Level

Level 1
7%

Level 2
20%

Level 4
29%

Level 3
44%

Key: Educational Levels are 1–4. Gender: M = Male and F = Female.

Questions:

1   How many women have Level 3 qualifications?

A. 250,000   B. 200,000

C. 2,000,000   D. 2,500,000

Answer [   ]

2   What percentage of students have Level 2 or better qualifications?

A. 93%   B. 83%

C. 63%   D. 73%

Answer [   ]

3   If the ratio of males to females with Level 4 qualifications is kept constant, but these qualifications make up 39% of the total, approximately how many more students will now have Level 4 qualifications?

A. 250,000   B. 500,000

C. 750,000   D. 1,000,000

Answer [   ]

The Example 14 questions are quite typical of numerical critical reasoning tests as they involve the use of one or more charts and then a calculation. As you can see it is important to understand how the charts are labelled, in particular that the 'Qualifications by Level and Gender' chart has a scale marked in 10,000s. The answer to question 1 is obtained by reading off the value and multiplying it by 10,000, which gives C. Question 2 relates to the pie chart with the answer being A. Lastly, there are a number of ways of working out the answer to question 3, but if 29 per cent is equal to three million then 39 per cent must be equal to about four million. This gives a difference of one million, which is answer D.

Uses

Numerical tests, especially those based on question formats like Examples 11 to 13, are used in selection whenever there is a need to assess numeracy or an aptitude for data manipulation. This covers many clerical and administrative jobs, as well as those in the banking and financial services sector. Graduates and managerial applicants can look forward to completing numerical critical reasoning tests with questions like those in Example 14.

As numerical reasoning tests are so commonly used there are many to choose from. In the UK the most popular include *Working with Numbers, Number Skills, Numerical Computation, Numerical Reasoning, Numerical Estimation, Interpreting Data, Numerical Analysis* and *Numerical Critical Reasoning*, all published by Saville & Holdsworth Limited. Other names to look out for are *Numerical Awareness* and *Numerical Estimation* (*Modern Occupational Skills Tests*), and the numerical component of the *Graduate and Managerial Assessment* and *First Graduate Assessment*, all published by Pre Visor; and the latest aptitude and Swift tests from Saville Consulting.

Hints

Make sure you are capable of performing simple calculations without a calculator. You can practise these when you go shopping by working out how much you will need to pay for your purchases, the real cost of discounted goods, the cost per minute of leaving your car in a car park and so forth. It's also a good idea to practise with tables of information such as bus or train timetables, tables of currency exchange rates and the financial information contained in newspapers.

In terms of mathematical knowledge you will find it useful to understand:

● factors and multiples, eg powers and roots of numbers;

● fractions, ratios, proportions and percentages;

● different types of graphs, eg bar charts, pie charts and line graphs;

● simple statistics, eg how to work with frequencies or calculate an average.

If you are unsure about any of these aspects of mathematics consult a textbook, especially any general text covering GCSE or equivalent level maths.

Perceptual reasoning

Perceptual reasoning is about understanding and applying information presented in a diagrammatic form. Most tests of this nature are based on perceptual analogies, or involve the interpretation of diagrammatic rules. In both cases the answers can only be worked out by determining the visual logic of the information provided. Indeed they are deliberately designed so that a visual problem-solving strategy will work better than any other approach.

Example 15: Perceptual analogies

Answer [   ]

Answer [   ]

Example 16: Diagrammatic interpretation

What will happen to the shape if the commands are applied?

A   ■ ⇨ 3 ⇨ 6 ⇨ 4 ⇨ ?   A. ■   B. ▼   C. ♥   D. ▲

Answer [   ]

In Example 15, analogy 1 is a simple case of the different orientations of an arrow. The answer can only be worked out visually and is A and E. In 2 you are presented with a series of clock faces, and the answer this time is B and D. The quickest way to the solution is to realize that the difference between the two starting clocks is that the hour hand has rotated through 180 degrees, and to look for two other clock faces where this has happened. In Example 16 you are forced to imagine what will happen to a shape when it is transformed in various ways. Again this can only be done visually, and the answers are C, D and B.

Uses

Perceptual tests are often used to select for scientific, computing, engineering, design and technical craft positions. As with verbal and numerical tests they are also good predictors of performance in general managerial, administrative and office-based jobs. The same designs of tests are used with candidates applying for jobs at all levels. However, the tests can be made more complicated by introducing additional variables, eg in Example 16 there could have been additional commands that changed the size of the shapes, the colour, or which only worked in combination with other commands.

A classic example of a perceptual reasoning test is the *Perceptual Test* (part of the *General Ability Tests*), published by The Morrisby Organization. Others include the *Diagrammatic Reasoning* and *Diagrammatic Thinking* tests from Saville & Holdsworth Ltd.

Hints

The best form of practice for perceptual analogies is to buy a book containing plenty of examples and to work out the relationships between the shapes or diagrams. You will discover that the relationships you find are similar to those used in abstract reasoning tests, and some verbal analogies. They will include changes in size, colour or orientation; and the membership of groups of shapes, which get progressively more complicated, but which share similar features.

For tests based on diagrammatic interpretation, practise by producing your own diagrams that explain how a system works, eg draw a flow diagram which explains how to programme a video recorder. Any game involving sequences of moves can also be good practice; this would include any board game based on strategy.

Spatial reasoning

Spatial reasoning tests measure your ability to manipulate shapes in two dimensions, or to visualize solid objects presented as two-dimensional patterns. In the first case the test often presents you with a pattern that has some missing components, and you have to decide which of a number of alternate pieces will complete the pattern, or maybe just how many pieces are required. Other tests present two-dimensional objects that have been rotated or reflected, and you have to decide what has happened, eg whether or not a shape has been turned over. In those tests requiring the visualization of a solid object, a number of patterns are presented that could be folded to make an object. Your job is to imagine which of the patterns would work in practice.

All spatial tests rely on you being able to imagine what would happen 'in your mind's eye'. This is something that many people find difficult to do, and some cannot do it at all. Thus, about 5 per cent of the adult population will find it impossible to imagine a two-dimensional shape moved through a third dimension. Psychologically speaking this is an interesting finding as it probably means that spatial ability is something that gets wired into the brain quite early in life or, at the very least, by the end of the teenage years.

Example 17: Spatial components

L-shape

How many of the L-shapes are required to fill the large square, without leaving any gaps?

A. 3   B. 4   C. 5   D. 6   E. Cannot be done

Answer

Example 18: Spatial rotations and reflections
All of the shapes below are the same, but they have been rotated into different positions. In addition *one* of them has been turned over, which one?

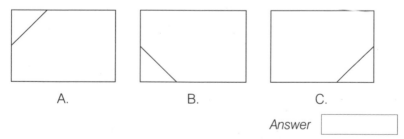

A.   B.   C.

Answer

In Example 17 you will find that there is only one way of completing the square without leaving any gaps and this requires five of the L-shaped pieces – answer C. The solution is to fit one piece around the black square in the top left-hand corner so that you end up with a complete small square, and then to fit two further L-shapes on the corner of that square so that you complete a diagonal going from the top left to bottom right. The remaining gaps are both L-shaped, and require two further pieces. The best way to work out the answer to Example 18 is to look for the one shape that has been turned over like the page of a book. Alternatively, you could look for two shapes, which when rotated will sit exactly on top of each other, making the remaining shape the one that has been turned over. Whichever strategy you use you should get B as the answer.

The last example measures advanced spatial reasoning and requires the ability to imagine patterns assembled into three-dimensional objects. Questions like this can involve the visual 'assembly' and 'disassembly' of objects; objects that have been rotated in space, or which are viewed from different angles (eg from above, below, the side, the back); and objects that have different colours or markings on their surfaces. The last variety are the hardest to deal with as they require an ability to imagine shapes moved in three-dimensional space, *and* the ability to work out the relative position of the markings on their surfaces.

Example 19: Spatial assembly

 Which of the following patterns will fold to make the cube?

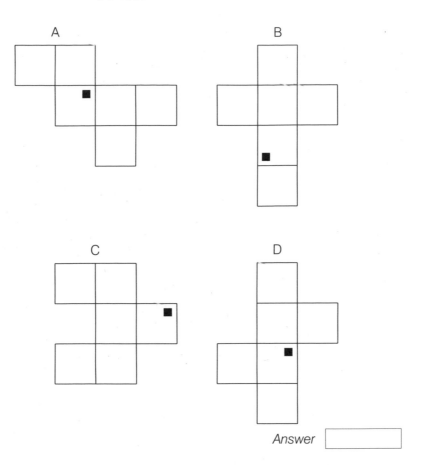

A

B

C

D

Answer

In order to answer Example 19 you first need to establish which of the patterns will fold to make the cube, and then which will have the small black square in the correct position. If you look at the patterns carefully you will see that A, B and D will all fold to make a cube. In this case they will also all produce the cube illustrated.

Uses

Spatial reasoning tests are used in selection for jobs where it is necessary to have a good eye for how things fit together, or to be able to cope with different shapes and patterns. This includes many practical jobs such as carpentry, decorating, floor-laying and sewing. Good spatial ability is also required in many production, technical and design activities where plans and drawings are used extensively. Thus, you would expect surveyors, architects, engineers and designers to have this sort of ability. It is also an ability that can be used in conjunction with modern 'visualization' tools such as computer-aided design (CAD) packages.

Spatial reasoning tests are used less frequently than the other sorts of tests mentioned so far, but they do measure an ability that is a key component of many jobs. The tests on the market include the *Shapes Analysis Test*, published by Hogrefe; and the *Shapes Test*, from The Morrisby Organization. Other frequently used examples are the *Spatial Reasoning* and *Spatial Recognition* tests from Saville & Holdsworth Ltd.

Hints

Spatial reasoning is a very practical sort of ability and so it is best practised by assembling and making things. For example, you could build models or assemble jigsaw puzzles. In fact these days there are three-dimensional puzzles that provide very good practice in imagining how complex parts fit together. If you are artistic you can also try drawing plans of objects from different angles, or try cutting out and assembling the sort of patterns illustrated in Example 19. Finally, if you have access to a computer drawing or CAD package you can draw objects that you can instruct the computer to move in three-dimensional space. This will allow you to see objects in any orientation and from any angle.

Mechanical reasoning

Mechanical reasoning tests are designed to assess your knowledge of basic mechanical and physical principles. They usually contain questions that do not require any specialist knowledge, but which rely on you being able to work out what is happening. However, that's not to say that some knowledge of physics or mechanics, or practical everyday experience of simple machines and devices, would not be of help.

Example 20: Mechanical reasoning

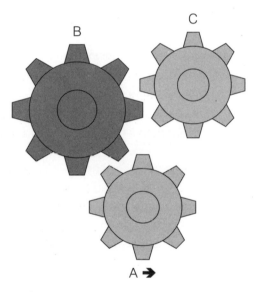

In which direction will C turn if A turns anti-clockwise?

A. Clockwise   B. It will jam

C. Anti-clockwise   D. Backwards and forwards

Answer [   ]

In virtually all mechanical reasoning tests you are presented with a question and a diagram. You have to determine what principle is being illustrated and select the correct answer from the options provided.

The answer to Example 20 is determined by imagining the effect of A on B, and then of B on C. In this way, even in this straight-forward example, it involves step-by-step problem solving. If you approach the task in this way you will find that C is the correct answer. Looking at the other options, obviously D is incorrect, and so is B. If you were tempted to answer B you were adding additional information to the diagram, eg by thinking that the cogs were too close together, or that friction would stop them turning. This is a common mistake with mechanical questions that can only be answered on the basis of the information provided, even if you think you know better!

Uses

Mechanical reasoning tests are used to assess people for practical jobs requiring a working knowledge of mechanical principles. These are often positions that involve assembling components or running and maintaining machinery. As a consequence, mechanical tests are often used to select mechanics, technicians and production workers.

One of the best-known mechanical reasoning tests is *Bennett's Mechanical Comprehension Test*, published by Pearson. This was developed in the 1940s, and is still widely used throughout the world. Other more modern tests include the *Mechanical Test* from The Morrisby Organization and *Mechanical Comprehension* from Saville & Holdsworth Ltd.

Hints

If you are interested in maintaining any form of machine, including a motor car, you are probably already practising this ability. Likewise, if you undertake 'do-it-yourself' projects, or repair things around the home, you are giving yourself scope to exercise your mechanical competence. Other things you can do are to work with construction kits (eg Technical Lego or Meccano); or simply to take household devices apart and put them back together again.

Research has shown that men are generally better at mechanical reasoning tests than women, so if you are female it's even more important that you understand the principles involved. However, whatever your gender, useful additional sources of information are GCSE level physics or technology textbooks. You will find that these give details on:

- *mechanisms*, eg balances, levers, linkages, gears, cranks and pulleys;

- *structures*, eg the effects of compression, stress and strain;

- *energy*, eg the transmission of heat, light and power;

- *forces*, eg gravity, and rotational effects such as centrifugal and centripetal force.

Other ability tests

The other main types of cognitive ability tests that you might encounter are concerned with checking detailed information. These are known as checking, data checking or classification tests. They are generally short in duration and present you with a number of tables of information, which you have to check against each other. The function of this sort of test is to measure how quickly and accurately you can detect errors in data. This is an ability that is important in any job where detailed records are kept, eg banking, accounting, telephone sales and retailing.

Example 21: Data checking

Look at the two tables of data below. Check each row and mark any differences you find between Table A and Table B.

Table A				Table B		
Code	Number	Band		Code	Number	Band
127/34	2510	XA		127/34	2510	XA
128/35	2505	LM		128/53	2505	LM
129/36	2543	BA		129/36	2534	AB
218/43	3671	LM		218/43	3671	LM
218/44	3762	AB		218/44	3762	AB
218/45	3892	XA		219/54	3892	XA

In Example 21 there are differences in three of the rows. However, consider how much more difficult this test would be if there were 40 rows and 6 columns per table; and a mixture of numbers, letters, numbers and letters, and names and addresses – all to be checked in a matter of minutes.

Uses

As already mentioned, this sort of test is used to select people for clerical checking and data input jobs. Most of the major publishers produce tests that are a variation on the theme illustrated; with the *Speed and Accuracy Test* from The Morrisby Organization and *Clerical Checking* from Saville & Holdsworth Ltd being good examples.

Hints

Data checking tests require an eye for detail and patience. One way to practise is to cross-reference codes and other details in catalogues and timetables, or to check accounts or balance sheets. In short, use any form of detailed information that you can check for its accuracy.

Manual dexterity tests

Finally, if you apply for jobs that require speed and accuracy with the hands, you may be asked to take a manual dexterity test. These are often in the form of wooden pegboards on which you are asked to place combinations of metal pins and washers in holes. Sometimes there are a series of tasks to complete in different ways, such as just using your left or right hand, both hands, or a pair of tweezers. More complex forms of dexterity test may require you to assemble a number of different types of components in a given time. These often look like construction kits, and involve the use of your hands and some tools. Commonly used dexterity tests include the *Peg Board* and *Fine Dexterity Tests*, both available from The Morrisby Organization and Hogrefe.

Future test developments

In the short term you are likely to encounter more tests based on so-called business learning experiences. These are work simulation exercises in which you take the role of an employee in a fictional company or organization. The tests work by teaching you what you need to know in order to complete a range of tasks, and then by finding out how good you are at applying your learning in practice. A typical scenario might be that you have just taken over a customer service desk, and your supervisor has briefly introduced you to the product and customer databases, and to a procedures manual. Your first customer arrives with a query…

Business learning exercises differ from traditional tests, which measure specific abilities, in that they present complete problem scenarios. In this way they present more realistic problems, and allow an employer to see more directly how you would perform in a real job. Arguably, these exercises are a fairer method of selection because they make no assumptions about your existing knowledge and, also, because they sample real job situations, they allow for a degree of self-selection. The last point is important because it saves time for employer and candidate alike.

Over the next few years more of these tests will be used, in particular for selecting potential middle and senior managers, and customer service and sales personnel. The pioneers in this area are Oxford Psychologists Press, who publish tests such as the *Aptitude for Business Learning Exercises (ABLE)*.

Example 22: Business learning exercise

Instructions

You have just started a job in the marketing department of a large travel group. Your first task is to update some new holiday brochures. This involves putting the details of three holidays into the brochures for 18–30 year olds and 50+ year olds, respectively.

To help you decide which holidays go in which brochures you have information on a number of existing packages.

For 18–30 year olds:

Extreme Adventures: A collection of adventure holidays in exotic locations. Customers need to be physically fit and enjoy a challenge. These are holidays for the individualist and prices start in the medium range.

Sun Worshippers: Holidays for those who want to soak up the sun. Based mainly in Mediterranean resorts, these packages represent good value for money, with many priced in the economy range. Special deals are available for groups of friends wishing to holiday together.

After Dark: All-action weekend breaks in the major European capitals. Ideal for those who like music, dancing and partying the night away. These are breaks for people who want to have fun! Prices start in the economy range.

For 50+ year olds:

Golden Cruises: Sophisticated luxury cruises to islands in the West Indies. Customers need to enjoy group excursions, although there are opportunities for individual activities. All cruise prices fall in the expensive price range.

Great Cities: Two- or three-day breaks in famous European cities. The package includes accompanied tours of major museums, art galleries and sites of architectural interest. Prices fall in the economy and medium price ranges.

Craft Breaks: Ideal for people who want to learn a new craft such as pottery or weaving, these holidays include accommodation, travel, food and expert tuition. All aro based in the UK and most are priced in the economy range.

Task

Which holiday goes in which brochure? In each case the answer is 18–30, 50+ or 'Cannot Tell'.

1   *Condor Trek.* A week-long break in South America exploring ancient jungle ruins. The highlight is a hang-gliding adventure from the top of the highest ziggurat. Not for the faint hearted! The price falls in the expensive range.

Answer [   ]

2   *Berlin Beer Festival.* A long weekend at the most famous beer festival of them all. Ideal for singles and groups, there is time to explore the cultural side of the city and to sample the beers to the early hours. The price falls in the economy range.

Answer [   ]

3   *Polar Adventure.* A unique opportunity to travel beyond the Artic Circle and experience the Polar Region. This cruising holiday is hosted aboard the luxurious *SS North Star* and the price falls in the expensive range.

Answer [   ]

Given the information you have on the different holiday packages the answer to question (1) is 18–30, question (2) is 'Cannot Tell' and question (3) is 50+.

The other two main developments in ability testing concern the move to more novel formats, and so-called Cognitive Process Profiling. A good example of the first is *Fastrack* from Saville & Holdsworth Ltd. This is a test for high-ability graduate and management candidates that is designed to assess problem-solving and analysis. It helps an employer decide how well a person is likely to apply his reasoning and judgement when making decisions, particularly when he is faced with new information.

The candidate is given information on a variety of different situations. This is presented on a number of cards that reflect the way in which we naturally receive information – from a range of different sources. The candidate then has to sort through the material, identify what is important, link together the different pieces of information, and use what has been discovered to solve problems.

In some ways, *Fastrack* is similar to the ABLE tests described previously, as both are trying to simulate aspects of business decision making and learning.

Cognitive Process Profiling

Cognitive Process Profiling is designed to look at your cognitive style (how you think), learning potential, strengths and limitations, and most appropriate working environment. This is a new technique and the best current example is the *Cognitive Process Profile* from PreVisor.

The Cognitive Process Profile is a computer simulation exercise that measures a person on 10,000 'mouse-click' points. It is a self-administered assessment in the form of a simulated card game that takes about two hours to complete.

As a selection tool, it provides information on how consistently a person approaches new and difficult problems, and their cognitive style. Are they analytic, structured, impulsive, random, or do they show the characteristics of any one of 16 different styles? Intriguingly, the assessment also provides a guide to someone's ideal work situation. The situations or 'environments' are:

- *Operational:* dealing with concrete, well defined tasks one by one. For example, clerical or production work.

- *Diagnostic:* accumulating information and using this to understand and overcome anticipated problems. For example, sales or educational work.

- *Alternative:* dealing with a whole operating system, optimizing all the available resources. For example, legal or medical work, senior management.

- *Parallel processing:* co-ordinating interacting programmes of activity, operating in parallel. For example, general managers or professional partners.

- *Strategic:* 'big systems' thinking, creating new structures and dealing with large-scale change. For example, CEOs of large organizations.

The key point about Cognitive Process Profiling is that the concern is not necessarily over getting the 'right' answers, but in describing the route a person uses to reach an answer. The profile approach also measures improvements in problem-solving from one item to another, and so provides an index of learning potential.

Virtual reality (VR)

Other developments include the use of VR to put you 'inside' a test. Thus, by wearing the appropriate equipment it will be possible to place you in a world of tests in which you can 'see' and 'feel' the questions. This may sound like science fiction but a number of systems do already exist, and VR-based exercises are already used for selection and training by the US Airforce and the British Royal Navy.

The pace of technological change is such that within the next 10 to 20 years it is reasonable to suppose that a combination of new test designs, VR and the world wide web will allow any person anywhere in the world to be assessed using a realistic simulation of any job.

Computer gaming systems also give us a clue as to how things may develop. It is only necessary to think about innovations such as Nintendo® Wii. This has a wireless controller that can be used as a pointing device, which can also detect motion in three dimensions. Clearly this technology could easily be used to develop a new range of spatial ability or manual dexterity tests.

Ten more ways to improve your performance

The details and hints given for each type of ability test will help you to prepare for most forms of testing. The key points listed at the end of Chapter 2 also provide important guidance on how to prepare for a test session. However, as you will see, there are a number of additional tips that can also help.

Tip 1: keep going!

As I have suggested elsewhere, the best policy is to try and complete as many questions as you can in the time allowed. However, you will find that different tests have different time limits. For example, here are the timing ranges for the tests covered in this chapter:

- *Abstract reasoning*   30–40 minutes
- *Verbal reasoning*   15–20 minutes
- *Verbal critical reasoning*   30–40 minutes
- *Numerical reasoning*   15–20 minutes
- *Numerical critical reasoning*   30–40 minutes
- *Perceptual reasoning*   15–20 minutes
- *Spatial reasoning*   10–20 minutes
- *Mechanical reasoning*   15–20 minutes
- *Data checking*   8–10 minutes
- *Manual dexterity*   5–8 minutes

Clearly, while it's good advice not to waste time on questions that you find difficult, you have more scope in some tests than in others to go back to a question you have not answered. As a rule of thumb, if a test is under about 10 minutes long it's better just to answer as

many questions as you can, and not to return to those you may
have left out.

Tip 2: double-check your answers

It is often suggested that when you attempt to answer the questions
in a test that your first impressions are usually correct. This implies
that if you have the time it is better to try and answer any questions
you have left out, rather than change any of your existing answers.
Interestingly, research has shown this to be an incorrect assump-
tion, with one US study indicating that you may be three times as
likely to change a wrong answer to a right one, than to make a right
answer wrong. This suggests that any time you spend double-
checking is time well spent.

Tip 3: guess with intelligence

If you do not know the answer to a question, should you guess? The
two things to consider are how you're going to guess, and whether
or not the test is negatively scored. When tests are negatively scored
you have marks deducted for incorrect answers. This may or may
not be announced at the beginning of the test, but if the instructions
say that you should not guess then it is actually better to leave questions out. Conversely, if the instructions suggest that you should not
leave any questions out, then it is probably safe to guess.

On the subject of how to guess, it is better to guess the answers
to questions about which you have some knowledge. For example,
if there are five options and you can completely eliminate two of
them, you have a one-third chance of hitting the right answer. These
are obviously better odds than a pure guess, which would give you
a one-in-five chance of picking the correct response. However, you
should bear in mind that if you are forced to guess a lot of the
answers, even if you can reduce each to a one-in-three chance,
then you are unlikely to score a very high mark. The reason is that
your chance of correctly guessing the first question is one-in-three,
and of the second question is one-in-three, but of correctly guessing

both of them your chance is one-in-nine (one-third *times* one-third). The more you guess, the worse are the overall odds. Even so, informed guesswork is much better than randomly picking the answers.

Tip 4: read the questions twice

Many people work out the correct answer to a problem and then fill in the answer sheet incorrectly. A common mistake is to mix up the answer choices. Consider the following example:

Example 23: Verbal sequences
What is the next word but one in the following sequence?

Century...   Decade...   Year...   Month...   ?
A. Hour   B. Minute   C. Day   D. Week   E. Second

Answer [   ]

It's easy to look at a question like that and to decide correctly that C is the right answer, but to mark D instead. That's because you have confused 'D' with the first letter of 'day'. Another thing that people do is misread the question. In this case not to notice that the question asks for *the next word but one.* This would mean that while you fully understood the sequence you would answer D again, which of course is incorrect. The moral of the story is always to pay very close attention to the questions, otherwise you will lose marks even when you actually know the correct answers.

Tip 5: estimate your answers

In most numerical tests the questions are usually designed so that you do not have to work out the answers exactly in order to choose the correct responses. This would imply that it is better to work out rough answers and check them against the options rather than spend time calculating things precisely.

Tip 6: don't be afraid of numbers

An ability to deal with numbers is a key requirement in many jobs. If you don't like mathematics the *only* way you are going to improve is to face your fear head on. Go to a library or a bookshop, find a maths book you understand, and work through some examples.

Tip 7: watch out for distractors

When test questions are written the designer will include different types of answer choices. Naturally, one of these will be the correct answer, but the others will be distinct sorts of incorrect answers. Here are some examples:

- If the correct answer is '67.5' a number of 'distractors' will be included such as '6.75', 675 and 6750. The estimation approach suggested in Tip 5 should help you to avoid picking any of these by accident.

- Body is to food as engine is to: A. spark B. wheels C. fuel D. exhaust.
  The correct answer is C, but it's surrounded by distractors, all of which are related to the word 'engine'.

The trick with distractors is to realize that they are there in the first place, and not to be seduced by things like near misses, or word associations.

Tip 8: think about the question order

It makes sense to answer the questions you find the easiest first. This means that it is not always advisable to answer the questions in the order presented. However, if you do adopt this tactic, make sure you do not get out of sequence on the answer sheet. Also, if you read the questions as you go along you will find that your unconscious mind has a chance to work on them, and sometimes you will find it much easier to get the answer when you return for a second time.

Tip 9: use all your time allowance

Even if you are finding a test hard going, use all the time you are allowed, and work right up to the last second. If you finish early double- and triple-check your answers.

Tip 10: practise, practise, practise!

Sometimes a few more marks will make all the difference. It pays to put as much energy as you can into preparing yourself for psychometric tests.

Key points

- There are about 50 different abilities that can be measured, but most assessments are based on combinations of only 6 types of test.

- The most frequently used tests measure abstract, verbal, numerical, perceptual, spatial and mechanical reasoning.

- Other types of test measure psychomotor abilities like hand–eye co-ordination; physical abilities like static strength (the ability to use continuous muscle force to lift, push and carry – important in jobs like firefighting); and sensory abilities, such as correct colour vision (important for designers, electricians, chemists and pilots).

- Each type of ability test has characteristic types of questions. Extensive details have been given in this chapter.

- There are exercises you can do to prepare for any test that is based on knowledge or experience (attainment tests). You can also improve your performance on other types of tests by following the hints provided.

- Preparation is the key to test success. No employer will expect you to be an authority on tests, or test taking, but intelligent preparation in the weeks before a test session will help to give you an edge over the other candidates.

● In those cases where employers use cut-off scores (see Chapter 1), a few extra marks can make the difference between success and failure. Ensure that you do not make avoidable mistakes.

● There are many sources of valuable information and practice material, such as textbooks, quiz books and books containing example questions. These can all be bought in large bookshops, or are available from libraries.

CHAPTER 4

Practice tests (technical, clerical and graduate)

Introduction to SHL® practice tests

This chapter contains three sets of practice tests. These have been supplied by Saville & Holdsworth Ltd and are the type of practice tests you will encounter before a real session. Tests like these are used in selection and assessment, as well as in careers guidance and development.

Each test comes with a set of instructions and a guide to the time you should spend answering the questions. It is important to stick to the suggested times, as this will give you an idea of the pace required for full-length tests of this type.

Series 1 contains six different tests. These are Working with Words, Working with Numbers, Working with Diagrams, Checking Information, Recognizing Shapes and Mechanical Understanding. The first four are basic-level assessments, the shapes and mechanical tests are applicable to all levels of ability.

Series 2 presents three rather harder tests concerned with Interpreting Written Information, Interpreting Data and Interpreting Diagrams. These would be used with candidates who had a good basic level of education.

Series 3 contains the hardest tests and focuses on Verbal Reasoning, Numerical Reasoning and Diagrammatic Reasoning. Tests of this sort are aimed at those with a good post-16 education. The format is also quite typical of graduate-level tests.

The best way to use these practice questions is to start with those that you think are the correct level. When you have completed the appropriate series move on to the others and see how they feel in comparison. The answers are provided at the back of the book.

Series 1

Test 1: working with words

This test looks at your ability to understand written instructions. Use the information given in the passage to answer the questions that follow. For each question, you have to select the correct answer from the five choices given, and fill in the appropriate circle.

Time guideline: See how many questions you can answer in **3 minutes**.

Start when you are ready.

Local drama group

Are you interested in acting? If you are, please come to a meeting about the Amateur Dramatics Society's next play. You don't need any experience of acting – so give it a try! The meeting will take place in the local Community Centre on 10th June between 3 and 5 pm.

We also need about 20 musicians to play music during the play. Musicians do not need to attend the meeting, but should contact Ms Patel at the Community Centre before the 17th June to arrange an audition.

People who are interested in decorating the stage set or providing technical assistance should contact the Amateur Dramatics Society direct.

Rehearsals will take place every Tuesday evening. Performances are planned for the 18th and 30th of August.

1 Who should attend the meeting on the 10th June?

A   Anyone with an interest in acting.

B   About 20 musicians.

C   Only people with experience of acting.

D   Only people without experience of acting.

E   All members of the Amateur Dramatics Society.

2 When will the rehearsals take place?

A   17th June.

B   Every Tuesday evening.

C   18th and 30th August.

D   10th June.

E   None of these.

3 What should any musicians do?

A   Make sure they go to the meeting on the 10th June.

B   Wait for Ms Patel to contact them.

C   Contact the Amateur Dramatics Society.

D   Ring Ms Patel at home.

E   None of these.

Vending machine – operating instructions

To obtain a drink follow these instructions:

- Remove plastic cup from dispenser and place directly under spout for drink required.
- Insert exact coins or tokens available from Reception.
- Press selected button once and wait until spout has completed pouring before lifting safety cover and removing cup.
- Sugar and milk powder can be dispensed without charge by placing cup under appropriate spout and pressing button once or twice as required.

Any faults in operation of machine should be reported immediately to the Maintenance Supervisor. Refunds can then be obtained from Reception.

---

4   What is the first stage in obtaining a drink?

A   Insert the exact coins.

B   Press the selected button.

C   Take a plastic cup from dispenser.

D   Insert the token and press the selected button.

E   Obtain a plastic cup from Reception.

5   What is available free of charge?

A   Only drinks.

B   Only sugar and milk powder.

C   Only plastic cups.

D   Only drinks, sugar and milk powder.

E   Only sugar, milk powder and plastic cups.

6   How can you obtain a refund?

A   By contacting the Maintenance Supervisor.

B   By pressing the 'refund' button.

C   By inserting another token.

D   From Reception (after reporting the fault).

E   None of these.

Answer sheet 1

1 Ⓐ Ⓑ Ⓒ Ⓓ Ⓔ
2 Ⓐ Ⓑ Ⓒ Ⓓ Ⓔ
3 Ⓐ Ⓑ Ⓒ Ⓓ Ⓔ
4 Ⓐ Ⓑ Ⓒ Ⓓ Ⓔ
5 Ⓐ Ⓑ Ⓒ Ⓓ Ⓔ
6 Ⓐ Ⓑ Ⓒ Ⓓ Ⓔ

Test 2: working with numbers

This test looks at your ability to make quick and accurate calculations. Identify the number which should replace the '?' in each question, and fill in the appropriate circle.

Time guideline: See how many questions you can answer in **3 minutes**, without using a calculator.

Start when you are ready.

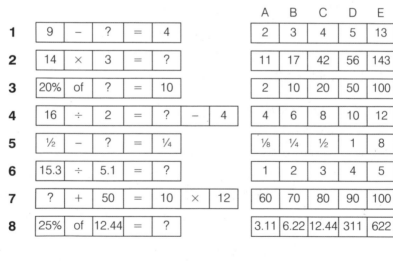

								A	B	C	D	E
1	9	−	?	=	4			2	3	4	5	13
2	14	×	3	=	?			11	17	42	56	143
3	20%	of	?	=	10			2	10	20	50	100
4	16	÷	2	=	?	−	4	4	6	8	10	12
5	½	−	?	=	¼			⅛	¼	½	1	8
6	15.3	÷	5.1	=	?			1	2	3	4	5
7	?	+	50	=	10	×	12	60	70	80	90	100
8	25%	of	12.44	=	?			3.11	6.22	12.44	311	622

Answer sheet 2

1 Ⓐ Ⓑ Ⓒ Ⓓ Ⓔ
2 Ⓐ Ⓑ Ⓒ Ⓓ Ⓔ
3 Ⓐ Ⓑ Ⓒ Ⓓ Ⓔ
4 Ⓐ Ⓑ Ⓒ Ⓓ Ⓔ

5 Ⓐ Ⓑ Ⓒ Ⓓ Ⓔ
6 Ⓐ Ⓑ Ⓒ Ⓓ Ⓔ
7 Ⓐ Ⓑ Ⓒ Ⓓ Ⓔ
8 Ⓐ Ⓑ Ⓒ Ⓓ Ⓔ

Test 3: working with diagrams

This test looks at your ability to follow instructions coded as symbols.

In this test columns of shapes are presented in BOXES. You have to change these shapes using commands that are shown as symbols contained in CIRCLES.

A complete list of these commands and what they do is given below.

Work down the column starting at the top, and change the shapes according to the command symbols given.

Select the answer that would result from applying the commands, and fill in the appropriate circle.

Time guidelines: See how many questions you can answer in **3 minutes**.

Commands

Ⓝ Turn the shape upside down

Ⓩ Remove the contents of this box

Ⓠ Swap the shape in this box with the shape in the box below

Ⓧ Cancel the previous command

Ⓘ Present all shapes in the column in REVERSE order

Start when you are ready.

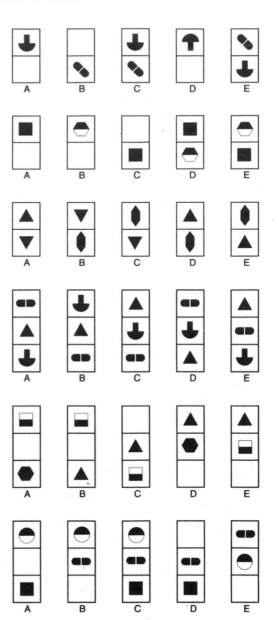

Answer sheet 3

1 Ⓐ Ⓑ Ⓒ Ⓓ Ⓔ
2 Ⓐ Ⓑ Ⓒ Ⓓ Ⓔ
3 Ⓐ Ⓑ Ⓒ Ⓓ Ⓔ
4 Ⓐ Ⓑ Ⓒ Ⓓ Ⓔ
5 Ⓐ Ⓑ Ⓒ Ⓓ Ⓔ
6 Ⓐ Ⓑ Ⓒ Ⓓ Ⓔ

Test 4: checking information

This test looks at your ability to check information quickly and accurately. You are given two lists of reference numbers, the original handwritten list on the left, and the final typed list on the right. You have to look for any differences (errors) between the two lists. Fill in the circle for any column where you find a difference. If there are no differences (errors) in a line, fill in circle E. Remember there can be more than one error in the line, so you may have to fill in more than one circle for a question.

Time guideline: See how many questions you can answer in **2 minutes**.

Start when you are ready.

	A	B	C	D	A	B	C	D
1	12	KT	3D	47–98	22	KT	3D	47–98
2	91	PM	C5	62–64	91	PM	C5	62–64
3	3	AJ	B4	L55–57	3	JA	B4	L51–55
4	17	AM	S5	B7–22	18	PM	S5	B7–12
5	11	ZZ	PO	M9–10	11	ZZ	PO	M9–10
6	89	SR	X8	F14–16	98	XR	Y9	F14–16
7	34	XX	K7	35–38	34	YY	K7	35–39
8	87	KP	M6	A12–13	87	M6	KP	A12–13
9	7	JZ	K2	H8–9	7	JZ	K2	H8–9
10	69	JI	S5	K66–69	96	IJ	5S	K64–66

Answer sheet 4

1 Ⓐ Ⓑ Ⓒ Ⓓ
2 Ⓐ Ⓑ Ⓒ Ⓓ
3 Ⓐ Ⓑ Ⓒ Ⓓ
4 Ⓐ Ⓑ Ⓒ Ⓓ
5 Ⓐ Ⓑ Ⓒ Ⓓ
6 Ⓐ Ⓑ Ⓒ Ⓓ
7 Ⓐ Ⓑ Ⓒ Ⓓ
8 Ⓐ Ⓑ Ⓒ Ⓓ
9 Ⓐ Ⓑ Ⓒ Ⓓ
10 Ⓐ Ⓑ Ⓒ Ⓓ

Test 5: *recognizing shapes*

This test looks at your ability to recognize identical shapes. Study the shape on the left, and after viewing all the choices, decide which of the shapes on the right is the same. Note that while the shapes may be turned around on the page, they are not flipped over.

Time guideline: See how many questions you can answer in **2 minutes**.

Start when you are ready.

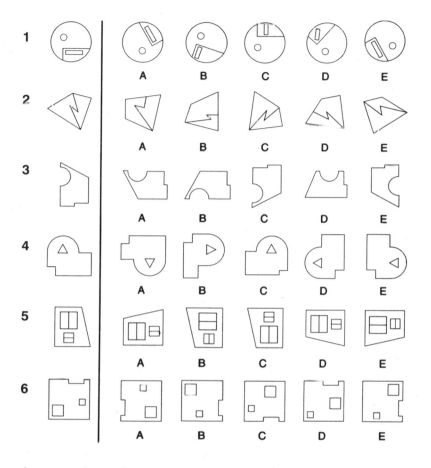

Answer sheet 5

1 Ⓐ Ⓑ Ⓒ Ⓓ Ⓔ
2 Ⓐ Ⓑ Ⓒ Ⓓ Ⓔ
3 Ⓐ Ⓑ Ⓒ Ⓓ Ⓔ
4 Ⓐ Ⓑ Ⓒ Ⓓ Ⓔ
5 Ⓐ Ⓑ Ⓒ Ⓓ Ⓔ
6 Ⓐ Ⓑ Ⓒ Ⓓ Ⓔ

Test 6: mechanical understanding

This test looks at your ability to understand mechanical principles and practical problems. Each problem consists of a question that refers to a drawing. Look at each drawing and answer the question that follows, filling in the appropriate circle on the Answer Sheet panel.

Time guidelines: See how many questions you can answer in **2 minutes**.

Start when you are ready.

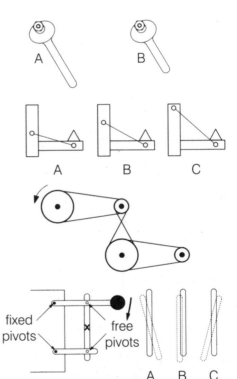

1 Which spanner makes it easier to undo the nut?

If equal, mark C.

2 Which shelf should support the heaviest load?

3 How many pulleys turn clockwise?

A   B   C
1   2   3

4 How will link 'X' move when the handle is operated as shown?

Answer sheet 6

1 Ⓐ Ⓑ Ⓒ
2 Ⓐ Ⓑ Ⓒ
3 Ⓐ Ⓑ Ⓒ
4 Ⓐ Ⓑ Ⓒ

Series 2

Test 1: interpreting written information

This test looks at your ability to understand written passages and evaluate the logic of written argument. The test consists of a series of passages, each of which is followed by several statements. Your task is to evaluate each statement in the light of the passage and to mark the appropriate circle, following the rules given below.

Mark Circle A
if the statement is **TRUE**, given the information or opinions contained in the passage.

Mark Circle B
if the statement is **FALSE**, given the information or opinions contained in the passage.

Mark Circle C
if you **CANNOT SAY** whether the statement is true or false without further information.

The test assesses your ability to reason with written information. It is not a test of your general knowledge and you should only base your answers on the information contained in the passage.

Time guideline: See how many questions you can answer in **5 minutes**.

Start when you are ready.

Many organizations find it beneficial to employ students during the summer. Permanent staff often wish to take their own holidays over this period. Furthermore, it is not uncommon for companies to experience peak workloads in the summer and so require extra staff. Summer employment also attracts students who may return as well-qualified recruits to an organization when they have completed their education. Ensuring that the students learn as much as possible about the organization encourages their interest in working on a permanent basis. Organizations pay students on a fixed rate without the usual entitlement to paid holiday or sick leave.

1   It is possible that permanent staff who are on holiday can have their work carried out by students.

2   Students in summer employment are given the same paid holiday benefits as permanent staff.

3   Students are subject to the organization's standard disciplinary and grievance procedures.

4   Some companies have more work to do in the summer when students are available for vacation work.

Most banks and building societies adopt a 'no smoking' policy in customer areas in their branches. Plaques and stickers are displayed in these areas to draw customers' attention to this policy. These notices are worded in a 'customer friendly' manner, although a few customers may feel their personal freedom of choice is being infringed. If a customer does ignore a notice, staff are tolerant and avoid making a great issue of the situation. In fact, the majority of customers now expect such a 'no smoking' policy in premises of this kind. After all, such a policy improves the pleasantness of the customer facilities and also lessens fire risk.

5   'No smoking' policies have mainly been introduced in response to customer demand.

6   All banks and building societies now have a 'no smoking' policy.

7   There is no conflict of interest between a 'no smoking' policy and personal freedom of choice for all.

8   A 'no smoking' policy is in line with most customers' expectations in banks and building societies.

Answer sheet 1

1   Ⓐ   Ⓑ   Ⓒ
2   Ⓐ   Ⓑ   Ⓒ
3   Ⓐ   Ⓑ   Ⓒ
4   Ⓐ   Ⓑ   Ⓒ
5   Ⓐ   Ⓑ   Ⓒ
6   Ⓐ   Ⓑ   Ⓒ
7   Ⓐ   Ⓑ   Ⓒ
8   Ⓐ   Ⓑ   Ⓒ

Test 2: interpreting data

This test looks at your ability to understand graphs and statistical tables and to draw appropriate conclusions from them. You will be using facts and figures presented in various ways to answer a range of questions. In each question you are given five answers to choose from. One and only one of the answers is correct in each case.

Time guideline: See how many questions you can answer in **5 minutes**.

Start when you are ready.

MACHINE PRODUCTION

1   How many machines were produced in the first three months
    of the period?

A	B	C	D	E
900	1000	1100	1200	None of these

2   If the trend of the last 3 months continues, how many machines
    will be produced in July?

A	B	C	D	E
1100	1200	1300	1400	Cannot say

3   In which month did machine production figures show the
    greatest percentage change, relative to the previous month?

A	B	C	D	E
February	March	April	May	June

4   What was the combined readership of *Home Hints, Travel Plus*
    and *Leisure Time* in 1983 (in millions)? (See page 89.)

A	B	C	D	E
7.2	16.5	20.8	37.3	None of these

5   What percentage of copies of *Computer News* were sold in
    specialist computer shops in 1993?

A	B	C	D	E
12%	34%	42%	66%	Cannot say

MAGAZINE READERSHIP

Magazine title	Estimated no of readers (millions)		Percentage of copies sold in 1993, by outlet:	
	1983	1993	Subscription	Newsagents
Home Hints	4.8	2.4	47%	13%
Business Tomorrow	1.1	1.4	58%	24%
Computer News	2.3	4.6	34%	24%
Travel Plus	8.5	6.1	25%	44%
Leisure Time	7.5	8.0	28%	47%

6   If 1.0 million copies of *Travel Plus* were sold by subscription, how many copies were sold overall in 1993 (in millions)?

A	B	C	D	E
1	2.9	4	6.1	8.5

Answer sheet 2

1 Ⓐ Ⓑ Ⓒ Ⓓ Ⓔ
2 Ⓐ Ⓑ Ⓒ Ⓓ Ⓔ
3 Ⓐ Ⓑ Ⓒ Ⓓ Ⓔ
4 Ⓐ Ⓑ Ⓒ Ⓓ Ⓔ
5 Ⓐ Ⓑ Ⓒ Ⓓ Ⓔ
6 Ⓐ Ⓑ Ⓒ Ⓓ Ⓔ

Test 3: interpreting diagrams

This test looks at your ability to recognize rules within logical sequences, and to apply them to given problems. You are shown a number of diagrams in which figures in **boxes** are altered by commands (letters) in **circles**.

The commands alter a figure by changing its size, colour or shape in general or specific ways.

Paths through each diagram are identified by black or white arrows. You must follow paths that only include one type of arrow.

In this test, you have to work out what each command does and then answer the questions immediately below each diagram.

Now look at the first diagram.

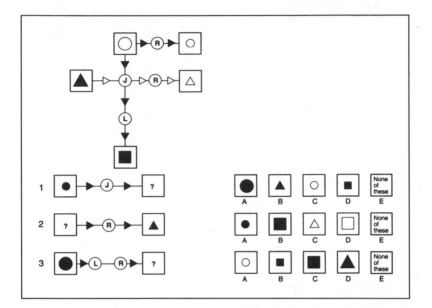

In the first diagram, it can be seen that command **R** reduces the size of the figure in the box; it changes a large circle into a small circle.

Following the white arrows across, we can see that **J** and **R** together, reduce the size of the figure and change its colour, here from black to white.

Since we know that **R** reduces the size of the figure, we can now say that **J** changes its colour.

Working down, **J** and **L** together change the colour, this time from white to black, and also the shape of the figure, from a circle to a square. Having established that **J** changes colour, we can now say that **L** changes the shape of a figure.

Now applying these commands to the first question, we have seen that **J** changes the colour of the figure, therefore producing a small white circle, answer C.

In question 2, **R** reduces the size of a figure, so we can say that what is missing is a large black triangle, answer E.

In question 3, **L** changes the circle into a square, and **R** reduces its size, so the result is a small black square, answer B.

Now, make sure that you understand these answers and then go on and do the next set of questions, 4 to 6, by yourself.

Time guideline: See if you can do Questions 4 to 6 in **3 minutes**.

Start when you are ready.

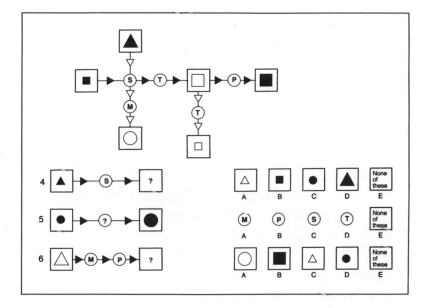

Answer sheet 3

1 Ⓐ Ⓑ Ⓒ Ⓓ Ⓔ
2 Ⓐ Ⓑ Ⓒ Ⓓ Ⓔ
3 Ⓐ Ⓑ Ⓒ Ⓓ Ⓔ
4 Ⓐ Ⓑ Ⓒ Ⓓ Ⓔ
5 Ⓐ Ⓑ Ⓒ Ⓓ Ⓔ
6 Ⓐ Ⓑ Ⓒ Ⓓ Ⓔ

Series 3

Test 1: verbal reasoning

This test looks at your ability to understand and reason with written information. The test consists of a series of passages, each of which is followed by several statements. Your task is to evaluate each statement in the light of the passage which precedes it and to mark the appropriate circle, following the rules given below.

Mark Circle A

if the statement is **TRUE** or follows logically, given the information or opinions contained in the passage.

Mark Circle B

if the statement is **FALSE** or the opposite follows logically, given the information or opinions contained in the passage.

Mark Circle C

if you **CANNOT SAY** whether the statement is true or false without further information.

This test is not a test of your general knowledge and you should only base your answers on the information contained in the passage.

Time guideline: See how many questions you can answer in **5 minutes**.

Start when you are ready.

A principal objective of the Health and Safety at Work Act 1974 is to involve everybody in the workplace. The promotion of health and safety is an essential function of good management in all areas. The employer, however, also has a duty to protect other persons on the premises. The term 'premises' includes all workplaces, and in particular, includes any vehicle, vessel, aircraft, or any other installation on land. Regulations may be made exempting certain employers from the necessity to provide all employees with written copies of the Act.

1   The Health and Safety Act is the sole responsibility of the employee.

2   All installations on land, and vehicles are subsumed under the heading 'premises'.

3   The Act states that all employees must receive written copies.

4   There were no health and safety rules before 1974.

The government has attempted to integrate the environmental clean-up of industry under one umbrella. To minimize environmental damage, the volume of pollutants emitted from a plant has to be authorized by an official pollution control inspectorate. Industry has complained repeatedly about the time and cost of getting operations approved under the new system. The inspectors maintain, however, that industry often has itself to blame for delays, as many applications provide insufficient data. Industry has also worried about public access to the information it supplies to get authorization. Information can only be withheld from public registers on the grounds of commercial confidentiality, if a company can prove it would be disadvantaged by disclosure.

5   The new pollution control system was set up to reduce the number of toxins used by industry.

6   Obtaining authorization on operations results in having to divulge confidential information to competitors.

7   Industry has not welcomed the introduction of the official pollution control inspectorate.

8   There would be no environmental destruction if there were no pollutants.

Answer sheet 1

1   Ⓐ   Ⓑ   Ⓒ
2   Ⓐ   Ⓑ   Ⓒ
3   Ⓐ · Ⓑ   Ⓒ
4   Ⓐ   Ⓑ   Ⓒ
5   Ⓐ   Ⓑ   Ⓒ
6   Ⓐ   Ⓑ   Ⓒ
7   Ⓐ   Ⓑ   Ⓒ
8   Ⓐ   Ⓑ   Ⓒ

Test 2: numerical reasoning

This test looks at your ability to understand facts and figures presented in various ways and to draw appropriate conclusions from them. You should base your answers only on the information contained in the tables and graphs and not on any prior knowledge. In each question you are given five answers to choose from. One and only one of the answers is correct in each case. You can use a calculator to help you.

Time guideline: See how many questions you can answer in **5 minutes**.

Start when you are ready.

NEWSPAPER READERSHIP

	Readership (millions)		Percentage of copies sold in Year 2, by outlet:	
Daily newspapers	Year 1	Year 2	Subscription	Newsagents
The Daily Chronicle	3.6	2.9	47%	37%
The Daily News	14.8	10.0	50%	33%
The Tribune	1.1	1.4	43%	43%
The Herald	8.4	10.9	29%	55%
The Daily Echo	4.8	4.9	30%	60%

1   What was the combined readership of *The Daily Chronicle*, *The Tribune* and *The Daily Echo* in Year 2 (in millions)?

A	B	C	D	E
9.2	9.5	18.7	31.8	None of these

2   Which Daily Newspaper showed the largest percentage change in readership from Year 1 to Year 2?

A	B	C	D	E
The Daily Chronicle	The Daily News	The Tribune	The Herald	The Daily Echo

3   If 4.5 million copies of *The Daily News* were sold by Subscription, approximately how many copies (in millions) were sold by Newsagents in Year 2?

A	B	C	D	E
1.5	2.3	3	6	Cannot say

4   What was the selling price for Mountain Bikes if the sales income for this product was £140,000 in January? (See chart below.)

A	B	C	D	E
300	350	400	450	500

RENAISSANCE CYCLE COMPANY

5 What was the percentage increase in the selling price of Racers between January and June?

A	B	C	D	E
0%	10%	20%	50%	Cannot say

6 If Racers sell for twice as much as Mountain Bikes, in which month was the total sales income highest?

A	B	C	D	E
February	March	April	May	June

Answer sheet 2

1 Ⓐ Ⓑ Ⓒ Ⓓ Ⓔ
2 Ⓐ Ⓑ Ⓒ Ⓓ Ⓔ
3 Ⓐ Ⓑ Ⓒ Ⓓ Ⓔ
4 Ⓐ Ⓑ Ⓒ Ⓓ Ⓔ
5 Ⓐ Ⓑ Ⓒ Ⓓ Ⓔ
6 Ⓐ Ⓑ Ⓒ Ⓓ Ⓔ

Test 3: diagrammatic reasoning

This test looks at your ability to recognize rules within logical sequences, and to apply them to given problems. You are shown a number of diagrams in which figures in **boxes** are altered by commands (symbols) in **circles**.

The commands alter a figure by changing its size, colour or shape in general or specific ways.

Paths through each diagram are identified by black or white arrows. You must follow paths that only include one type of arrow.

In this test, you have to work out what each command does and then answer the questions immediately below each diagram.

Now look at the first diagram.

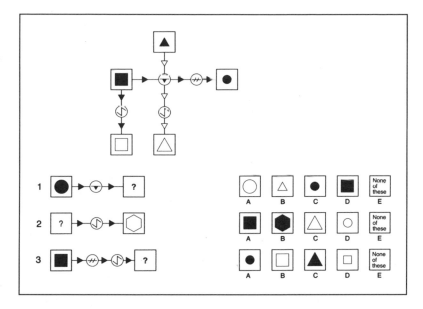

Working down from the black square in the first diagram, it can be seen that command ⓓ changes a black square into a white square.

Following the white arrows down, we can see that the two commands ⓥ and ⓓ together, increase the size of a triangle, and **also** change its colour from black to white.

We already know that ⓓ changes the colour of the figure; therefore ⓥ must change its size, here from small to large.

Working across, ⓥ and ⓦ together **reduce** the size of the figure and also change its shape, from a square to a circle. We can now say that ⓥ **reverses** the size of the figure, therefore ⓦ changes its shape.

Now applying these commands to the first question, we have seen that ⓥ reverses the size of the figure therefore producing a small black circle, answer C.

In question 2, ⓓ changes the colour of a figure from black to white, so we can say that the missing figure is a large black hexagon, answer B.

In question 3, ⊕ changes the square into a circle, and ⊕ changes its colour from black to white. The result is a large white circle, answer E.

Time guideline: See if you can do Questions 4 to 6 in **3 minutes**. Start when you are ready.

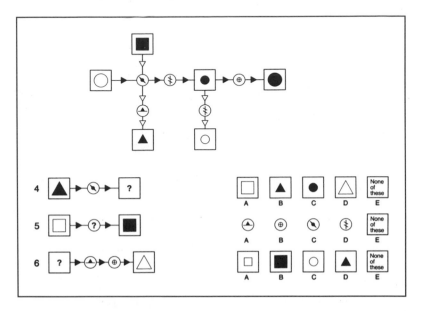

Answer sheet 3

1 Ⓐ Ⓑ Ⓒ Ⓓ Ⓔ
2 Ⓐ Ⓑ Ⓒ Ⓓ Ⓔ
3 Ⓐ Ⓑ Ⓒ Ⓓ Ⓔ
4 Ⓐ Ⓑ Ⓒ Ⓓ Ⓔ
5 Ⓐ Ⓑ Ⓒ Ⓓ Ⓔ
6 Ⓐ Ⓑ Ⓒ Ⓓ Ⓔ

CHAPTER 5

Practice tests (graduate and university admissions)

Introduction to Team Focus practice tests

Team Focus Ltd are a firm of occupational psychologists that specialize in the development of online assessment tests and questionnaires. Over the last few years they have designed an impressive range of ability and personality tests and other measures that are all available via the internet. These tests and questionnaires are used by employers and universities for selection and development purposes. For example, it is useful to know how your thinking skills compare with those of other job applicants or potential students, or to explore learning style and career preferences.

Each of the online tests and questionnaires on offer takes about 15 minutes to complete, and results are returned instantly by e-mail. The following section includes some genuine practice material from Team Focus for you to try, with the answers provided at the end of the book. The tests look at abstract, verbal and numerical reasoning.

It is rare for test publishers to offer 'open' access to a range of full-length, professionally developed tests and questionnaires. If you would like to complete the actual tests and questionnaires, they can be accessed easily at **www.profilingforsuccess.com**; or if you are interested in university entrance tests, at **www.drtest.co.uk**. You can complete a single test or questionnaire, or a combination.

It is also possible to complete a 'taster' assessment that has been devised to go with this book. If you would like to try this free test, which includes a feedback report, go to **www.profilingforsuccess.com/kogan-page**.

Practice material

Test 1: abstract reasoning

The abstract reasoning items look at your ability to identify relationships between shapes. This ability is related to skills such as generating ideas and problem-solving.

For each set of items you will see two sets of shapes, labelled Set A and Set B. All of the shapes in Set A are similar in some way, as are the shapes in Set B. Set A and Set B are not related to each other.

You have to work out how the shapes in each set are related to each other. You then have to work out whether each of six further shapes belongs to Set A, Neither set, or Set B.

Time guideline: See how many questions you can do in **4 minutes**.

Start when you are ready.

3

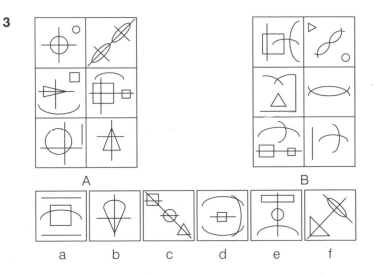

A   B

a   b   c   d   e   f

Answer sheet

	Mark the correct answer		
1a	Set A	Neither	Set B
1b	Set A	Neither	Set B
1c	Set A	Neither	Set B
1d	Set A	Neither	Set B
1e	Set A	Neither	Set B
1f	Set A	Neither	Set B
2a	Set A	Neither	Set B
2b	Set A	Neither	Set B
2c	Set A	Neither	Set B
2d	Set A	Neither	Set B
2e	Set A	Neither	Set B
2f	Set A	Neither	Set B
3a	Set A	Neither	Set B
3b	Set A	Neither	Set B
3c	Set A	Neither	Set B
3d	Set A	Neither	Set B
3e	Set A	Neither	Set B
3f	Set A	Neither	Set B

Test 2: verbal reasoning

The verbal reasoning items test your ability to think logically about written information. Below are passages of text, each followed by five statements. Your task is to read carefully each passage and then decide whether each statement follows logically from the information in the passage.

For each statement there are three options to choose from: True, False and Can't Tell.

- *True* – this means that, on the basis of the information in the passage, the statement is true or logically follows from the passage.

- *False* – this means that, on the basis of the information in the passage, the statement is false.

- *Can't tell* – this means that you cannot tell from the information in the passage whether the information is true or false.

When deciding whether a statement is true, false or you cannot tell, it is important to base your answer only on the information in the passage and not on any other knowledge you may have. Your task is simply to judge whether or not the statement follows logically from the passage.

Time guideline: See how many questions you can do in **4 minutes**.

Circle the correct answers and start when you are ready.

1   Want to find out more about flying? ... then join our cabin crew

You don't have to sign up for life – initially you start on a fixed-term contract, beginning with a comprehensive training programme which gives you a chance to see if this is really for you. To join us, you will need to demonstrate a high level of personal presentation, excellent communication skills and the ability to recognize, identify and respond to individual customer needs. Age doesn't matter – as long as you're over 20 and under 60 – but you must be fit, resilient and well-organized. So, if you enjoy using your initiative and welcome the chance to acquire new skills, this is the opportunity for you.

A. Before you join the airline, you must be sure that this is the right occupation for you.

B. This job requires some good 'people skills'.

C. The advert tells you how to apply to join the airline's cabin crew.

D. Age is not a factor in the airline's selection criteria.

E. The airline selects cabin crew at the end of the training programme.

2   Directions for taking cough medicine

Adults and children over 12 years: Two 5 ml spoonfuls four times a day.

Children 6–12 years: One 5 ml spoonful four times a day.

Children 2–5 years: One 5 ml spoonful twice a day.

X   Not to be given to children under 2 years.

X   Avoid alcoholic drink.

X   Do not exceed the stated dose.

A. An adult should take 40 ml of the cough medicine per day.

B. Alcohol prevents the cough medicine from working.

C. A child of 7 can take the cough medicine as often as an adult.

D. If taken as directed, the cough medicine has no side effects.

E. Adults and children over 12 can take twice the daily amount of cough medicine as children aged 2–5 years.

3   Pennywise Bank has written the following letter to its customers:

I am writing to let you know that the interest we pay on your Super Savings account has been reduced. You will find the new rate in the enclosed leaflet. The leaflet gives the interest rates for all our investment accounts as well as the previous rates which applied.

As you know, we always write to tell you whenever we change the interest rate on your account because we are committed to the Banking Code. This voluntary code sets standards of good practice for banks and building societies in dealings with their personal customers. As well as writing to you, we will continue to use national newspapers to advertise rates on all our accounts, and we will display this information in your local branch.

A. Banks and building societies must abide by the Banking Code.

B. Pennywise Bank has reduced the interest rates on all its investment accounts.

C. The Banking Code does not apply to the bank's business customers.

D. You can find out how much interest Pennywise Bank charges on personal loans from the leaflet enclosed with this letter.

E. From the information leaflet, you could calculate the overall change in interest rate on your Super Savings account.

Answer sheet

	Mark the correct answer		
1A	True	False	Can't tell
1B	True	False	Can't tell
1C	True	False	Can't tell
1D	True	False	Can't tell
1E	True	False	Can't tell
2A	True	False	Can't tell
2B	True	False	Can't tell

2C	True	False	Can't tell
2D	True	False	Can't tell
2E	True	False	Can't tell
3A	True	False	Can't tell
3B	True	False	Can't tell
3C	True	False	Can't tell
3D	True	False	Can't tell
3E	True	False	Can't tell

Test 3: numerical reasoning

The numerical reasoning items look at your ability to solve numerical problems. For each set of items you will see some numerical information. Below this are five questions, each followed by five possible answer options, labelled 'a', 'b', 'c', 'd' and 'e'.

Work out the correct answer using the numerical information provided, then select one of the five options. Please note that you should not use a calculator for this test.

Time guideline: See how many you can do in **4 minutes**.

Circle the correct answers and start when you are ready.

1 The table below shows the annual cost of breakdown cover with two motoring organizations. The figures are given in pounds.

	Motoring organization	
Type of cover	**Blue Star**	**Green Arrow**
Gold	75	90
Silver	65	60
Bronze	40	30

A. Next year, you intend to change from Blue Star Silver to Green Arrow Bronze cover. How much will you save?

a) £5　　b) £10　　c) £25　　d) £30　　e) £35

B. Green Arrow offer 10% discount on the total cost of cover if you take out breakdown cover for more than one car. What is the cost of having two cars with Green Arrow Bronze cover?

a) £46   b) £54   c) £60   d) £66   e) £72

C. Three members of a family share equally the cost of Silver cover for one car with Green Arrow. How much does each person pay?

a) £20   b) £25   c) £30   d) £60   e) £180

D. What is the ratio of the cost of Silver cover with Green Arrow to Gold cover with Green Arrow?

a) 1:3   b) 2:3   c) 3:2   d) 2:1   e) 3:1

E. If the cost of Blue Star Bronze cover increases to £50, what percentage increase is this?

a) 10%   b) 20%   c) 25%   d) 50%   e) Can't tell

2   The letters p to u are used to represent coins as shown:

p	1p
q	2p
r	5p
s	10p
t	20p
u	50p

A. How much is p + q + r + t?

a) 17p   b) 18p   c) 19p   d) 20p   e) 28p

B. How much is 5u + s?

a) 35p   b) 65p   c) 100p   d) 260p   e) 300p

C. How much is (s + t)/5?

a) 2p   b) 4p   c) 6p   d) 14p   e) 35p

D. What is the value of $2u/(r + t)$?

a) 2p   b) 4p   c) 5p   d) 20p   e) 40p

E. If $z = p + q + r + s$, which of the following is true?

a) $t = z$ b) $t > z$ and $t - z > 5p$ c) $t > z$ and $t - z < 5p$

d) $t < z$ and $t - z > 5p$ e) $t < z$ and $t - z < 5p$

3 Two surveys were conducted, asking people which political party they would vote for. The results are shown in the table below.

	Survey A	Survey B
Party 1	48,000	16,000
Party 2	36,000	22,000
Party 3	6,000	2,500
Party 4	2,000	6,000
Don't Know	8,000	3,500

A. In Survey A, what is the ratio of those intending to vote for Party 1 to those who responded 'Don't know'?

a) 12:1   b) 8:1   c) 6:1   d) 5:1   e) 4:1

B. In Survey B, what is the difference in the number of people intending to vote for Party 2 and Party 4?

a) 3,500   b) 14,000   c) 16,000   d) 19,500   e) 30,000

C. In Survey B, what percentage of people said they would vote for Party 3?

a) 5%   b) 10%   c) 15%   d) 20%   e) Can't tell

D. What is the difference between the two surveys in the percentage of people intending to vote for Party 4?

a) 2%   b) 4%   c) 8%   d) 10%   e) 12%

E.   Which party is in the lead according to the survey results?

   a) Party 1   b) Party 2   c) Party 3   d) Party 4   e) Can't tell

Answer sheet

	Mark the correct answer				
1A	a	b	c	d	e
1B	a	b	c	d	e
1C	a	b	c	d	e
1D	a	b	c	d	e
1E	a	b	c	d	e
2A	a	b	c	d	e
2B	a	b	c	d	e
2C	a	b	c	d	e
2D	a	b	c	d	e
2E	a	b	c	d	e
3A	a	b	c	d	e
3B	a	b	c	d	e
3C	a	b	c	d	e
3D	a	b	c	d	e
3E	a	b	c	d	e

University admissions tests

One of the growth areas for psychometric testing is in university admissions. This is a result of the enormous increase in popularity of some university courses, coupled with the increasing number of candidates who achieve top grades in their examinations. To put this in perspective, over the last five years the number of students applying to study medicine has increased by 88 per cent. And for medicine, and for that matter, dentistry, this means that the ratio of applications to acceptance is now approaching 10:1. Other courses such as veterinary science, law, and Oxbridge history, mathematics, physics and modern languages are also highly competitive.

The consequence is that admissions tests like the UK Clinical Aptitude Test (UKCAT), BioMedical Aptitude Test (BMAT) and Law National Admissions Test (LNAT), plus various Oxford and Cambridge tests, like the Thinking Skills Assessment (TSA), have been introduced. The results from these tests are used alongside other information, such as examination grades and personal statements, to make more balanced selection decisions.

The tests are designed to measure a variety of things. Some have an attainment component and rely on knowledge of a particular subject. For example, one of the questions in the BMAT practice paper is based on a diagram of the blood flow between the major organs of the human body. The task is to determine the path of the blood passing from the kidneys to the liver. Other tests, like the LNAT, have an essay section. In this you are asked to address a question such as: Sport is 'war minus the shooting'. Do you agree?

However what all these tests have in common is a critical thinking component. Indeed, the main part of the UKCAT is composed of four critical thinking sub-tests. What this means is that if you are to prepare for most university admissions tests it is wise to practise with the same sort of tests that are used to select graduates for jobs. Use the example tests in this book and visit some of the websites listed in Chapter 7.

Also, to give you an idea of what to expect, try the example test that follows. The questions are from the TSA which is used by many colleges at Cambridge University to help select students for computer science, natural sciences, engineering and economics courses.

Thinking Skills Assessment

What follows are six questions from the TSA demonstration test. For each question, five possible answers, A, B, C, D and E, are provided. Choose the **one** answer you consider is correct and record your choice on the answer sheet at the end of the section.

Time guideline: See how many questions you can do in **10 minutes**.

Start when you are ready.

1   Every motorist pays the same amount for road tax, regardless of how much they use the roads: someone who covers as little as 1,000 miles pays the same as someone who covers 20,000. This is unfair. Road tax should be scrapped and the money raised by an increase in the tax on car fuel. Making this change would ensure that those who use the roads more would pay more. This would not only be a fairer system, but could also bring in more revenue.

   Which of the following best illustrates the principle underlying the argument above?

   A. People should receive free medical treatment only if they cannot afford to pay for it.

   B. People who travel to work every day by train should pay a lower fare than those who travel only occasionally.

   C. People who earn more than double the average wage should be made to pay much higher charges for dental treatment.

   D. Television channels should be paid for by subscription so that only those people who watch them should be made to pay.

   E. Telephone charges should be higher for business customers than for domestic customers because they are using the system only to make money.

2   When a sky diver leaves the aircraft, they fall faster and faster until they reach a maximum steady speed known as terminal velocity. The sky diver falls at this speed until the parachute opens. The parachute slows them down until a much smaller steady speed is reached. This speed remains constant until the sky diver touches the ground.

Which of these graphs could show this information?

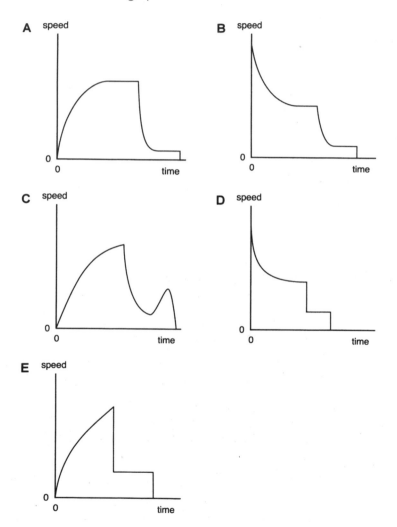

3   Jonathan is planning to use a 10 acre field to supply winter silage for his cattle and hay for his sheep. He reckons to get 100 bales of hay from each acre. Before cutting the hay he will first cut an acre round the edge of the field as silage – this allows him to manoeuvre his hay making machinery. After making his hay in June he will cut the whole field as second cut silage in August and again as third cut silage in September. His farm manual provides the following information.

	As silage	**As hay**
First cut	7 bales per acre	100 small bales per acre
Second cut	5 bales per acre	Not applicable
Third cut	4 bales per acre	Not applicable

How many bales of silage will Jonathan have at the end of his harvest?

A. 16

B. 90

C. 97

D. 157

E. 160

4   Tanya has 2 pigs. She estimates the weight of one as being 85 kg and the other as about 72 kg. She has ready access to a cheap source of potatoes but wishes to feed her pigs a 50/50 nutritional mix of potatoes and meal. Two tables from her feed book are reproduced below.

State of pig	Amount of meal to feed each day (for feeding meal alone)	Nutritional equivalents to 1 kg of meal	
80 kg – bacon weight	2.5 kg	Carrots	8 kg
60 kg–80 kg	2.0 kg	Comfrey	5 kg
50 kg–60 kg	1.8 kg	Grass	5 kg
40 kg–50 kg	1.6 kg	Kale	7 kg
30 kg–40 kg	1.4 kg	Potatoes	5 kg
20 kg–30 kg	1.0 kg	Skim milk	6 litres
Weaners: 8–10 weeks	Up to 1.0 kg	Swedes	8 kg
Weaners: 6 weeks to weaning	250–350 g	Whey	9–10 kg

How much meal should Tanya feed her pigs each day?

A. 2.25 kg

B. 2.50 kg

C. 4.50 kg

D. 11.25 kg

E. 22.50 kg

5   Ever since Uranus was discovered in 1781, astronomers have thought there might be more planets to be discovered in the Solar System. Because of small deviations in the orbits of Uranus and Neptune – deviations which would occur if another planet existed – some astronomers think there must be an undiscovered planet – Planet X. But the search for Planet X is futile, because these deviations would occur if the orbits had been wrongly predicted. Since Uranus and Neptune take many decades to circle the sun, astronomers must rely on old data in order to calculate their orbits. If this data is inaccurate, the calculated orbits are wrong. If the calculated orbits are wrong, Uranus and Neptune will deviate from them even if there is no Planet X.

Which of the following is the best statement of the flaw in the argument above?

A. From the fact that the old data is inaccurate, it cannot be inferred that the calculated orbits are wrong.

B. From the fact that the data about the orbits is old it cannot be inferred that it is inaccurate.

C. From the fact that deviations occur which would occur if Planet X existed, it cannot be inferred that Planet X exists.

D. From the fact that the calculated orbits are wrong, it cannot be inferred that Uranus and Neptune will deviate from them.

E. From the fact that Planet X has not been discovered, it cannot be inferred that the search for it is futile.

6   The diagram shows a square piece of paper with identical semicircles cut out half way along three of its edges.

Which of the following is not a possible view of the paper after it has been folded along one of the dotted lines?

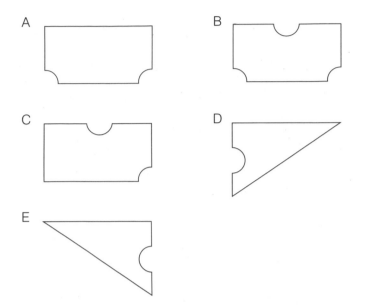

Answer sheet

	Mark the correct answer				
1	A	B	C	D	E
2	A	B	C	D	E
3	A	B	C	D	E
4	A	B	C	D	E
5	A	B	C	D	E
6	A	B	C	D	E

From the Thinking Skills Assessment (*www.tsa.cambridgeassessment.org.uk*).
Reprinted by permission of the University of Cambridge Local Examinations Syndicate.

CHAPTER 6

Personality questionnaires

Personality, like ability, is a key influence on how a person performs at work. It's particularly important in all those situations that involve interaction and co-operation with other people; namely all managerial, supervisory, customer oriented, team or group based activities.

Personality is usually measured by using a self-report questionnaire. This is a 'test' that directly asks *you* about aspects of your own personality, allowing for a consistent and objective measure of things like how you cope with pressure, your preferred way of dealing with other people and your general behavioural style. In this way personality is really the characteristic way in which you respond to situations, or your preferred way of behaving in particular circumstances, or towards other people.

It has recently been estimated that there are 1,200 self-report questionnaires on the UK market alone, and that they are used by over 50 per cent of medium- to large-sized organizations. Their popularity is no doubt due to the speedy and objective way in which they can give a detailed picture of what a person is like, and the ease with which this 'profile' can be matched against the *behavioural* requirements of a job. However, whatever the use, it's important that the aspect of personality that is measured is genuinely part of you, rather than merely the consequence of a particular situation; and also something that allows predictions to be made across a range of different activities. For example, knowing that you are an extrovert, but that you behave in completely different ways in different social situations, wouldn't be of much use.

Another critical thing about personality is that it does not change dramatically over time. This does not mean that it never changes, rather that it's stable enough to be measured in a meaningful way. Again, it wouldn't be very useful to ask you to complete a questionnaire one day, only to get a completely different result if you did the same questionnaire a week later. This is obviously rather important from an employer's point of view as employment is a long-term business. As such it's valuable to know how you are likely to behave over the months and years you will be with a particular organization, not just on the day you happen to have been tested.

To summarize, personality questionnaires are a standard and objective way of discovering your preferred ways of behaving and relating to other people. They allow an employer to see if you fit the behavioural requirements of a particular job; or, conversely, if you're already in a job, to identify your training and development needs. From a purely selfish point of view they also allow you to 'choose' work that better suits you temperamentally, and which you will find more interesting and satisfying.

Different personality questionnaires

There are many different designs of personality questionnaire, but the vast majority fall into only one of two psychological camps. These are those that assign you to a specific personality *type*, and those that are based on a *trait* approach – a trait being an aspect of personality that you possess to a lesser or greater extent.

Type questionnaires

There are a number of commonly used personality questionnaires that are based on a type approach, yet they all owe their basic structure to the work of the Swiss psychologist Carl Jung. He developed a theory to describe the *predictable* differences between the ways in which people behave in different situations. The crux of his argument was that the variations in our behaviour are caused by the way we prefer to use our minds. The use of the word 'prefer' is important here because the Jungian approach is rooted in an either/or way of looking at personality, ie you take this approach *or* that approach, not a bit of both.

In terms of preference, the two options we have when our minds are active are to receive information (perceiving), or to process it and come to a decision (judging). Moreover, if the focus is on perceiving, then there are only two ways of taking on board information, sensing and intuition; likewise, judging splits into thinking and feeling. Thus, there are four key processes that we use to understand the world around us, the only further modification being our orientation towards the world, either extroverted or introverted. The former shows a concern for social interaction with other people, and a desire to understand and experience the world at large. The latter shows a fascination for the 'inner world' of thinking, feeling and reflecting.

To summarize, the type approach allows your personality preferences to be expressed on 4 double-ended scales, giving a total of 16 main types. However, that's not to say that you're 'stuck' with one of 16 particular ways of behaving, rather that you have a natural and comfortable way of behaving. An analogy that is often used is that of having to write with your 'wrong' hand. If you do this it feels unnatural and clumsy, and requires concentration, whereas if you use your preferred hand your writing is automatic and you don't have to think about it. In the same way we all have a definite preference, say, for perceiving or judging; and if we are able to use our preferred approach we are generally more confident *and* competent.

This method of personality classification does not imply that there are 'good' or 'bad' personalities. Thus, 'extrovert' does not equal 'good with other people', or 'introvert' 'shy' and 'retiring'. People simply differ in their approaches and, if you happen to have a similar approach to another person, you will tend to share similar sorts of behaviours and attitudes. These may be more or less useful, strengths or limitations, depending on what you are trying to do. The other thing to realize is that type can be independent of ability, in that the sort of 'intelligence' you have does not dictate the sort of person you are.

The type approach is mostly used in an intrapersonal sense, that is for development and exploration of the self. It can also be used to select people for jobs, but usually only if the questionnaire is designed so that direct comparisons can be made between people in terms of the *amounts* of particular characteristics they possess (a normative approach – see Chapter 1). This being said, question-naires based on the type system are completed by millions of people every year. In consequence it makes sense to spend a little more time exploring the 'preferences' in more detail.

Extroversion–introversion

Extroverted people are concerned with the world that surrounds them. They like to interact with other people, and are fond of talking and debating. In social situations they tend to take the initiative, and to search out other people. However, sometimes their enthusiasm leads them to say things without thinking, and they may inadvert-ently hurt others. In a work context, extroverts are active and people oriented; and they do not like slow, repetitive jobs.

Those who are introverted tend to be more involved in their own private world. They like to analyse what they are going to say before they say it, and may prefer to communicate in writing. There is a 'self-contained' air to their dealings with other people, and they may sometimes be regarded as being a little too cool and detached. At work introverts need quiet so that they can concentrate (they don't like open-plan offices), and are quite happy to work alone.

Judging-perceiving

Those who prefer a judging style live in a structured and orderly way. They like to have plans and schedules, and work to a time-table. Their whole life is organized, controlled, and executed in a precise manner. In the workplace they need order and a plan of action, and work best when they can organize their time thoroughly. They also like to follow a task through to an obvious and tangible conclusion.

In contrast the perceiving person reacts in a flexible and spontaneous manner, and adapts to what is going on rather than attempting to control it. This casual approach often manifests itself in last-minute planning and an 'open-ended' approach to life. Unlike the judging person, the perceiver feels positively claustrophobic if things are planned to the last detail. At work this can cause problems, especially with jobs that need to be completed within tight deadlines. However, many perceiving people would claim that they produce their best work at the eleventh hour!

Sensing-intuition

This aspect of personality is concerned with how you prefer to receive information, with sensing people concentrating on the information that flows from their senses of sight, hearing, taste, touch and smell. Such people are usually practically oriented and assess things in a step-by-step way. They tend to trust what they sense, and are rooted in the 'here and now'. In the work context, this manifests itself in a preference for dealing with facts, and sensing people can usually be relied upon to be right about matters of detail.

The intuitive person has a more abstract approach and is interested in the interconnections between things, not necessarily the things themselves. The concern is more with the 'big picture' and how information fits together in different patterns. Indeed, the truly intuitive person may be particularly good at developing new insights and working out different ways of doing things. From a work point of view this means that intuitive types tend to follow their noses, and may actually overlook certain facts. There is also a tendency to work in short, inspirational bursts, rather than make steady, continuous progress.

Thinking–feeling

A preference for thinking indicates a detached and logical approach to problem solving. The style is characterized by the search for cause and effect, and a reduction of situations to their component parts. There is little room for fancy, and such an analytic and impersonal style is perhaps best described as 'scientific' (and for fans of the TV programme *Star Trek* is perhaps most akin to the Vulcan objectivity of Mr Spock). At work the thinker is firm minded and principled, but may tend to overlook the human side of things.

In stark contrast the feeling person bases decisions on their likely impact on other people. The mentality is one of identifying with the thoughts and feelings of others, and of adopting the most sympathetic approach. This is sometimes described as 'tender-mindedness', as the aim of any action is to take the most compassionate line. Thus, feeling individuals are distinguished by their understanding and supportive style, and are usually driven by a strong sense of the value of the individual. In a work scenario this translates into a desire to please other people, and to ensure a harmonious working environment.

Questionnaire formats

The questions in a personality questionnaire can be presented in a number of different ways. A format that is often used in type questionnaires is one that forces you to choose between two options, or to rank a number of statements in terms of how true they are of you.

Example 1: Forced choice
Do you prefer to:

A.   plan what you do in advance; or

B.   react to things as they happen?

If you answered B to the above question you would be saying that you like to wait and see what happens rather than organize yourself before events. That's because the two parts of the question score on different personality scales. However, the big problem with this approach is that you have not been able to indicate how true you believe *either* of the statements to be. In reality you may be neither very organized nor very reactive; indeed you may be a combination of both depending on the circumstances. What this means is that tests constructed in this way can only broadly comment on you as an individual; and they cannot (unless used very judiciously) be applied to selection situations. The following example should make this point even clearer.

Example 2: Ranking
Rank in order of interest, 1 to 3, the following sports:

Golf   [   ]
Football   [   ]
Tennis   [   ]

Supposing we both answered *Example 2*, we might both order the sports (1) Tennis, (2) Golf, (3) Football. However, in practice, you might be a professional tennis player and a keen golfer, and I might just enjoy watching them all on the television. So what this sort of approach cannot do is show the strength and application of a particular interest or, in the personality sense, the different amounts of a particular characteristic. This is a very important consideration for employers who are interested in the relative balance of characteristics between potential employees.

How are type questionnaires used?

Type questionnaires are widely used in organizations for development and training purposes. They can help to show the sort of environments in which people prefer to work, the way in which they are likely to go about their work, and the ideal personality of any colleagues with whom they would work best. This last concern has become more important in recent years with the increase in work teams, groups or cells. Indeed, the team approach is now common in most areas of employment from manufacturing plants, such as those producing cars and aircraft, to retail businesses like banks, supermarkets and shops.

By far the most widely used type questionnaire is the *Myers–Briggs Type Indicator*® (*MBTI*®), with over 3.5 million people taking it throughout the world each year. It is published by Consulting Psychologist Press Inc in the USA, and is also available from Oxford Psychologists Press in the UK. Other type questionnaires include the *Type Dynamics Indicator* from Team Focus Ltd, the *Jung Type Indicator*, published by Psytech International Ltd, and the *Occupational Type Profile* produced by Selby Mills Ltd.

Trait questionnaires

Trait questionnaires are concerned with the differing amounts of personality characteristics that all people possess. So these questionnaires are designed to measure how much of a certain trait you possess, eg how extroverted you are compared to another candidate for a job, or how stable you are compared to people in general. The traits that are measured are assumed to influence the ways in which we behave, and so are predictive of behaviour. Indeed, those who design questionnaires that measure traits, such as the famous American psychologist Raymond Cattell, have defined personality as 'that which permits a prediction of what a person will do in a given situation'. However, before we move on to look at the different sorts of traits that can be measured, it is useful to think about the difference between a trait and a state. This isn't just of academic interest as it's important that a questionnaire is measuring a stable and enduring aspect of a person's personality, rather than just the current state of that person. After all, we pass through different mental states during the day, with our mood changes depending on the situations in which we find ourselves. Naturally, most questionnaires attempt to concentrate on the measurement of traits, but there are some that assess both trait and state. Thus, whether or not you are an anxious person can be measured, alongside an indication of whether or not you were anxious at the time you completed the questionnaire.

There are about 20,000 words in the English language that label traits. Obviously many of these relate to the same underlying traits, but even so that still leaves a considerable range of different characteristics. As such it should come as no surprise that questionnaires have been designed that measure anything from 3 to 30 or more aspects of personality. This may sound confusing but not all questionnaires are attempting to measure every part of someone's personality, and many are actually concentrating on what are recognized as the five key dimensions of personality. These are known as the 'Big Five', or the 'Five Factor Model', and are reckoned to be the primary personality dimensions that underpin all observable behaviour! I should say, however, that there isn't universal agreement on this question and many psychologists would argue that there are as few as three main dimensions. This being said, the 'Big Five' are worth exploring in some detail. Incidentally, along the way you will notice that there are some similarities with the type descriptions given in the last section, demonstrating that both type and trait approaches are covering more or less the same ground.

The 'big five'

A great deal of research points to the fact that personality can be broken down into five main dimensions or domains. These concern how people approach situations and tasks (action); the style of their reasoning (thinking); how they behave towards other people (relating); the underlying nature of their emotions (feeling); and how they regulate their actions (conformity).

Action

This concerns an individual's attitude towards other people in a work or personal context. In many questionnaires it is either referred to as 'tough-mindedness' or as 'agreeableness'. The tough-minded person is someone who is primarily results orientated, and who may disregard other people's feelings in pursuit of a particular goal. Those who are very tough-minded have little time or patience for those who need support, and tend to work best with other like-minded colleagues.

It is, of course, possible to possess the complementary personality characteristics and be a tender-minded person. This suggests a warmer, more people-focused individual who has a genuine concern for the feelings of other people. This sort of person is also more likely to achieve results by listening to different viewpoints, and to adopt a co-operative, trusting and consensual style. In this way those wishing to discuss sensitive and personal issues are far more likely to approach this sort of person than their tough-minded, results-driven counterpart.

Thinking

This is about the structure and organization a person brings to a situation. It also relates to self-discipline and, characteristically, to attention to detail. The 'structured' person places great value on order and control. This manifests itself in a very tidy and systematic way of approaching tasks. For example, projects are often planned to the last detail, and organized in a precise and meticulous manner. Thus, a highly structured person leaves nothing to chance, and is always conscious of what to do and how long it will take. In extreme cases this can appear somewhat obsessional (especially to a 'low structure' individual), or overly perfectionist.

A 'low structure' person tends to have a more relaxed and casual approach to life. As long as jobs are completed, such people do not worry about formal structures or schedules. They are not particularly concerned with personal organization and can sometimes appear somewhat disorganized. In many cases they may miss important details or, because they are less ordered, be late for appointments or meetings. In a managerial sense they have a greater preference for the overview or the strategic approach, rather than the detail or tactical level of a project.

Relating

Classically, this refers to how a person relates to other people in the environment. It is the personality dimension that is most used by the layperson when describing other people as it concerns extroversion and introversion.

The extroverted individual is sociable, outgoing and attracted to other people. Such a person is energetic and enthusiastic, and is prepared to voice an opinion and to become involved in most things. At work, people-centred and high-profile roles have the most appeal, especially those relying on the skills of negotiation and persuasion. However, extroverts can be rather impulsive and sometimes take risks without properly weighing up the odds. They can at times also appear rather domineering, and find it difficult to believe that others do not share the same enthusiasms they do.

The introverted character is less concerned with other people and tends to be more introspective. In general there is a less excitable and more moderate outlook, and a tendency to take a more cautious and restrained approach to work. Introverts are also far less likely to want to be 'in charge' or to seek the limelight. In many ways the attitude is one of personal challenge (the inner game), rather than an open competition with other people. In terms of analogy it's like wishing to break a personal best time in athletics, rather than race against other people.

Feeling

This relates to the level of confidence you have as an individual. It is sometimes also referred to as neuroticism, anxiety or emotionality. However, basically it concerns how self-assured you are as a person.

Those with high self-confidence tend to be relaxed and optimistic. They enjoy responsibility and like to be put to the test. When they are put under pressure they react in a calm and organized way, and have faith in their own ability to cope. At work they are able to deal with unexpected events with ease, and put their views forward with confidence and conviction. Other people are likely to see them as being highly personally competent and assertive.

Those with low confidence, or high emotionality, have difficulty coping with stress and pressure. While they *can* take on responsibility, they may find it places a considerable emotional strain on them. They also tend to question their abilities, and are generally more pessimistic and cautious than those who are confident. In the work sense they prefer predictability and tend to shy away from complex, open-ended situations. This suggests that routine jobs in large, supportive organizations are likely to suit them the best.

Conformity

This refers to a person's need for variety, or the way in which an individual responds to change. It is also sometimes called creativity, independence or openness to experience.

The conforming person works within existing rules and regulations, and usually deals with problems using well-established methods. The approach is measured and conservative, and can be described as being 'by the book'. Such individuals are also practically minded and more comfortable with implementing plans rather than creating them. The conforming person is happy operating within the status quo and does not have a burning ambition to be seen as creative.

In contrast the non-conforming person is concerned with individual expression. This frequently indicates an unconventional and creative thinker, who actually resents structure and order. Thus, non-conforming people actively seek out and enjoy discovering new ways of doing things, and like to have variety in their work. At work the non-conformer is seen as being innovative and change oriented. There is a resistance to the traditional way of doing things, and a preference for risk taking. The latter can sometimes prove dangerous for an organization as uncontrolled risk taking can lead to business failure. However, modern management thinkers do suggest that some non-conforming people are desirable in an organization as they provide the catalyst for change or, as it is sometimes described, the grit in the oyster. This is a useful expression as it's the grit that ultimately leads to the pearl.

Trait questions

There are two main ways in which the questions in trait questionnaires are arranged. These involve either rating a list of statements, or indicating choices between a number of statements.

Example 3: Rating

Mark the [1] if you strongly agree with the statement; the [2] if you agree; the [3] if you are unsure; the [4] if you disagree; and the [5] if you strongly disagree.

1 I enjoy social gatherings	[1]	[2]	[3]	[4]	[5]
2 I am always late for appointments	[1]	[2]	[3]	[4]	[5]
3 I avoid taking risks	[1]	[2]	[3]	[4]	[5]
4 I like playing team games	[1]	[2]	[3]	[4]	[5]

Note: Sometimes the questions appear in the form of lists of adjectives (creative, dominant, tense, active, social, sensitive etc), rather than statements. In this case all you do is indicate your level of agreement, 1–5, with a series of words.

Example 4: Two from four choice

For each block of four statements indicate which one is most like you [M], and which one is least like you [L]. Leave the other two statements blank.

I am ...

1 A highly organized person	[M]	[L]
Anxious when meeting new people	[M]	[L]
The 'life and soul' of the party	[M]	[L]
An energetic person	[M]	[L]
2 Even tempered	[M]	[L]
Skilled at practical problems	[M]	[L] etc

Example 5: One from two choice

For each statement indicate whether you think it is true [T] or false [F]:

1 I like to try new ways of doing things   [T] [F]

2 I find it difficult to relax after a hard day's work   [T] [F]

3 I am an optimistic person   [T] [F]

4 I enjoy organizing meetings and gatherings   [T] [F]

Example 6: One from three choice

For each statement indicate whether you think the statement is true [T]; false [F]; or if you are unsure [?]:

1 People should sort out their own problems   [T]   [?]   [F]

2 I can get more done when I can work alone   [T]   [?]   [F]

3 I like telling people funny stories   [T]   [?]   [F]

4 I show my emotions easily   [T]   [?]   [F]

All the above are common ways of presenting questions and, as you can see, some allow more choice than others. In particular one of the biggest differences is between those questionnaires that allow you to respond 'unsure' [?], and those that force your choice between a number of options. You may feel that you don't want to be forced to answer one way or the other; however, questionnaires are designed like this to stop you being indifferent to everything. That's because if you were unsure, or couldn't make your mind up about most of the statements in a questionnaire, it would be impossible to produce an accurate picture of your personality.

How are trait questionnaires used?

Trait questionnaires are used for selection and development purposes. Unlike type questionnaires they can be used to select people for jobs because they allow an employer directly to compare one person with another. Therefore it is possible to say that person A is more extroverted than person B, and also how much more extroverted A is than B.

Questionnaires of this design are used in most of the large companies in the UK and the USA. Variations are also available in most European and Asian countries, translated into the appropriate languages. Virtually all measure the 'Big Five' personality dimensions, although in practice they usually do this by breaking the five main components down into a number of sub-scales. So, for example, in the UK, the most popular questionnaires contain 16 and 32 scales respectively.

The names to look out for are the *Sixteen Personality Factor Questionnaire*™ (*16PF*), published in the UK by Oxford Psychologist Press; *Global Personalities Inventory* from PreVisor; the *Occupational Personality Questionnaire*® (*OPQ*®), published by Saville & Holdsworth Ltd; and the *California Psychological Inventory*™ (*CPI*™), published by the Consulting Psychologists Press Inc, and distributed by Oxford Psychologists Press. Other questionnaires you might come across are Saville Consulting's *Wave*, the *Rapid Personality Questionnaire* (*RPQ*), *Manchester Personality Questionnaire* (*MPQ*), *Personal Profile Analysis* (*PPA*), and the *NEO Five Factor Inventory*™ (*NEO-FF*™). The first two were designed in the UK, while the others have their antecedents in the USA but are also widely used in the UK.

Emotional intelligence

An additional development in personality assessment is the Emotional Intelligence (EI) questionnaire. This looks at the traits that are thought to differentiate between average and high performers in a work setting. What this really means is a person's emotional and interpersonal competence, or how we 'manage' our own personality. One way of looking at it, is that EI is the practice of 'thinking about feeling' *and* 'feeling about thinking'. EI questionnaires measure things like:

- *Self-awareness:* our understanding of our own feelings and how we control them.

- *Emotional resilience:* our ability to perform under pressure and to adapt to new situations.

- *Motivation:* the drive and energy we have to achieve results and to work towards goals.

- *Interpersonal sensitivity:* the degree of respect we have for others' needs.

- *Influence and persuasion:* our ability to bring other people around to our point of view.

- *Intuitiveness:* the process of being able to come to a clear decision when we only have incomplete or ambiguous information.

- *Conscientiousness and integrity:* our ability to display commitment and match words with action.

The traits measured by EI questionnaires have been chosen because they are predictive of likely success in given roles, particularly in the management arena. However, many are measured by standard personality questionnaires (albeit in the 'being' rather than the 'doing' sense), and they also have much in common with some of the 'competencies' described at the end of this book – see the Appendix.

As an example of the output from an EI questionnaire, read the following extract from a real report:

While generally aware of your feelings and emotions in work situations, there are some situations in which this is not so. You might find that occasionally, even though you are aware of your feelings and emotions, you are unable to control their impact on the way in which you behave as much as you would like. In order to develop this element further, you might find it helpful to reflect on specific situations in which you have felt in control of your feelings and emotions. In thinking about these situations you may be able to identify specific actions that were helpful. You could then apply these in a broader situation that arouses strong feelings and emotions. (Emotional Intelligence Questionnaire report, ASE)

Having read the extract above, you will see that the report describes a person's typical behaviour and also provides some pointers on how to develop self-awareness.

There are many EI questionnaires on the market, including an option with the *Occupational Personality Questionnaire®* from Saville & Holdsworth Ltd; the *Emotional Intelligence Questionnaire* from Pre Visor; and the *Emotional Competence Inventory* from HayGroup.

Personality and the 'dark side'

Finally, one of the latest ideas in personality is to look at personality disorders and to see how these relate to 'normal' functioning. For example, problems often arise if a person is too arrogant, melodramatic, aloof, or even perfectionist. But that's not to say that a small measure of some of these attributes cannot be good – it's when there is too much of one of them that things can go wrong. This, in . the current jargon, can be potentially *derailing*.

Questionnaires like the *Hogan Development Survey* (HDS), distributed by Hogan Assessment Systems, aim to measure these derailing factors, or what is also termed, the 'dark side' of personality. The HDS has 11 scales and looks at things like Enthusiastic – Volatile, Shrewd – Mistrustful, Careful – Cautious, Vivacious – Dramatic, and so forth. Note that the words on the left-hand side of each scale are generally thought to indicate positive attributes; those on the right, what this attribute turns into when it's in excess.

To help to make the point, let's look at two 'flawed' personality types which link to an HDS scale. Histrionic people need to be the centre of attention and enjoy making a drama out of any sort of crisis. What's more, they often demonstrate seductive, and often provocative behaviour in their dealings with other people. They also tend to look and dress the part, and use exaggerated expressions of emotion. You may recognize this description as being like that of the melodramatic theatrical 'luvvie'. Unfortunately it is also some-times attached to those in managerial and leadership roles.

The obsessive–compulsive type is totally obsessed with details, plans, rules and schedules. They are sticklers for doing things 'right' and their perfectionism often gets in the way of things that need to be done. Such people are often workaholics and highly driven, and so can be of genuine benefit to an organization. However too much attention to detail can mean that they find it difficult to delegate, and come across as highly controlling. There are many bosses like this and they can be difficult to work for, not least because someone who spends an excessive amount of time at work often thinks that other people should do likewise.

So in short, 'dark side' personality questionnaires are attempting to measure the type of dysfunctional behaviour that erodes the trust, loyalty and enthusiasm that is critical to successful management and leadership.

How to complete a personality questionnaire

At present, most personality questionnaires come in the form of a question book and a separate answer sheet. Thus, your task is simply to read the questions and complete the answer sheet using a pencil. However, many questionnaires are becoming available on computer and so you may find yourself using a keyboard to respond to ques-tions presented on a computer screen. There are also a number of other less common variations (see Chapter 2), but irrespective of how the questions are physically presented they will always be in one of the formats described previously. In addition, it's worth remember-ing that if you are tested by computer you will not be expected to be a keyboard expert (it's your personality that is being assessed, not your typing skills); and you will always have the opportunity to prac-tise and to ask questions before the assessment begins.

There follows some general guidelines on how to approach any personality questionnaire:

- *Be as honest as you can.* The best advice is to give the most straightforward answer to any question. Do not look for trick questions or be tempted to give the answers you feel will do you the most good, but which are untrue. The reasons are that it is difficult to 'bend the truth' consistently when you may be answering up to 200 questions; and you may also inadvertently emphasize one aspect of your personality at the expense of another. Likewise, you do not know the ideal profile for a particular job, and you may actually distort your personality results in the wrong direction.

  In addition, many questionnaires contain special scales that are designed to detect those who are presenting themselves in an overly positive light. These are called 'impression management' or 'motivational distortion' scales, and contain questions to check how honest and consistent you are being. For example:

I have never been late for an appointment	True	False
I have never told a 'white lie'	True	False

  Some questionnaires also contain scales that can help to identify potential criminal behaviour, or addictive personalities. Clearly such information can be of value to employers in the retail and financial sectors, although it should be stressed that no questionnaire can produce a foolproof indication of such behaviour. This being the case they are always backed up by other sources of information, eg personal references.

- *Think about a typical day.* The questions you will be asked relate to how you usually behave at work. If you don't have a job just think about how you deal with other people in social situations, or how you deal with situations at school, college, or wherever you spend your time.

- *Trust your first impressions.* Although most questionnaires have no time limit, it is better to answer the questions quickly rather than agonize over each one. The reason is that in this case, unlike ability tests, your first thoughts are usually the most accurate. It's also a good idea to work quickly because it will often take you between 30 and 40 minutes to finish a questionnaire even when you are trusting your first impressions. That's not to say that every questionnaire will take this long, as some are quite short, and will only take about 10 minutes to finish. The latter are often used to recruit people for customer service or sales positions.

● *Read the questions carefully.* If you study the questions it is often possible to determine which broad aspects of personality are being measured. For example, extroversion or *relating* questions frequently refer to sociability, risk-taking, impulsiveness, lack of responsibility and high levels of emotional energy. In contrast, introversion questions often cover the opposite characteristics such as a dislike for social occasions and more thoughtful decision making.

In a similar vein, tough-mindedness or *action* questions often concern achievement orientation, competitiveness, assertiveness, manipulation and a lack of sympathy for other people, whereas tender-mindedness questions focus on a feeling, trusting and co-operative style, or on an empathic way of behaving.

Likewise, questions concerning anxiety or *feeling* will be based on issues such as low self-esteem, obsessive behaviour (such as repeatedly checking things or always having to be early for appointments) and a lack of personal autonomy. The contrasting confidence questions will concern things like being able to respond in crises, being able to take criticism, not worrying over mistakes, and generally taking a relaxed view of life.

The thinking or *structure* questions will relate to how organized a person is in everyday life. So high-structure questions will tap behaviours such as ordering and controlling people and things, and anything relating to detailed planning and organizing tasks in advance. The low-structure items will then cover a dislike for organization and planning, and especially things like a poor sense of time or lack of personal discipline.

Finally, *conformity* questions will concern practicality, conservatism, tried-and-tested methods and conscientiousness. Their low-conformity counterparts will cover creative and divergent thinking, a frustration with rules and regulations, a need to be able to express individuality, and a search for variety and mental stimulation.

In describing the content of questions like this, the argument is that if you understand what the questions are asking, you will be able to give better and more genuine responses.

- *Answer all the questions.* It's important that you answer all the questions or it will not be possible to get a valid picture of your personality. Also, don't get stuck on questions you don't feel are relevant, but just give the best and most immediate answer you can. A related problem is 'arguing' with the questions, ie over-analysing the questions to such an extent that you don't know what is being asked. Unfortunately, some questions will appear rather ambiguous but, as before, the most profitable thing to do is just give your first reaction.

- *Know yourself.* The more self-knowledge you have the easier it will be to present an accurate picture. Remember that personality questionnaires are really only asking you to report on yourself, and so it makes sense to be as aware as you can of your own personality. You can do this by consulting self-test books (look in a good bookshop), or by asking other people to describe how they see you. In fact, one of the most interesting things you can do is to write down, say, 10 adjectives that you feel sum up your personality, and then get someone who knows you well to do the same thing. If you then compare the two lists you may get a few surprises!

- *Know the job.* Just as it's useful to know something about your personality before you complete a questionnaire, it's also beneficial to know about the job for which you are applying. What sort of a person are they looking for? You will get some clues from the job advertisement and also any other literature you can study before the assessment session. For example, you may find that an advert refers to particular 'competencies' (see the Appendix for more details), or that a company publishes a house magazine or newsletter. Do these give a feel for the ideal employee? What impression do you get of the organization? Perhaps it's large and traditional, and favours 'middle-of-the-road', detail-conscious and stable workers. Or is it small, fast moving and creative? Does this suggest more dynamic, risk-taking and extroverted individuals?

Finally, always follow the directions printed in the front of the questionnaire booklet, and pay particular attention to any instructions given by the test administrator. It should also be a comfort to remember that personality questionnaires are designed to assess you in a fair and objective way, and to help you choose the work to which you are most suited. Clearly there's little point in fulfilling all the requirements of a job in terms of ability and experience, only to find that you cannot cope with the people aspects of a particular position.

Leadership Style questionnaire

To provide some experience of completing a self-report question-naire what follows is a fully working Leadership Style questionnaire. This is based on the work of Daniel Goleman and the Hay Group into what characterizes highly effective leaders, in particular the six distinct managerial styles. Effective managers use a combination of these styles, at the appropriate time, to build a positive working environment for their teams.

Practice questionnaire

Introduction

The Leadership Style Questionnaire (LSQ) contains 30 pairs of statements. The statements ask about how you think, feel and deal with the people with whom you work. When you have completed the questionnaire you will be able to identify the sort of style, or styles, that you use when managing or leading other people.

Instructions

For each question decide which of the two statements is most like you. Then put a cross in the appropriate box.

Example

		A	B	C	D	E	F
1	I feel that people should always be involved in decisions, or						
	I expect people to do what I have told them do				x		

When you answer the questions, bear the following points in mind:

- Try and be as honest as you can when answering the questions.

- Don't spend too long thinking about each question; just give the first answer that comes into your mind.

- Make sure that you answer all of the questions, even if some of the statements are difficult to choose between.

- There is no time limit, but try to complete the questionnaire as quickly as you can.

- Don't look at the scoring system until you have completed the questionnaire!

Start when you are ready.

		A	B	C	D	E	F
1	I think the key to success is through meeting people's needs, or	☐					
	I like to give people a clear direction to follow		☐				
2	I help people to identify their strengths and weaknesses, or			☐			
	I insist on excellence						☐
3	I think that you need to tell people what to do, or				☐		
	I include everyone in decision making					☐	
4	I am good at selling a 'vision' of where we need to go, or		☐				
	I encourage people to work on their own development needs			☐			
5	I concentrate on promoting harmony amongst people, or	☐					
	I prefer to lead by example						☐
6	I give people feedback on their work performance, or			☐			
	I expect people to do what I say				☐		
7	I organize meetings to decide what needs to be done, or					☐	
	I think that my main job is to complete things to a high standard						☐
8	I pay attention to the whole person and their happiness, or	☐					
	I tailor my support to the needs of the individual			☐			

		A	B	C	D	E	F
9	I persuade people by explaining what needs to be done, or		☐				
	I trust people to work out how to do their job				☐		
10	I closely monitor the work that people are doing, or				☐		
	I often find that to get something done I have to do it myself						☐
11	I am good at listening to other people, or			☐			
	I reward the whole team if it has done well					☐	
12	I give people constructive feedback, or		☐				
	I get people to comply instantly because it raises standards			☐			
13	I always look for opportunities to give positive feedback, or	☐					
	I prefer to reach decisions by consensus					☐	
14	I provide a clear idea of long term direction, or		☐				
	I only delegate to people I know will do a good job						☐
15	I reward the person as much as their job performance, or	☐					
	I think people need to know exactly what is expected of them				☐		
16	I believe in creating a warm and caring atmosphere, or	☐					
	I let people know when they are doing well		☐				

		A	B	C	D	E	F
17	I think that you sometimes need to learn from failure, or			☐			
	I take responsibility away from people who do not perform						☐
18	I insist on procedures so that people know what to do, or				☐		
	I believe in building commitment from all involved					☐	
19	I delegate tasks to people with clear instructions, or		☐				
	I help people to see that learning is a continuous process			☐			
20	I see my role as looking after other people, or	☐					
	I think that you often have to demonstrate how to do things well						☐
21	I take time to discover people's aspirations for the future, or			☐			
	I think that you must always keep on top of what is going on				☐		
22	I believe in involving everyone in issues affecting them, or				☐		
	I give people precise details on what to do						☐
23	I want people to feel valued as individuals, or	☐					
	I look for opportunities to enhance people's development			☐			

		A	B	C	D	E	F
24	I set standards which everyone can understand, or		☐				
	I am good at organizing and running meetings					☐	
25	I think people respect you if you can also do their job well, or				☐		
	I set high standards and expect others to reach them						☐
26	I think the main thing is people's long term development, or			☐			
	I am concerned with getting everyone's contribution					☐	
27	I ask people for their ideas on how to achieve goals, or		☐				
	I think people need to be told when they are not doing well				☐		
28	I believe that to work together we must all like each other, or	☐					
	I wait until everyone has had their say before making decisions					☐	
29	I am good at explaining the 'big picture' to people, or		☐				
	I always act to put things right as quickly as possible						☐
30	I think that welfare comes before organizational goals, or	☐					
	I swiftly point out when people have deviated from the rules				☐		

Scoring the questionnaire

Simply add up all the crosses in each of the six columns, A–F, and record the totals in the table below.

Column	Total	Style
A		Affiliative
B		Authoritative
C		Coaching
D		Coercive
E		Democratic
F		Pace-setting

What the styles mean

The styles show you what you think you do as a manager or leader, and what you consider to be important. Look at the one or two styles with the highest total scores. What do the results tell you? Should you use these styles less? Contrast with the style with the lowest score: is this an area for development? Should you use this style more?

Affiliative

This is all about creating a peaceful and harmonious working environment and building strong emotional bonds with other people. It rests on empathy, paying attention to relationships and good communication skills. It's useful when there are fault lines in teams, or to motivate people during difficult periods.

Overall it has a positive effect on organizational 'climate' in that it frees people to be more creative, increases sense of ownership and responsibility, clarity of purpose and commitment. However one possible problem is that it can often look like avoiding the difficult problems, especially those concerned with poor performance.

Authoritative

An authoritative approach is concerned with selling a 'vision'. It relies on self-confidence, a persuasive style, and the ability to act as a catalyst of change. It comes into its own when change requires a new vision of the future, or when a clear and unambiguous direction is needed.

In terms of climate this has the most strongly positive effect and is the style to adopt for maximum impact on the working atmosphere. If there is a downside it's that it can sometimes backfire when team members are highly competent and capable, and they actually know best!

Coaching

This focuses on developing people for the future. The underlying emotional competencies are empathy, self awareness and a concern for empowering others to grow and develop. It is of particular value when the concern is over improving performance and on developing long-term strengths and capability.

As with the Affiliative and Authoritative styles it has a positive effect on organizational climate. Yet it should be recognized that the coach sometimes needs to trade a short term drop in performance for a long term increase in capability.

Coercive

This is about compliance and getting others to immediately do what they are told. It is driven by the need to achieve, self-control and initiative and is the style that works best when there is a crisis, or when a problem needs a kick-start.

It should be used sparingly because in terms of climate it has a negative effect. It can stifle creativity and decrease sense of ownership and responsibility. It's also not particularly useful when the need is to communicate the 'big picture' or a guiding strategy.

Democratic

The democratic style is about deciding things together and creating a sense of common purpose. It draws on the competencies of collaboration, communication and team building. This style is useful when there is a need to get people to buy in to a course of action, or to get the right sort of input from the most capable members of a team.

In terms of climate it's another style that has a positive effect, alongside the Authoritative and Affiliative approaches. However it's not a good style to use in a crisis when there is no time for meetings or discussions.

Pace-setting

This centres on standards and is mostly concerned with setting targets for performance. The underpinning competencies are conscientiousness, drive to achieve and initiative. It works best where there is a need to get quick results from a team that is already highly motivated and competent.

Along with the coercive style this is one that should be used on a limited basis. It should be recognized that it is a quick fix and not a style that will help teams to deliver to a high standard over the long term.

Other self-report questionnaires

There are a number of other aspects of human temperament that can be measured apart from personality. These include qualities such as values, motivation, integrity and interests. All of these additional factors are assessed at one time or another, and the next section deals with each in more detail.

Values

These are the 'personal concepts' that we hold, which determine how we deal with everyday life. They are the standards or principles that guide our behaviour towards other people. In practice, of course, it's difficult to differentiate between values and aspects of personality; but, unlike personality, values are influenced more by the culture in which we live.

Values questionnaires are often used to complement personality assessments, and are usually focused on how you cope with everyday problems and/or your relationships with other people.

The questionnaires are generally designed in a forced-choice format (see Example 1: Forced choice) and measure values such as:

- honesty;

- self-respect;

- equality;

- goal orientation;

- self-control;

- independence;

- altruism;

- social support.

Values questionnaires are often used in assessment programmes for middle and senior managers. The best-known example is probably the *Global Gordon's Personal Profile Inventory* (*Global GPP-I*) distributed by PreVisor.

Motivation

Motivation is closely related to the issue of values and is one of the most important things to assess during the selection process.

However, it's also one of the hardest to measure as we all claim to be highly motivated when we apply for jobs; in particular we are likely to put on a great show of interest during the interview.

In practice, motivation can be defined as the energy that we are likely to bring to bear on work tasks. This is useful for an employer to know as it is essential to select people who are genuinely motivated, and committed to making a success of a job. It's also important to know what a person wishes to strive towards, and those activities or circumstances that both increase *and* decrease motivation.

Motivation questionnaires are often used with managerial, professional and supervisory staff, and aim to identify the range of factors that energize and support individual behaviour. For example, people are often motivated by some of the following:

- high workload and tight deadlines (**pressure**);
- responsibility and authority (**power**);
- exceeding personal goals and targets (**achievement**);
- working as part of a close-knit team (**affiliation**);
- competing against other people (**competition**);
- self-development and personal learning (**growth**);
- praise and recognition from other people (**recognition**);
- earning a good salary (**reward**);
- having a stable and dependable job (**security**);
- working in a well-organized business (**structure**);
- working for a well-respected organization (**prestige**);
- being able to maintain high personal values (**ethics**);
- having a good position (**status**);
- being able to move up an organization (**progression**);
- having control over work activities (**autonomy**);

- the desire to succeed (**achievement**);

- the work ethic, or work itself (**drive**);

- creative and varied work activities (**interest**).

You may have noticed that some of these motivational factors are the same as the values mentioned previously. This goes to show that it is actually quite difficult to untangle values from motivation, and that in all probability they interact with each other. So, if you're the sort of person who places great value on independence you may well be motivated by having control over what you do (**autonomy**), and being able to develop your personal competence and extend your repertoire of skills (**growth**).

Employers find that motivation questionnaires are a good way of comparing job applicants or current employees against job demands; and also against the management style of an organization. The latter is of increasing importance as many businesses are starting to pay attention to their organizational 'culture'. For example, if you have a strong need for structure, clear paths of progression, and security, you might find it difficult to work for a small organization with little in the way of hierarchy or long-term promotion prospects.

An example of a motivation questionnaire is *Motive-A*, published by Hogrefe. Other popular questionnaires are the *Motivation Questionnaire (MQ)* distributed by Saville & Holdsworth Ltd and the *Values-based Indicator of Motivation* from Team Focus Ltd.

Integrity

Integrity is the weasel word used by psychologists when they are talking about honesty; and so integrity tests are designed to discover if you are likely to be an honest and reliable employee. At present, most of these come from the USA and are the result of the adverse publicity generated by polygraph tests. If you are unfamiliar with the polygraph approach it is a lie detector test, which is based on the fact that the electrical resistance of your skin varies when you are telling a lie. This is measured by placing a series of electrical pads on your fingers or hands. It is clearly a rather worrying way of assessing honesty, and also a method that is unacceptable in a selection context.

In consequence, modern integrity tests are questionnaire based and are designed to indicate those aspects of a person's potential work behaviour that may give cause for concern. In many integrity tests the questions relate to how you would respond to a variety of common situations involving money, 'time-theft' and tardiness; and your attitude towards rule breaking and criminality in others. Here are some examples:

- If you found £50 in the street would you hand it in at a police station?

- Would you take a day off 'ill' if you felt you had been overworked?

- If you received too much change in a shop would you give it back?

- Do you know anybody who steals regularly?

These are fairly obvious questions, but even so they can be quite instructive in showing someone's potential (dis)honesty. Interestingly, there are differences between the sexes in the way that they reply, and also between different countries. Thus, recent research by a major firm of UK test publishers has shown that women are far more likely to return excess change in a shop and that, culturally, of all the European nations, the Spanish are the least likely to give money back. Needless to say these sorts of variations have to be taken into account when applying integrity tests.

Integrity tests are used by retail organizations and other businesses that rely on personal honesty, eg the police, security services, financial organizations and airlines. An example of an integrity test is *Giotto* published by Pearson.

Interests

Interest questionnaires are constructed so that they indicate your workplace preferences, or those activities that you feel you would enjoy. Thus, the two main types of interest questionnaires that you will encounter are those assessing management interests; and the more general variety, which measure general occupational interests.

Management interest questionnaires focus on the balance of management functions that are of interest. For example, you will find yourself indicating your level of interest in areas of management such as:

- production and manufacturing;

- technical support and services;

- research and development;

- transport and distribution;

- sales and marketing;

- personnel and training;

- finance and accounts;

- administration and control;

- legal and management services;

- IT and computer systems.

In addition, some questionnaires compare your interest in, say, producing accounts and managing the finances of a business, with the amount of experience you have of doing such a job. This allows an employer to compare your interest, or enthusiasm for something, with your actual experience.

Management questionnaires can also measure your interest in distinct work activities, especially those relating to the day-to-day control of a business. For example:

- written communication;

- oral communication;

- decision making;

- problem solving;

- developing and training;

- negotiating and persuading;

- predicting and forecasting;

- information collection and analysis;

- organizing people and resources.

Such questionnaires are routinely used to assess existing or future managers. However, as with measures of values, they are usually used alongside other sources of information such as personality questionnaires and ability tests.

An example of a management interest questionnaire is the *Management Interest Inventory* (*MII*), published by Saville & Holdsworth Ltd.

General occupational interest questionnaires are often used with school leavers, graduates and others to assess interests over the entire range of work activities. One of the best-known systems is that produced by the American psychologist, John Holland, who developed a way of breaking down people's work interests into six main types: **R**ealistic, **I**nvestigative, **A**rtistic, **S**ocial, **E**nterprising and **C**onventional.

- *Realistic* people prefer activities in which they can use practical ways of solving problems. They value concrete things and prefer tangible rewards for their endeavours such as money or status. Realistic people can be described as being genuine, hard-headed, practical and persistent.

- *Investigative* people prefer activities involving a systematic and analytic way of working. They also like tasks involving an observational and scientific approach. Investigative people can be described as being critical, rational, intellectual and curious.

- *Artistic* people place value on individual expression and enjoy language, art, music, drama and writing-based activities. They can be described as being aesthetic, cultural, emotional, intuitive and imaginative.

- *Social* people prefer activities that allow them to influence other people, and to be involved in helping, caring, managing, training, developing and informing. The emphasis is on interpersonal skills, and so social people can be described as being persuasive, understanding, empathic and co-operative.

- *Enterprising* people are concerned with making things happen, and the manipulation of other people and resources to achieve personal success. They often perceive themselves as being aggressive and as possessing leadership abilities. The enterprising person can also be described as being ambitious, energetic, self-confident and adventurous.

- *Conventional* people prefer activities that involve the detailed and systematic use of information. They like to organize and use data in a precise and disciplined way. They can be described as being conforming, conscientious, methodical and thrifty.

Naturally, it is possible to be a mixture of the above types and to have more than one area of interest. Indeed, this is true of most people, although some combinations are less likely than others, eg conventional and artistic do not often go together, whereas enterprising and social do.

When this system is used in careers guidance the questionnaire yields a three-letter code that indicates your area of interest, eg SEI. This is then used to check against a dictionary of occupational codes containing well over 12,000 different jobs – from abrasive grinder and hassock maker, to uptwister tender and yeast washer. By the way, in the example given, SEI is the code for an occupational psychologist.

An example of an interests questionnaire based on the work of John Holland is the *Self-Directed Search* (*SDS*), which is published by Psychological Assessment Resources Inc in the USA. Other interest questionnaires include *Passport* and the *Rothwell-Miller Interest Blank*, both distributed by The Morrisby Organization, and the *General* and *Advanced Occupational Interest Inventories* (*GOII; AOII*), published by Saville & Holdsworth Ltd.

Finally...

In this chapter the intention has been to introduce you to the idea of personality and the various ways in which it can be measured. Some of you may believe that reducing personality to four or five dimensions is a gross oversimplification. However, before coming to such a conclusion consider the following analogy used in the marketing of a leading US personality questionnaire:

> *... there are only three primary colours and yet they allow us to produce every single colour, tone and hue in the world...*

In a similar way the 'big five' personality dimensions allow us to describe the complete spectrum of personality, because when each dimension is broken down into its component scales there are literally millions of different combinations.

Key points

- There are about 1,200 different personality and other self-report questionnaires available to psychologists and employers.

- Type questionnaires place you in a fixed personality category, and are used for development and training purposes.

- Trait questionnaires measure how much of a personality factor you possess. They are used for selection and assessment as they allow you to be directly compared with other people.

- Research has indicated that there are five main dimensions of personality. These cover action, thinking, feeling, relating and conforming.

- There are six main types of questions in personality questionnaires. These include those that force your choice, and those that allow you to rate or rank a series of statements.

- There are a range of strategies that will help you complete any personality questionnaire. These involve being honest (and not second guessing the questionnaire designer); placing your answers in the appropriate context; trusting your first impressions; reading the questions properly; and knowing yourself and the job for which you are applying.

- Some questionnaires contain scales to detect whether you are bending the truth. While there is nothing wrong with presenting yourself in the most positive way, it is very difficult to disguise your real self. The best advice is just to be as honest and straightforward as you can.

- There are many other types of questionnaires apart from those that directly measure personality. For example, questionnaires that assess personal values, integrity, motivation and interests are also common.

- In order to present a strong and consistent picture of your personality you must be positive, open-minded and truthful in your answers. Remember that personality questionnaires are designed to help you find the right job; getting a position on the grounds of inaccurate results is only likely to lead to low performance, and ultimately a great deal of stress.

CHAPTER 7

Top 100 practice test websites

Practice test websites

If you type the phrase 'psychometric test' or 'psychological test' into an internet search engine it will return the addresses of thousands of websites. Unfortunately many of those that claim to provide genuine tests and questionnaires are of extremely low quality. However there are a good number that provide useful practice material if you know where to look!

The websites listed in this section provide thousands of high quality test practice questions, quite apart from a variety of insightful questionnaires. In addition much of this material is available at no cost, or for a small fee.

Top 100 practice websites

General

These websites provide background information on psychometric testing, and what the test-taker can expect to happen in the job application and recruitment process.

- *British Psychological Society Testing Centre* (official BPS site): http://www.psychtesting.org.uk.

- *Chartered Institute of Personnel and Development* (useful articles): http://www.cipd.co.uk.

- *European Test Publishing Group* (A–Z of testing): http://www.etpg.org/c-doftesting.htm.

- *People and Organisations @ Work* (useful articles): http://www.pow-bps.com.

- *Royal National Institute for the Blind* (testing and visual problems): http://www.rnib.org.uk.

- *Saville & Holdsworth Ltd* (best practice guidelines): http://www.shl.com/ourscience/bestpractice/default.aspx.

Ability tests

Many websites cover ability tests, for example:

- *Profiling for Success* (unique ability test linked to this book): http://wwwprofilingforsuccess.com/kogan-page.

- *Assessment Day* (range of different tests): http://www.assessmentday.co.uk.

- *3 Smart Cubes* (range of different tests): http://www.3smartcubes.com.

- *Aviac* (ability tests for pilot selection): http://www.aviac.com.

- *Criterion Partnership* (verbal and numerical tests): http://www.criterionpartnership.co.uk/test_samples.

- *Cubiks* (graduate level tests): http://practicetests.cubiks.com.

- *Diagonal Thinking* (lateral thinking test): http://www.diagonalthinking.co.uk

- *Efinancial* (numerical test): http://www.efinancialcareers.co.uk.

- *EPSO* (EU civil service 'competition' tests): http://europa.eu/epso.

- *HSBC* (verbal and numerical tests): http://www.jobs.hsbc.co.uk/graduates/useful-tools/psychometric-test.aspx.

- *Irish Army* (numerical test): http://irisharmy.shlsolutions.net/nmg1.htm.

- *MAT* (analogy tests): http://www.matexampractice.com.

- *Military* (US military tests): http://www.military.com/asvab.

- *Morrisby Organization* (set of six basic aptitude tests): http://www.morrisby.com.

- *Practice tests* (range of tests): http://www.practicetests.co.uk.

- *PSL/Kenexa* (graduate level tests): http://www.psl.com.

- *Psychometric Success* (range of different tests): http://www.psychometric-success.com.

- *Qantas Pilot tests* (ability tests used to select pilots – pdf format): http://www.qantas.com.au/infodetail/about/employment/qtests.pdf.

- *Royal Air Force* (aptitude test): http://www.raf.mod.uk/careers/aptitude/aptitude.html.

- *Saville Consulting* (set of six new practice tests – pdf format): http://www.savilleconsulting.com/products.

- *Saville & Holdsworth Ltd* (official SHL practice test site): http://www.shldirect.com.

- *Test Grid* (range of tests): http://www.testgrid.com.

- *Top Employers* (numerical tests): http://www.topemployers.co.uk/graduate-job-numeracy-game.html.

- *University of Kent Careers Service* (range of tests): http://www.kent.ac.uk/careers/psychotests.htm.

- *Wikijob* (range of tests): http://www.wikijob.co.uk.

IQ tests

If you want to complete a test that will give you an idea of your IQ, then try one or more of the following:

- *Mensa* (Mensa 'workout'): http://www.mensa.org.

- *High IQ Society* (IQ tests and puzzles): http://www.highiqsociety.org.

- *GIQ test* (full length IQ test): http://www.giqtest.com.

- *Get IQ* (full length IQ test): http://www.getiq.co.uk.

- *IQ Test Labs* (full length IQ test): http://www.intelligencetest.com.

- *Mental Testing* (adaptive IQ test): http://www.mental-testing.com.

- *Online IQ Test* (full length IQ test): http://online-iq-test.co.uk.

Personality and value questionnaires

There are plenty of websites that host personality and similar questionnaires. Here's a selection of some of the best:

- *BBC Science* (range of questionnaires): http://www.bbc.co.uk/science/humanbody/mind/index_surveys.shtml.

- *Enneagram Institute* (psychological type questionnaire): http://www.enneagraminstitute.com.

- *Human Metrics* (psychological type questionnaire): http://www.humanmetrics.com.

- *Keirsey Type Indicator* (psychological type indicator): http://www.keirsey.com.

- *Learn Myself* (psychological trait questionnaire): http://www.learnmyself.com.

- *Little Lab* (personality and faces): http://www.alittlelab.com.

- *NEO Personality test* (psychological trait questionnaire): http://www.personalitytest.net/ipip/ipipneol.htm.

- *Octogram* (values questionnaire): http://www.octagon.net.

- *People Profiler* (work attributes questionnaire): http://www.peopleprofiler.co.uk.

- *Personality Project* (psychological trait questionnaire): http://test.personality-project.org.

- *Psychology Today* (range of questionnaires): http://www.psychologytoday.com/pto/self-tests.php.

- *Reed* (psychological trait questionnaire): http://www.reed.co.uk/careertools/selfassessments.aspx.

- *Sam Gosling* (short psychological trait questionnaire): http://homepage.psy.utexas.edu/homepage/faculty/gosling/.

- *Signal Patterns* (psychological trait questionnaire): http://www.signalpatterns.com.

- *Strategic Business Insights* (values questionnaire): http://www.strategicbusinessinsights.com/vals/presurvey.shtml.

- *Talent Drain* (psychological trait questionnaire): http://www.findingpotential.com.

- *Team Technology* (psychological type indicator): http://www.teamtechnology.co.uk/mmdi-re/mmdi-re.htm.

- *Youniverse* (visual personality questionnaire): http://www.youniverse.com/personality/.

- *Wikipedia* (good introduction to 'big five' traits): http://en.wikipedia.org/wiki/big_five_personality_traits/.

Leadership and emotional intelligence questionnaires

Leadership and emotional intelligence questionnaires are often used in staff development programmes. Questionnaires that will help you explore your style are:

- *Cameron Change* (leadership style questionnaire): http://www.cameronchange.co.uk/question.com.

- *DTI Inspired Leadership* (government sponsored questionnaire): http://www.inspiredleadership.org.uk.

- *Formula 4 Leadership* (based on four key leadership types): http://www.formula4leadership.com/menu_questions.htm.

- *Institute for Health & Human Potential* (emotional intelligence questionnaire): http://www.ihhp.com/quiz.php.

- *My Skills profile* (leadership style questionnaire): http://www.myskillsprofile.com

- *Turknett Leadership Group* (emotional intelligence questionnaire): http://www.leadershipcharacter.com/eq_quiz2.htm.

Learning and thinking style questionnaires

An appreciation of your learning style is valuable if you are considering further education or training. Find out about your style using these questionnaires:

- *Brain Me Up* (general thinking styles questionnaire): http://www.brainmeup.com.

- *Brain Technologies* (brain dominance tool): http://www.braintechnologies.com/brainmap_intro.htm.

- *VARK* (based on four factor model of learning styles): http://www.vark-learn.com.

- *Memletics* (based on seven factor model of learning styles): http://www.learning-styles-online.com.

- *MIT* (based on five factor model of thinking styles): http://web.mit.edu/10.27/www.team-building/forms/thinksty.html.

- *University of Oxford* (learning needs analysis): http://tall.cented.ox.ac.uk/lnat.

Careers interest and career planning questionnaires

There are some really good careers interest and careers planning resources available, especially for younger people. Try some of these:

- *Career Key* (based on Holland model): http://www.careerkey.org.

- *Career Zone* (based on Holland model): http://www.nycareerzone.org.

- *Fast Track Me* (career planning tool):
  http://www.fast-track-me.com.

- *Life Works* (career interest questionnaire):
  http://science.education.nih.gov/lifeworks.nsf/careerfinder.htm.

- *Manifest Your Potential* (career planning tool):
  http://www.manifestyourpotential.com.

- *Oscar* (career interest and values questionnaire):
  http://www.ioscar.org/tx/oscar.asp.

- *Quest Career* (career interest questionnaire):
  http://www.questcareer.com/career_assessment_resources.html.

University admissions tests

For those who have to take a university admissions test there are a variety of useful practice resources. Some of these, such as Dr Test, also link to material that is valuable in preparing for graduate and managerial job applications.

- *Dr Test* (best site for all admissions tests):
  http://www.drtest.co.uk.

- *BioMedical Admissions Test* (BMAT): http://www.bmat.org.uk.

- *Dental Admissions Test* (DAT): http://www.ada.org/prof/ed/testing/dat/demo/index.htm.

- *Graduate Medical School Admissions Test* (GAMSAT):
  http://www.gamsat.co.uk.

- *Health Professionals Aptitude Test* (HPAT):
  http://www.hpat.org.uk.

- *History Aptitude Test* (HAT): http://www.history.ox.ac.uk.

- *Law School Admission Council* (LNAT practice):
  http://www.lsac.org.

- *Learning Matters* (QTS practice):
  http://www.learningmatters.co.uk/questions/intro.htm.

- *Modern and Medieval Languages test* (MML):
  http://www.mml.cam.ac.uk.

- *National Admissions Test for Law* (LNAT): http://www.lnat.ac.uk.

- *Ozimed* (GAMSAT practice): http://www.ozimed.com.

- *Personal Qualities Assessment* (PQA): http://www.pqa.net.au.

- *Physics Aptitude Test*: http://www.physics.ox.ac.uk.

- *Sixth Term Examination Papers* (STEP):
  http://www.maths.cam.ac.uk.

- *Training & Development Agency for Schools* (QTS tests):
  http://www.tda.gov.uk/skillstests.aspx.

- *Thinking Skills Assessment* (TSA): http://www.tsa.ucles.org.uk.

- *UK Clinical Aptitude test* (UKCAT): http://www.ukcat.ac.uk.

- *University College London* (BMAT practice):
  http://www.ucl.ac.uk/lapt/bmat.

Brain training

There are an increasing number of brain training websites, for example:

- *Funky Fogey Brain Gym* (brain training):
  http://www.funkyfogeybraingym.com.

- *Lumosity* (brain training): http://www.lumosity.com.

- *Smart Kit* (brain training): http://www.smart-kit.com.

360-degree feedback

Finally another area worth exploring is 360-degree feedback. This is the process whereby you rate yourself against a set of competencies, and then people who know you well (friends, colleagues and managers) also comment on your competencies. Have a look at:

- *Reactive 360* (360-degree feedback): http://www.reactive360.com.

- *Appraisal 360* (360-degree feedback): http://www.appraisal360.co.uk.

- *Track Surveys* (360-degree feedback): http://www.tracksurveys.co.uk.

Note: The lists in this chapter are based on a regularly updated web page that can be found at:

- www.markparkinson.co.uk/psychometric_links.htm.

You can also try new tests and questionnaires, which are currently under development, at:

- www.profilingforsuccess/freepsychometrictesting.htm.

Competencies

The word 'competency' is widely used in business and personnel psychology, and refers to the behaviours that are necessary to achieve the objectives of an organization. A competency is also something you can measure; and lists of competencies form a common language for describing how people perform in different situations.

Every job can be described in terms of key competencies. This means that they can be used for all forms of assessment, including appraisals, training needs analysis and selection. In fact, it is in the selection context, especially in advertisements, that you are most likely to come across competencies. For example, the following were recently used in a recruitment campaign for a major UK car retailer:

> You will have good **interpersonal** and **communication skills**, and have substantial personal **impact**. Also familiar with IT systems, you will enjoy **problem solving**, and make the best use of your **analytic skills** … This is a job that requires an **innovative** approach, coupled with a commitment to **teamwork**. You will be **quality focused**, and committed to building on our enviable reputation in the industry.

This is quite a typical list containing eight different competencies. It is these sorts of competencies that personnel professionals aim to detect by examining your application details, and through assessment processes such as psychometric testing and interviewing.

Different competencies

The competencies that follow are all commonly used in job specifications, and form the criteria against which to assess people. I have described each one and indicated if it can be assessed using a psychometric test or questionnaire. You can use this list, in conjunction with job advertisements, to decide which aspects of your ability or personality may be assessed by the tests you are asked to complete. Surveys have shown that the most popular competencies asked for are communication, leadership, judgement, initiative, motivation, analytic skills, planning, innovation, interpersonal skills and numeracy.

Individual competencies – your personal attributes

- *Flexibility* – This is the ability to change direction, or modify the way in which you do something. It includes a willingness to try, adaptability and a positive outlook.
  Measurement: *Personality or Motivation Questionnaire.*

- *Decisiveness* – This is a readiness to act and to take decisions. It involves making a balanced judgement and taking the appropriate actions.
  Measurement: *Personality Questionnaire.*

- *Tenacity* – This is the ability to persevere and stick with a problem until it is solved. It is also marked by the ability to abandon a problem if it is unsolvable.
  Measurement: *Personality Questionnaire.*

- *Independence* – This is a willingness to question the accepted way of doing things; also the strength of mind to pursue a course of action based on your own convictions.
  Measurement: *Personality or Values Questionnaire.*

- *Risk taking* – The extent to which you are prepared to take calculated risks. An important factor in many jobs including sales and manufacturing.
  Measurement: *Personality or Values Questionnaire.*

- *Personal integrity* – The maintenance of high personal standards; also the implementation of appropriate ethical and moral norms in a work context.
  Measurement: *Personality, Integrity or Values Questionnaire.*

Interpersonal competencies – dealing with other people

- *Communication* – The ability to convey information clearly and accurately, both orally and in writing; also includes a recognition of the importance of actively listening to others.
  Measurement: *Verbal Reasoning Test (for written communication).*

- *Impact* – The skill of creating an immediate and positive first impression on other people. A vital ability for many managerial and selling positions.
  Measurement: *Personality Questionnaire.*

- *Persuasiveness* – The ability to persuade and influence others to your point of view. This also involves being seen as believable and authoritative.
  Measurement: *Personality Questionnaire or Specialist Sales Personality Questionnaire (if appropriate).*

- *Personal awareness* – This is being aware of other people and the environment in which they operate. It means taking into account other people's thoughts and feelings before acting.
  Measurement: *Personality Questionnaire.*

- *Teamwork* – This means contributing in an active and co-operative way with other team members. It includes supporting other people, and making decisions by consensus.
  Measurement: *Personality Questionnaire or Team Role Indicator.*

- *Openness* – This is being able to encourage different points of view without becoming defensive; also the ability to build on the contributions from other people.
  Measurement: *Personality Questionnaire.*

Analytical competencies – the elements of decision making

- *Innovation* – The ability to come up with imaginative and practical solutions to business problems.
  Measurement: *Personality or Creativity Questionnaire or specialist Ability Test.*

- *Analytic skills* – The ability to break a situation down into its component parts, recognize what needs to be done and plan a suitable course of action in a step-by-step way.
  Measurement: *Critical Reasoning Test.*

- *Numerical problem solving* – The ability to understand and analyse numerical information. This includes financial data and statistics presented in reports, tables, graphs, charts, etc.
  Measurement: *Numerical Reasoning Test.*

- *Problem solving* – The ability to evaluate a situation and to identify an appropriate solution that meets the customers' needs – the skill of 'turning a problem into a solution'.
  Measurement: *Critical Reasoning Test.*

- *Practical learning* – This involves being able to absorb and learn new methods, and then applying them to job-related activities.
  Measurement: *Specialist Ability Test or Learning Styles Questionnaire.*

- *Detail consciousness* – The ability to process large amounts of complex information. This includes all forms of written, verbal and visual data.
  Measurement: *Ability Test or Personality Questionnaire.*

Managerial competencies – taking charge of other people

- *Leadership* – This is being able to take the role of a leader and guiding the actions of other people accordingly. The focus is on achieving results by working through other people.
  Measurement: *Personality Questionnaire or Leadership Style Questionnaire.*

- *Empowerment* – This is the concern for developing other people, and giving them the authority and responsibility to act on their own volition.
  Measurement: *Specialist Personality Questionnaire or Values Questionnaire.*

- *Strategic planning* – This is the ability to maintain a broad overview ('helicopter' view) of business activities, which allows you to plan for the future.
  Measurement: *Personality Questionnaire or specialist Ability Test.*

- *Corporate sensitivity* – This is the demonstration of an understanding of where a business is going, and of its agreed goals and strategies.
  Measurement: *Personality or Interests Questionnaire.*

- *Project management* – The ability to define the requirements of a project and to lead a group of people towards a specified goal.
  Measurement: *Specialist Personality Questionnaire or Team Role Indicator.*

- *Management control* – The appreciation that businesses need to be controlled and that the work of subordinates needs to be organized.
  Measurement: *Specialist Personality Questionnaire or Management Interests Indicator.*

Motivational competencies – the things that drive you

- *Resilience* – The ability to 'bounce back' in the face of adversity or when things do not go according to plan.
  Measurement: *Personality Questionnaire.*

- *Energy* – The personal store of energy that you bring to work, which helps you maintain a high level of performance – your 'stamina' or 'drive'.
  Measurement: *Personality Questionnaire or Motivation Questionnaire.*

- *Motivation* – This is the ability to motivate yourself *and* those around you. It's also related to knowing when to take control of a situation, and when to issue orders to other people.
  Measurement: *Personality or Motivation Questionnaire.*

- *Achievement orientation* – This is the drive to achieve results, and to set targets that provide personal challenges.
  Measurement: *Personality, Values or Motivation Questionnaire.*

- *Initiative* – This is the ability to work in a proactive way to anticipate events, and to act on opportunities as they arise.
  Measurement: *Personality Questionnaire.*

- *Quality focus* – This is the commitment to getting a job done well, and to recognizing that the quality of a product or service is of critical importance.
  Measurement: *Specialist Personality or Values Questionnaire.*

The preceding list is by no means exhaustive but it should give you an idea of the sort of competencies required by employers. You should also recognize that some of these competencies are difficult to measure with psychometric tests alone (especially those that I have indicated as needing 'specialist' measures), and many are assessed using a combination of methods, eg tests, interviews and group exercises involving a number of candidates.

Group exercises

Group exercises are designed to assess your problem-solving abilities, and responses to other people, in typical work situations. In some ways they are similar to the business learning exercises described in Chapter 3, but they involve a combination of both interpersonal and analytical skills. The following example will give you an idea of what is involved.

The runway exercise

'You are a member of a group of four planning officers who have to decide on the location of a new runway for a major regional airport. You have at your disposal a range of maps, plans, costings, economic surveys and the results of a local planning inquiry.'

'The task is to decide which one of three options best balances the demands of the regional economy, the local population and the environment. The group has two-and-a-half hours to produce an argued recommendation.'

This sort of exercise typically produces a range of arguments both for and against all the options. For example, in this case some of the key issues include the following:

Option 1:   Easy access to motorway and rail systems
Strong support from regional businesses
Enthusiastic backing from local Member of Parliament

but ...

Most expensive (£2.5 million)

Will destroy habitat of rare bird species

Requires some compulsory land purchase

Option 2: Least expensive (£1.8 million)

Uses some existing derelict land

Preserves habitat of rare birds

but ...

May produce a slight noise problem

Location makes it most difficult to build

Opposition from local pressure groups

Option 3: Costs £2 million (£3 million minus £1 million grant aid)

Requires no compulsory land purchase

Has room for business park (creating 2,500 new jobs)

but ...

Is opposed by national conservation groups

Requires a 'greenfield' site

May create a long-term pollution problem.

Which option would you choose?

If you are ever faced with one of these exercises, the most important thing to remember is that there isn't one perfect solution. What the assessors are looking for are reasoned and logical arguments, which take into account all the information provided. It's also important that all members of the group agree on the solution, and consequently that decisions are made on a consensual basis. Should you require any further information on group exercises the best place to look is in books that include chapters on Assessment Centres, eg *How to Succeed at an Assessment Centre*, published by Kogan Page.

SHL® practice tests (technical, clerical and graduate)

Series 1

Test 1: working with words 1 = A, 2 = B, 3 = E, 4 = C, 5 = E, 6 = D.

Test 2: working with numbers 1 = D, 2 = C, 3 = D, 4 = E, 5 = B, 6 = C, 7 = B, 8 = A.

Test 3: working with diagrams 1 = A, 2 = E, 3 = C, 4 = A, 5 = B, 6 = D.

Test 4: checking information 1 = A, 2 = E, 3 = B, D, 4 = A, B, D, 5 = E, 6 = A, B, C, 7 = B, D, 8 = B, C, 9 = E, 10 = A, B, C, D.

Test 5: recognizing shapes 1 = A, 2 = C, 3 = B, 4 = D, 5 = C, 6 = B.

Test 6: mechanical understanding 1 = A, 2 = C, 3 = B, 4 = B.

Series 2

Test 1: interpreting written information 1 = A, 2 = B, 3 = C, 4 = A, 5 = C, 6 = B, 7 = B, 8 = A.

Test 2: interpreting data 1 = D, 2 = A, 3 = B, 4 = C, 5 = E, 6 = C.

Test 3: interpreting diagrams: 1 = C, 2 = E, 3 = B, 4 = A, 5 = D, 6 = E.

Series 3

Test 1: verbal reasoning 1 = B, 2 = A, 3 = B, 4 = C, 5 = C, 6 = B, 7 = A, 8 = C.

Test 2: numerical reasoning 1 = A, 2 = B, 3 = C, 4 = B, 5 = E, 6 = D.

Test 3: diagrammatic reasoning 1 = C, 2 = B, 3 = E, 4 = B, 5 = D, 6 = A.

TFL graduate tests and thinking skills assessment

Test 1: abstract reasoning. Question 1 = (a) B, (b) A, (c) Neither, (d) A, (e) B, (f) B; Question 2 = (a) B, (b) Neither, (c) A, (d) A, (e) A, (f) Neither; Question 3 = (a) Neither, (b) A, (c) A, (d) B, (e) Neither, (f) A.

Test 2: verbal reasoning. Question 1 = (a) F, (b) T, (c) F, (d) F, (e) CT; Question 2 = (a) T, (b) CT, (c) T, (d) CT, (e) F; Question 3 = (a) F, (b) CT, (c) T, (d) CT, (e) T.

Test 3: numerical reasoning. Question 1 = (a) e, (b) b, (c) a, (d) b, (e) c; Question 2 = (a) e, (b) d, (c) c, (d) b, (e) c; Question 3 = (a) c, (b) c, (c) a, (d) d, (e) e.

Thinking Skills Assessment:
Question 1 = (d); Question 2 = (a); Question 3 = (c); Question 4 = (a); Question 5 = (b); Question 6 = (b).

Further reading from Kogan Page

Testing series

- *The Advanced Numeracy Test Workbook*
- *Aptitude, Personality and Motivation Tests*
- *The Aptitude Test Workbook*
- *The Graduate Psychometric Test Workbook*
- *How to Pass Numerical Reasoning Tests*
- *How to Master the BMAT*
- *How to Master Nursing Calculations*
- *How to Master the UKCAT*
- *How to Pass Advanced Aptitude Tests*
- *How to Pass Advanced Numeracy Tests*
- *How to Pass Advanced Verbal Reasoning Tests*
- *How to Pass the British Army Regular Soldier, Officer and Territorial Army Selection Process*
- *How to Pass Data Interpretation Tests*
- *How to Pass Diagrammatic Reasoning Tests*
- *How to Pass the GMAT*
- *How to Pass Graduate Psychometric Tests*
- *How to Pass the Life in the UK Test*

- *How to Pass Numeracy Tests*
- *How to Pass the Police Selection System*
- *How to Pass Professional Level Psychometric Tests*
- *How to Pass the QTS Numeracy Skills Test*
- *How to Pass the UK's National Firefighter Selection Process*
- *How to Pass Verbal Reasoning Tests*
- *How to Succeed at an Assessment Centre*
- *IQ and Aptitude Tests*
- *IQ and Psychometric Tests*
- *The Numeracy Test Workbook*
- *Test your Emotional Intelligence*
- Ultimate Psychometric Tests

Careers

- *The A–Z of Careers and Jobs*
- *Disaster Proof your Career*
- *Great Answers to Tough Interview Questions*
- *How to Get into Medical School*
- *Knockout Job Interview Presentations*
- *Learn While You Earn*
- *Preparing the Perfect CV*
- *Preparing the Perfect Job Application*
- *Readymade CVs*
- *Readymade Job Search Letters*

1

WHY PERSONALIZED MEDICINE?

EARLY ONE MORNING Jonathan, twelve years old, wakes up and finds that his stomach hurts—hurts badly. But he has no temperature and is not nauseous; he's just in a lot of pain. His mother, Marianne, is not alarmed at first, only irritated that she can't go to work. She lets Jonathan stay home from school, assuming that all will be well come evening. But the pain persists. By evening, she thinks perhaps seeing the doctor is a good idea; by early morning, after a night of sitting by Jonathan's bed, listening to him moan, going to emergency has become a necessity. After an interminable wait in the emergency room, Jonathan is finally examined by a doctor. The doctor gently prods and probes Jonathan's abdomen and then starts to look worried. He orders a CT scan. Marianne, who is now very apprehensive, asks, "What's wrong?" The doctor is noncommittal: "Let's wait for the scan."

But bad news follows. There is a mass in Jonathan's stomach, the size of a golf ball. At this point, Marianne is having trouble holding herself together, and she calls her husband, Bill, who immediately races to the hospital. He feels sick at heart— the dreaded "cancer" word has not been spoken yet, but it is in the air.

The news gets worse. Jonathan is admitted to hospital, a biopsy is performed, cancer is diagnosed, and surgery followed by chemotherapy is advised. Jonathan's life is at stake. The surgery is as successful as it can be, but it is very rare that a surgeon can remove all of this type of cancer. Hence the chemotherapy, to try to kill any remaining cancer cells.

Jonathan reacts well to the first dose of chemotherapy. He feels tired but does not get sick. Bill and Marianne allow themselves to dream: maybe Jonathan will get through this, and life will become a little more normal again. But following the second dose, Jonathan becomes short of breath after walking only a few steps. Back to the emergency: this time, the doctor calls a cardiologist, who tests Jonathan's heart using an echocardiograph. The cardiologist returns, grim faced. "Your son has heart failure," he informs Marianne and Bill. It turns out that Jonathan is highly sensitive to one of the drugs in the chemotherapy used to treat him. The drug, doxorubicin, causes heart problems in some patients,[1] but the doctors have no way of knowing which patients are going to be affected.

In the space of a month, Jonathan has been transformed from a normal twelve-year-old to an invalid undergoing cancer treatment who also needs a heart transplant. How did this happen? The presence of a tumor the size of a golf ball indicated a cancer that had been growing for at least three years. Why couldn't it have been detected long before, when it would have been much easier to treat?

And why was Jonathan treated with a drug that caused his heart to fail?

These "adverse drug reactions" are common: every year more than 2 million North Americans are hospitalized because of adverse reactions to prescription drugs.[2] The reason why drugs work in some people and cause bad reactions in others can usually be traced back to differences in genetic makeup. Medicines that work for most people may not work for you. They may, indeed, harm you. So we need two things: first, we need ways of predicting and detecting disease well before it becomes life threatening; and second, we need medicines that work for you and your unique body.

Medicine has been trying to do these two things for millennia. While enormous progress has been made, it is still not good enough. And so it is that we are nearing the biggest revolution of our time—perhaps of all time.

This revolution has many names and guises. It is sometimes called personalized medicine, sometimes precision medicine, sometimes stratified medicine. It is a cousin of "evidence-based" medicine, a relatively new concept in medical practice. (Whoever came up with that name was clearly trying to make a point.) Whatever the name, what we will call personalized medicine—medicine based on the unique molecular makeup of our individual selves and a molecular-level understanding of whatever disorder we may have—is on our doorsteps. It promises to satisfy our need to know what is wrong with us and provide ways to treat our ailments that our species has been seeking since the beginning of recorded time. It will also mean that once and for all, we will leave behind the natural evolutionary forces that our ancestors endured and embark on a self-directed future.

We tend to view medical progress as some sort of continuum, along which we develop better drugs to fight whatever diseases are prevalent, better machines to image our insides and detect problems, better devices to use when joints wear out or eyes fail, better ways to treat pain or depression or loneliness; and we might be inclined to believe that the future holds more of the same. But it is not going to happen that way.

Medical progress to this point has been mainly based on advances that benefit the population as a whole rather than you as an individual. Two hundred years ago, the average life span in England was only about forty years, largely because two-thirds of all children died before age four.[3] Public-health initiatives leading to adequate diet and clean water have had a huge impact, and these, combined with other population-wide advances such as vaccination, sterile procedures during childbirth and surgery, and antibiotics to treat bacterial diseases mean that the average life span today is about eighty years or more. But population-based approaches to maintain human health and life have begun to fail.

The most obvious way current medicine has begun to fail is in the development of drugs. When Paul Ehrlich discovered arsphenamine, a drug to treat syphilis, in 1909 and introduced the concept of the "magic bullet" to cure our illnesses, and when Alexander Fleming followed up with the discovery of penicillin in 1928 to cure a wide spectrum of infectious diseases, we became seduced by the notion that other compounds could be found that would have similar magical effects on other diseases, ranging from cancer to the common cold. An enormous industry, the pharmaceutical industry, has sprung up as a result, and there are now more than a thousand commonly prescribed drugs to treat almost every disease you can name. The average family doctor in North America writes more than 20,000 prescriptions for these drugs every year. This practice has led to alarming levels of medication, with approximately 20 percent of North Americans over the age of sixty-five taking ten or more drugs every day. More than 50 percent of Americans take at least one prescription drug each day.[4] As a direct result, the fourth highest cause of death in North America is a bad reaction to a drug or drug regimen, resulting in more than 100,000 deaths per year.[5] Furthermore, it has been estimated that up to 90 percent of adverse drug reactions are not reported,[6] so the dangers associated with taking prescription drugs are likely much higher.

In addition to the potential for causing a bad reaction, many of these drugs simply do not work for the individual who takes them. The numbers are appalling. Approximately 75 percent of drugs for cancer treatment do not help the patient they are prescribed for. More than 70 percent of the drugs for Alzheimer's do not work on the patient they are prescribed for. Nearly 60 percent of drugs for incontinence are of little use to the patient they are prescribed for. Fifty percent of drugs for osteoporosis do not lead to stronger bones in the patient they are prescribed for. Rheumatoid arthritis, migraine, cardiac arrhythmia, asthma—more than 40 percent of the drugs used to treat these conditions do not work on the patient they are prescribed for. In general, less than 50 percent of prescribed drugs actually help the patient they are prescribed for.[7]

There are problems even with drugs that are hugely successful. Statins, "blockbuster" drugs used to treat high levels of blood cholesterol, have been found to reduce the risk of a heart attack by 54 percent and the risk of a stroke by 48 percent.[8] They have been instrumental in reducing deaths due to cardiovascular disease to the point where it is now no longer the leading cause of death in the Western world. On average, for most people, statins work very well.

However, the problem with statins and other blockbuster drugs is that many people aren't average. Some people metabolize statins too quickly: their bodies break down the medication before it gets a chance to work, and their cholesterol levels stay high, so they are still at increased risk of a heart attack or stroke. Others metabolize the drug too slowly, and it lingers in their systems, lowering cholesterol levels but also causing all sorts of uncomfortable, often painful, side effects. It has been estimated that 17 percent of statin users suffer from muscle pain and nausea.[9] The really unlucky ones can have serious reaction to the drug, statin-induced rhabdomyolysis,[10] a debilitating form of muscle damage, which can result in kidney failure.

Adverse drug reactions occur because most common drugs go everywhere in your body. Only a small proportion, usually far less than 1 percent, ends up at a disease site where it can have a beneficial effect. The other 99 percent can cause problems in previously healthy tissues. Doxorubicin, a commonly prescribed anticancer drug, is very effective for killing rapidly dividing cells such as cancer cells, but because it goes everywhere, it also kills rapidly dividing cells in your bone marrow, causing your immune system to be compromised; in your stomach lining, causing you to throw up; and in your hair cells, causing your hair to fall out. All this is in addition to the severely toxic effects it can have on your heart.

There are still more problems. One of the first major successes of cancer chemotherapy was in treating childhood leukemia. In 1950, a diagnosis of leukemia in childhood was an almost certain death sentence, with more than 90 percent of children dying within a year.[11] Now more than 90 percent of children who are diagnosed with acute lymphoblastic leukemia, the most common type of childhood cancer, are cured, judging by the number of patients who remain cancer free for five years after treatment. But these survivors often do not lead normal lives. More than 30 percent of children treated with the most effective drug cocktail go stone deaf, permanently.[12] Other "side effects" include infertility, retardation—the list goes on and on. The costs to the child are immeasurable, emotionally damaging, and career limiting. The costs to society are daunting: often more than $20,000 per child per year until adulthood to provide special resources.

This example is not an isolated one. The common chemotherapy protocol for treatment of solid cancers in children calls for doxorubicin. It is not unusual for a child being treated for such cancers to go into heart failure as a result of chemotherapy, which sometimes makes a heart transplant necessary. More often, the effects of a weakened heart persist through the survivor's lifetime.

Drugs to treat many conditions are hit or miss: a family practice physician, on being asked how he selects the best drug for patients suffering from depression, answered, "Well, I have a dartboard hanging behind my door. It depends what number I hit." There is no way for him to know in advance which drug will work best for which patient and which patient will suffer a nasty side effect. And so the patient and the doctor embark on a risky trial-and-error journey to find the best, most effective drug for him or her.

The problems arising from the variable efficacy of drugs and their toxic side effects on healthy tissues have made the development of new drugs an almost impossible task: getting a drug approved now costs more than $1 billion and may take more than fifteen years.[13] Even then, some adverse reaction that occurs in a small subset of people may cause the drug to be withdrawn from the market.

All these problems spring from a one-size-fits-all approach to medicine. This approach doesn't necessarily work, because what you have always thought about yourself is actually true: you really are different from everybody else. And you need to be treated appropriately. The medicine of the future is going to be much more personalized—designed specifically for you and the body you inhabit.

Doctors are often upset by the term personalized medicine. "We have always practiced personalized medicine!" they proclaim, meaning that they listen to and consult with their patients and diagnose and advise on an individual basis. And so they do. But how much do they actually know about you? Your doctor sees the macroscopic version of you and, on the basis of a physical examination and your symptoms, can often diagnose what is wrong quite efficiently. But your doctor does not know much about the microscopic version of you, where disease and your responses to treatment are first manifested. Your doctor does not know details of your genetic code and therefore cannot know how you will respond to a drug he or she may prescribe. Your doctor does not know the composition of molecules in your blood, which contain a huge amount of diagnostic information regarding diseases that you may have or be trending towards, whether the drugs you are taking are working to cure whatever disorder you are suffering from, or whether your diet is appropriate. Your doctor does not know the types and amounts of micro-organisms that are living in you and on you, which influence how well your immune system is working and play important roles in inflammatory diseases. In short, your doctor does not have access to a lot of important molecular-level information about you to guide many of his or her decisions. This can lead to wrong or delayed diagnoses and inappropriate therapeutic interventions.

The medicine of the future will be more personalized—and much more effective—because detailed molecular-level information about you and whatever disorder you may have is increasingly available. The lead example is your genome— your DNA (deoxyribonucleic acid), which codes for every physical feature you have and which makes you the individual you are, with all your strengths and weaknesses. Soon it will be normal for you to have your genome sequenced, to decipher the molecular code contained in the long strings of DNA found in your cells, and have this information stored as part of your medical record. The sequence of your genome contains detailed and accurate information on your risk for diseases ranging from heart disease to diabetes, to depression and dementia, as well as information as to which drugs might work best for you and which might produce harmful side effects.

However, the sequence of your genome does not give complete information about you. With the exception of genetic diseases such as cancer and inherited conditions, genomic sequences are not that useful for diagnosing disorders you actually have—and that's where proteomics, the next level of molecular analysis, kicks in. Your genome codes for the proteins that make you the animal that you are; and all the proteins in your body constitute what's called your proteome. We're getting pretty good at measuring your proteome—which is important, because an analysis of, say, 1,000 proteins in your blood or other bodily fluid will potentially provide an accurate diagnosis of any disease you actually have or are trending towards. Such analyses will also be able to tell you whether the therapy you're undergoing or the lifestyle change you're making is helping you to regain your health.

And so it goes on: an avalanche of molecular-level analyses of the bits and pieces that make up you is coming online. Within the next five years, increasingly comprehensive molecular tests will be available that will tell you, with ever-improving accuracy, what is wrong with you when you don't feel well or are in pain or are depressed or feel weak. A hypochondriac's heaven—or hell, depending on your point of view.

For those who want a monitored life, it is going to be heaven. Wristbands, implants, or a high-tech Band-Aid will be able to give you minute-by-minute reports of your physical status, and you'll be able to download these to your computer to see day-to-day and longer trend lines. This degree of monitoring means a big change in preventive health care, or maintaining wellness. Soon you will have data that tells you whether that probiotic stuff you hate is working as advertised, whether those three drinks a day you crave are doing any harm—or good—or whether that gym membership is worth it. Elite athletes will be early adopters: for those always training at a level just shy of doing themselves injury, a voice in their ear saying their left calf muscle is going to tear in five minutes if they don't slow down or that their energy reserves are good for another thirty minutes at that pace, but no longer, would be most welcome.

This future is not far away. Many of the technologies that will allow truly personalized medicine are either in place or close to it. You have probably heard about many of them—nearly every day we hear of some advance in determining the molecular basis of one cancer or another or the development of drugs that can cure patients with genetic diseases such as cystic fibrosis. These announcements are usually accompanied by a solemn pronouncement that "these findings could lead to new medicines to treat disease within five years" or some variant thereof, and then you never hear about it again.

We have become inured to such announcements, thinking that they will never apply to us. But they will—and soon.

2

FROM MAGICAL THINKING TO PERSONALIZED MEDICINE

WHEN PEOPLE DON'T understand things that are clearly important, they often resort to magical thinking, otherwise known as making stuff up. Inventing deities to explain the world around us was a favorite occupation of our ancestors. Mayans would sacrifice virgins at dawn as the sun rose over the Atlantic, blood-red from its battles in the underworld of night, to celebrate yet another victory of the sun god. For the Greeks, thunder and lightning expressed the displeasure of Zeus, the god of the sky. In Chinese mythology, clouds were the breath of the dragon kings. The Indian god Indra brought on the monsoon rains by defeating Vritra, the Demon of Drought, who held the "cloud-cattle" captive in his mountain fortress. Creation was explained by the Apache gods Tepeu and Gucumatz, who sat together and thought, and whatever they thought came into being. They thought "Earth!"—and there it was. And on it goes, every civilization inventing fascinating myths to explain everything from the origins of the universe to the stars in the sky and what happens after death.

Disease and pain are particularly effective for inducing magical thinking. In medieval Europe, Christians thought the bubonic plague to be a punishment for man's wicked ways. Self-flagellation, to atone for one's sins, was therefore seen as a logical means to avoid the Black Death. In fifteenth-century Japan, disease was believed to be caused by horrible little creatures living inside you. Dizziness and hot flashes were caused, for example, by an animal living in your spleen called Hizonomushi, which could cause problems by grabbing your muscles with its long arms and claws. Luckily, Hizonomushi could be tamed if you ate rhubarb. To ancient Egyptians, illnesses were caused by the presence of evil spirits. Cleansing the body by incantations, prayers to Sekhmet, the goddess of healing, and the injection of nasty-tasting medicines into various bodily orifices to drive the evil spirits out, were prescribed treatments.

We still indulge in remarkable levels of magical thinking when our health is threatened. Folk remedies for everything from treatment of the common cold to cancer are followed with zeal. Apple cider vinegar for treatment of allergies, acid reflux, gout, arthritis, headaches, yeast infections, psoriasis, you name it. Banana peels for warts, beets for constipation, Epsom salts for nail fungus—there are loyal proselytizers for all these "cures." Herbal remedies are used to treat depression, heart disease, insomnia, hypertension, and weight gain. Twenty thousand herbal medicines are available in the United States, and these are used by more than 80 million people. However, there is very limited evidence that even the ten most commonly used remedies are at all effective, and harmful side effects can be significant.[1] There are even believers in the benefits of homeopathic medicine, who strain credulity when they tell us that giving less of a therapeutic is somehow supposed to result in improved therapy.

This level of magical thinking is inconceivable in almost all other areas of our lives. You certainly wouldn't accept that a plane crash was caused by bad karma or that your boat sank because you offended the god of the sea. But when it comes to our health, we give our imagination full rein. There is good reason for this, of course: When there are no explanations or cures for things that are sometimes terribly wrong, what else can we do? We consult the high priests of medicine about our ailments; they consider, discuss, and prescribe; sometimes things work and sometimes they don't. We feel ourselves to be helpless cogs in a giant medical processing plant that we do not understand and are powerless to resist, and magical thinking is our only resort.

Personalized medicine, which we will also call molecular medicine, is the antithesis of magical thinking. It is driven by the conviction that every ailment you have has a cause at the molecular level and that once you understand the cause of your disorder, an appropriate molecular-level treatment can be devised that will work for you. It is also driven by the conviction that signals of disease are apparent well before the disease appears (at which point it may be too late). We simply need to recognize what those signals are.

The road from magical thinking to personalized medicine has been blazed by the development and application of modern science, an odyssey that began less than 500 years ago.

The story begins with Galileo Galilei, born in Pisa, Italy, in 1564. He is generally accepted to be the father of modern science. He was the first scientist to note that the universe is constantly changing, the first to observe that moons could orbit around planets, and the most effective in championing the view that the Earth could be orbiting the sun. Because of his inability to accept the magical thinking that put the Earth at the center of the universe, he was found "vehemently suspect of heresy" by the Roman Inquisition and put under house arrest by the Catholic Church for the last nine years of his life. Galileo was also the first to postulate in clear terms that mathematics is key to understanding the universe. Galileo stated that "the universe ... cannot be understood unless one first learns to comprehend the language and interpret the characters in which it is written. It is written in the language of mathematics ... without which it is humanly impossible to understand a single word of it; without which, one is wandering around in a dark labyrinth." This statement is fundamental to all progress that has been made since Galileo's death, in 1642, in determining what we are made of and how it works. There is little doubt that if there is a God, the language that He/She/It speaks is mathematics. Anyone who has experienced the eerie, unearthly, completely alien precision with which mathematics can be used to describe the universe from the beginning of time to the end of time, from the very smallest particle to the very largest galaxy, has a sense of this.

Isaac Newton was born in a small village near Cambridge, England, in the year in which Galileo died. He lived in Cambridge and London and during his lifetime, drove a dagger into the heart of magical thinking. He did it by taking Galileo's approach to heart, developing sophisticated mathematics that allowed him to marry mathematics with natural philosophy and thereby inventing modern physics. He invented classical mechanics and calculus to explain the motion of suns and planets and devised a theory of optics to explain how light works. Before Newton, everything was magic; but by using his classical mechanics, people came to understand that eclipses occurred because the moon gets between the Earth and the sun, that the sea rises and falls because of the gravitational pull of the moon and the sun, and that seasons happen because of the Earth's axial tilt. Furthermore, he proved that if you get accurate data, construct the right model, and do the mathematics correctly, you can predict when high tides will happen, when eclipses will occur, when comets will blaze across the sky, and when they will return. Magic reigned no more.

How does this apply to you? The classical mechanics Newton invented to understand the movement of planets, as well as apples falling from trees, also applies to the world of the very small, down to distances as little as one billionth of a meter (a nanometer), at which point quantum mechanics takes over. Since the molecules and cells in your body are bigger than a nanometer, classical mechanics can be used to describe and predict the ways the molecules in your body move and interact, which is basic to the construction and interpretation of you at the molecular level. But Newton's work is far more pro-found than that. By the time he died in 1727, we had the sure knowledge that we can understand natural phenomena by first measuring them very accurately, then building a theoretical, mathematical model that fits with these observations, and finally by conducting experiments to test other predictions of the theory to see if it is generally true. This approach is the most fertile discovery process the world has ever known.

Antonie van Leeuwenhoek was a contemporary of Newton's, although they never met. He was born in Holland in 1632 and was the first person to show that while you may think of your-self as a continuous whole, there are many little bits of you. Leeuwenhoek made powerful microscopes that could magnify by as much as 500 times, allowing him to see individual cells. In a series of reports to the Royal Society of London, he described the microscopic world for the first time, including bacterial cells he found in any body of water he looked at, the bacteria he found in his mouth and feces, blood cells he found in blood vessels, sperm cells he found in "recent ejaculate from a healthy man," the organized arrays of cells he found in muscle, and so on. Leeuwenhoek's discoveries showed that to understand you, we first need to understand what goes on in the cells you're composed of.

What *does* go on in the cells that you're made of? The initial steps to address this question were taken by a French Anthony, namely Antoine Lavoisier, who was born in 1743 in Paris, where he remained all his life. Lavoisier was interested in how things burned and why air is necessary for things to burn. Through a careful series of experiments that signified the start of modern chemistry, he determined that when things burn, a component of air is consumed to produce carbon dioxide. The component that is consumed is now known as oxygen, and as a result, the process of burning is often referred to as oxidation. Lavoisier then showed in a remarkably intuitive experiment that when an animal breathes, it produces exactly the same amount of heat per amount of oxygen consumed and amount of carbon dioxide produced as any other combustion process.

Thus was born the idea that a constant process of slow burning, or oxidation, takes place in our bodies, where the food that we eat is the fuel that we burn. This discovery explained why our bodies are warm and led to subsequent discoveries of how oxidation is used to provide power for movement, thought, and sight—in short, for all bodily functions. Lavoisier's contribution to understanding ourselves was profound; however, he had the misfortune to be a wealthy and influential man in Paris at the time of the French Revolution. He was guillotined in 1794 after being convicted of corruption on trumped-up charges. He was pardoned a year later, but by then it was a little too late.

Lavoisier was followed by another giant in the evolution of chemistry: John Dalton, who invented the atomic theory and the idea that elements combine to form molecules consisting of fixed ratios of these elements to make liquids, such as water, and gases, such as carbon dioxide. Dalton was born in 1766 in England and spent most of his life in Manchester, dying there in 1844, just after a statue was erected in his honor in the town square. The combined work of Lavoisier and Dalton gave rise to modern chemistry, including biochemistry, which describes the way that biological molecules, such as proteins coded for by your DNA, do their work inside cells.

Charles Darwin was also vitally important in the quest to understand what you're made of. He was born in 1809 and managed in his lifetime to establish the fundamental reality that humans and all other life forms are related to each other by a vicious selection process known as evolution, in which only those species most adapted to their environment survive. The concept of survival of the fittest permeates to the very heart of you: each molecule in your body has evolved through millennia to function as well as possible to ensure that species that preceded you could survive. Mechanisms that were honed over 4,000 million years of evolution in species ranging from bacteria, sponges, worms, fish, and vertebrates have been adapted in your body in more ways than you can imagine. For example, every cell in your body contains little fuel cells called mitochondria. Mitochondria perform the oxidation process first noted by Lavoisier and produce molecules called adenosine triphosphate (ATP) by burning molecules derived from the food you eat. The ATP, in turn, provides power for your body to function. Mitochondria are direct descendants of an early bacterium that evolved to live in a symbiotic manner in cells that were precursors of the cells making up your body. Without mitochondria, we could not exist.

Your ability to see depends on the evolution of proteins that can detect light. Vision evolved during a relatively short period of evolutionary time (400,000 years) from primordial light-sensing proteins that enabled unicellular organisms to orient towards the sun. When versions of these proteins were some-how incorporated into animals to enable them to see, organisms that couldn't see became lunch for animals that could.

Charles Darwin could have used some personalized medicine. The list of ailments that tortured him throughout his life are legion and include "malaise, vertigo, dizziness, muscle spasms and tremors, vomiting, cramps and colics, bloating and nocturnal intestinal gas, headaches, alterations of vision, severe tiredness, nervous exhaustion, dyspnea, skin problems such as blisters all over the scalp and eczema, crying, anxiety, sensation of impending death and loss of consciousness, faint-ing, tachycardia, insomnia, tinnitus, and depression."[2] There are tales that he suffered from uncontrollable flatulence that caused him to retire to his study for at least an hour after din-ner. Nonetheless, he was one of the giants, up there with Newton and Galileo, in the battle against magical thinking. His theory of evolution allowed us to discover ourselves by analyzing simpler organisms such as yeast, flies, and mice to see what makes them—and you—tick. This work has led to the discovery of DNA as the molecular mechanism whereby biologi-cal information can be passed on from generation to generation, the discovery and characterization of early versions of the cells and molecules that you are made of, and the discovery and development of all the ways we have to treat disease.

In parallel with the exploits of Leeuwenhoek, Lavoisier, Dalton, and Darwin in understanding the biological world, progress was also being made in understanding the physical world, again based on the example Newton set. An important example is electricity, which is not just vital to our civilization but also vital to every device we use to characterize you and to interpret the vast amounts of information that result. Two pioneering scientists who enabled us to use electricity were Michael Faraday and James Maxwell. Faraday discovered that electric currents were associated with magnetic fields. He made the first electrical motor when he showed that a changing electrical field could exert a force on a magnet in that field, and he hypothesized that magnets (and wires carrying electrical currents) had invisible fields associated with them, which he called lines of force.

James Maxwell, who was born in Edinburgh in 1831, was a direct intellectual descendant of Newton in that besides trying to understand natural phenomena, he was also one of the best mathematicians of his time. He invented the new mathematics required to understand the relationship between magnetism and electricity. He showed that Faraday's lines of force had a tangible reality that could be modeled theoretically. He came up with Maxwell's laws, which solved electromagnetic behavior for all time, and allowed us to generate and transmit electricity and to use it in all the electronic gadgets we are so familiar with today. His work also led to wireless transmission of information, ranging from radio to television, to the wireless connection your cell phone uses. Maxwell was only forty-eight when he died, but like Newton, he changed the world, moving electricity from the curiosity of static electricity or the drama of lightning into something we could understand, harness, and use. Aside from enabling the machines we use to characterize all the molecules that make you up, Maxwell's equations also apply to the electrical currents that are used by the nerves in your body to make your hands move on demand or your heart beat or your brain think.

There is another important stream of intellectual endeavor that has led to a greater understanding of our molecular selves:

technology, or the application of science to produce things of practical use. Galileo and Newton developed technology by grinding lenses and building telescopes so they could examine the heavens in detail and see whether their theories were compatible with observation. The tradition of building ever more sophisticated instruments to investigate natural phenomena has become deeply ingrained in science, particularly physics, and has led to every single one of the machines we use today. Technology received a decided boost when Maxwell found out how we could tame electricity and has since gone on to define our civilization.

But how does the development of technology apply to personalized medicine? The answer lies in the computers we use to collect and decipher the molecular information describing you, the machines we use to visualize what is going on inside you, and the ways in which we can transmit information about you.

Without computers, the notion of molecular medicine could not exist. Computers are used every step of the way, from controlling the instrumentation that we use to decipher your DNA, for example, to storing the immense amounts of data that we get from molecular-level analyses of DNA, proteins, and other biological molecules, to analyzing all this data so that we can use it to benefit you. But we haven't always had computers. How did they come to be? The imaginings of Charles Babbage and the brilliance of Alan Turing played a large part. Babbage was born in London in 1791 and is considered the "father of the computer," although he only ever had one working model, and it was very limited. Babbage had a great many interests, being a mathematician, philosopher, astronomer, economist, inventor, theologian, cryptographer, and engineer. He also wrote a variety of articles for popular consumption on "public nuisances" such as the abominable nature of street music to the role of drunkenness in women and boys as the cause of broken windows. Obviously, a lot of things, including many people, bothered Babbage.

One thing that particularly bothered Babbage was that mathematical tables necessary for navigation, the forecasting of tides, or computation were full of errors, as the numbers were derived by "computers"—which, at that time, were human beings. Babbage thought that one way to eliminate these mistakes would be to have the tables generated by machines designed for the task, and he set about designing such an instrument, drawing on his considerable engineering talents. The result was the "difference machine"—a mechanical computer having 15,000 parts and weighing 10 tons. The difference machine was, in fact, never built in Babbage's lifetime, but it was completed some 150 years later by following Babbage's original plans—and it worked.

Alan Turing, who was born in 1912 in London, had an enormous influence on the design of computers. In 1935, he published a scientific paper that demonstrated that any computation that can be reduced to a set of instructions can be done by a computer, subsequently called a Turing machine. He also played a major role in winning the Second World War by designing the early mechanical computers that broke the German cryptography codes. This allowed the British to read the transmissions of the German army, navy, and air force. Alan Turing and other cryptographers worked at Bletchley Park, north of London. As Winston Churchill put it, Bletchley Park was "the goose that laid the golden egg—and never cackled."

Turing did not receive much thanks for his amazing contributions. He was homosexual, which led to his arrest in 1952 on charges of gross indecency. His security privileges were revoked, and criminal charges were brought against him. He was given a choice of prison or chemical castration, and he chose castration. He committed suicide in 1954. The British Government gave an official apology to Alan Turing in 2009, but as with Antoine Lavoisier, it was a little too late.

The Turing machine envisioned and built by Alan Turing anticipated and led to all the computers we use today. The ones we use now, however, are a great deal more powerful, much more compact, much easier to make, much cheaper, and much more personal. How did this happen? It is here that we get into microtechnology and nanotechnology, and we can start to see how the grand design of nature's technology (the molecules and nanomachines that make up you)—which was arrived at by evolutionary forces—and the technology that arises from the findings of Newton, Maxwell, and Darwin are converging. Both the natural and the human-made technologies are aimed at perfecting machinery that functions in the world of the very small.

It is important to start to think in terms of the world of the very small. It is crucial to understanding how technology has evolved to produce all the devices we see around us, particularly the devices we use to store and process data about you. It is also vital to understanding yourself, as you consist of an enormous number of exquisitely designed nanomachines. The computers we design are decreasing in size as we cram more and more functions into smaller and smaller spaces. This trend was predicted by Richard Feynman in 1959 when he gave a lecture that signaled the start of the information age. The lecture was entitled "There's Plenty of Room at the Bottom," a brilliant title for a deeply profound insight into nature. Richard Feynman was one of the most influential thinkers of the twentieth century. He played a key role in the Manhattan Project, which produced the atomic bomb, and he won a Nobel Prize in 1965 for his work on quantum theory. Fellow physicists held Feynman in awe because of his remarkable computational abilities and his unique ways of solving problems. When asked how Feynman solved problems, one colleague commented, "Well, he thinks really, really hard and then tells you the answer." He was an unusual person—his favorite hobbies were cracking safes and playing bongo drums, and he found the atmosphere of a local strip bar to be most beneficial for productive thought.

Feynman certainly pointed out that very large amounts of information could be stored and analyzed in very small devices. Through a simple series of calculations, he demonstrated that without breaking any of the laws of nature, it should be possible to store the entire contents of the Library of Congress, together with addresses indicating where that information is stored, in a particle smaller than a speck of dust. The computers and smartphones we use now illustrate how far we have come in realizing this goal: compared with early computers such as Colossus—which was built in 1944 and was the size of an average office—today's laptop is at least a billion times more powerful. And we still have a long way to go before we hit the limits that Feynman identified.

The key to making computers smaller was the invention of the transistor. Until 1950, the only way we could control electrical currents to make devices such as radios or TVs was by using glass vacuum tubes that housed electrical circuits that regulated the flow of electricity through the tube. These tubes were large, the size of a shot glass or bigger, and lots of them were required—which resulted in computing machines the size of Colossus, with enormous energy demands. William Shockley, in partnership with John Bardeen and Walter Brattain, invented the transistor in 1947, which changed everything. Shockley also demonstrated that brilliant people are not necessarily that enlightened: he had distinctly bigoted views. He believed, for example, that the human race was being degraded because poorer people with limited intellectual capabilities were having too many children. The transistor, however, was an enormous contribution. Transistors can be configured to be in an "on" state (current can flow through) or an "off" state (no current flows through), and are therefore ideally suited to storing information in the binary code (zeros or ones) that all computers use today. In addition, the main component used in transistors is silicon, also known as sand, so costs can be low. Finally, the circuits that make up transistors can be miniaturized so that massive amounts of processing power and information can be stored in very little space.

The first transistor was very large by current standards—about the size of a small postage stamp. Today, a single transistor can be more than a thousand times smaller. By putting transistors together in appropriate ways, the functions of complete circuits can be achieved, and by putting a lot of these circuits together as one physical entity, integrated circuits that perform specific functions (such as detection of radio waves, amplification, data storage, and so on) can be made. Interestingly, the length scale of the circuitry in today's integrated circuits is approaching the length scale of the machinery in your body's cells, which operates on the nanometer scale. In 1990, the smallest circuit components had dimensions of 500 nanometers, which were reduced to 45 nanometers by 2010 and are now approaching 10 nanometers. We are nowhere near being able to match the complexity of biological nanotechnology, which has been honed by eons of evolution, but we are getting closer.

So Newton's work led to Maxwell's insights, Shockley's transistor, and Feynman's predictions, which in turn led to Bill

Gates, Steve Jobs, and the computers, smartphones, and other devices we know and love. Thanks to this progression, we now have ways of storing and analyzing enormous amounts of information. And Lavoisier, Dalton, and Darwin laid the groundwork for modern biochemistry, and thus a molecular-level understanding of living organisms began to evolve.

Still, how is it that we have found ways of detecting, characterizing, and measuring all the molecules that make you up? It's through application of all the technology we've developed to make everything from computers to smartphones, to the cars we drive, to the movies we watch. This technology is now sufficiently advanced that it can be used to decipher you at the molecular level.

The application of technology to biology started slowly but is now ramping up to warp speed. Early examples were the microscopes invented by Leeuwenhoek, but it wasn't until the discovery of X-rays by Wilhelm Röntgen in 1895 that things really took off. The discovery of X-rays led to many things, two of which are vital to personalized medicine. First, X-rays provided a way to look inside you—as was noted by Röntgen. The first X-ray picture ever taken was one by Röntgen of his wife's hand. On seeing the skeletal structure, she exclaimed, "I have seen my death!" Today, you take the ability to image things inside your body for granted, but up until 1900, it was impossible. X-ray machines have been used for all sorts of things, including by shoe stores to see how well your shoes fit—definitely not the most inspired of applications. Now we have all sorts of ways to look inside ourselves, including sophisticated X-ray machines called computed tomography (CT) scanners, which give remarkable three-dimensional visualizations of bones, tissues, and tumors in your body; magnetic resonance imaging (MRI) machines, which give images with excellent resolution for soft tissues such as the brain; and ultrasound imaging, which allows you to look at your baby before it is born.

The second way that X-rays are vital to personalized medicine is that they can be used to determine the structure of the molecules you are made of. Linus Pauling, one of only four people who have won two Nobel prizes, was the first to develop this application. Pauling became a professor at the California Institute of Technology in 1927 and was a polymath who excelled at everything he did, although he did perhaps oversell the benefits of vitamin C, which he proposed as a cure for cancer and the common cold. Pauling not only used quantum mechanics to understand how atoms in molecules were joined together but also took it upon himself to develop the use of X-ray techniques to understand the structure of the proteins that make up your body. In the process, he was the first to identify the root cause of a genetic disease. He showed that sickle-cell disease occurred because the structure of hemoglobin in people with the disease is slightly different from that of normal hemoglobin. This anomaly was later traced to one difference in the genetic code for hemoglobin in people with sickle-cell disease, which leads to one difference in the amino-acid composition of hemoglobin. This difference produces a hemoglobin molecule that tends to crystallize within blood cells, causing them to adopt a sickle shape, which has many unpleasant consequences, such as an enhanced tendency for stroke as well as priapism—erections that won't go away.

The concept that differences in protein structure, which arise as a result of mutations in your DNA, can cause disease is essential to understanding the importance of a personalized approach to medicine. Protein structure determines ways that you differ from everybody else. If a mutation creeps into your genome that leads to a slightly different structure for a protein, serious genetic diseases can result. For example, individuals who have cystic fibrosis have mutations in their DNA that lead to missing components—and an ineffective structure—in a protein that transports chloride ions across cell membranes. This leads to salty skin, buildup of mucus in the lungs, and other, more serious problems. One in 200 people have genetic mutations that lead to structural defects in proteins that pump ions across the membranes of your heart cells,[3] causing your heart to beat irregularly. Sometimes the first evidence that you have of these mutations is sudden death, so it's important to know if you carry that gene before you die at age nineteen after a particularly intensive session on the basketball court.

X-ray technology also allowed James Watson and Francis Crick (with the considerable assistance of Maurice Wilkins and Rosalind Franklin) to unlock the structure of DNA, revealing the iconic double-helix structure for the first time. This achievement was a culmination of the discoveries of Darwin and the technology made possible by Newton, and it set the path for fifty years of research that would lead to the beginnings of personalized medicine. In research published in 1954, Watson and Crick showed that the structure of DNA led to a logical method by which the sequence of the four "bases" that make up DNA could code for the proteins that do all the work in your body. During a celebration of this discovery at the Eagle Pub in Cambridge, Crick is reported to have exclaimed, "We have discovered the secret of life!" And he was right. To make that relevant to you, however, to unravel the secrets in your genome, methods of determining the sequence of your DNA and proteins it codes for are needed.

Sequencing began with the genius of Fred Sanger, who worked in Cambridge all his professional life, first at the Department of Biochemistry of the University of Cambridge and then the Laboratory of Molecular Biology of the Medical Research Council. It was his genius, as it is with most geniuses, to recognize the obvious. In his case, the obvious was that if proteins do all the work and if the structure of proteins determines how they do that work, it was pretty important to develop ways to discover the sequence of proteins to understand the molecular composition that determines their structure and, therefore, their function. Having solved this problem and won one Nobel Prize, he did the next obvious thing, which was to say that if the sequence of proteins is determined by the sequence of the DNA that codes for the proteins, it was pretty important to sequence DNA too. So he did that as well and won a second Nobel Prize. Thus was born the science of sequencing, which has grown increasingly, unbelievably rapidly over the last twenty years. In 2000, it took ten years and cost $3 billion to complete the first sequencing of a human genome. Now it costs around $1,000 and takes a day or two.[4]

Our ability to measure everything else has grown at equal speed. There are thousands—probably more than 10,000—proteins in your blood. Many of these originate from your brain, your heart, and other organs in your body, and measuring their levels in your blood can potentially diagnose the health of the organ they came from. A technique called mass spectrometry can now be used to rapidly determine the levels of hundreds of different proteins in a drop of blood. The same sequencing techniques used to decode your genome can be applied to characterize the different bacteria in your body by rapidly sequencing the bacterial DNA to determine which bacteria are present. These are the fundamental advances that have given rise to personalized medicine: suddenly we have the ability to measure what you are made of, at the molecular level, for the first time in human history. Contained in all this information are "biomarkers" that are diagnostic for every facet of your being, including what your risks of disease are, what diseases you may actually have, and what diseases you may be trending towards.

Soon, within five years or probably less, all these tests will be available for you as a consumer to buy and use. It is likely that the cost will be less than $100 for each molecular profile, and you will have far more reliable data about yourself than anybody has ever had before. Properly interpreted, this data will provide accurate information about what may be wrong with you and provide strong clues as to how to put it right. Magical thinking will reign no more.

THE
MOLECULAR
YOU

AS A RESULT of the efforts of Newton and Maxwell and Darwin and a legion of other scientists and clinicians, we now have the ability to measure a lot about ourselves, not just at the level of organs such as our heart or lungs, not just at the level of the cells that make up the organs and tissues in our bodies, but now at the level of the molecules that make up our cells. These molecules are the most basic determinants of our identities. It is this amazing advance that is fueling the personalized medicine revolution.

Knowledge of yourself at the molecular level is going to have a huge impact on you because you have a fundamental problem. When you were born, you were given a unique body, possibly the most complicated organism on the planet, but you were not given an operator's manual. To use a car as a metaphor, you were not even given very many instruments to monitor how well your body is functioning, and you weren't given any information on the best fuel you should feed your body, whether it should be premium or regular, or whether ethanol can be used as an additive. A number of us seem to run quite well on ethanol, also known as alcohol; but others, not so much. You weren't given any early warning lights to tell you that a life-threatening disease is starting somewhere in your body or that your immune system is going off-kilter, or that some behavior or environmental exposure will lead to arthritis in the future. You have no instrumentation to tell you whether any of those lifestyle changes you make to better your health actually work, and you are usually not quite sure whether the medication you take to fix your aches and pains is doing what it is supposed to do.

In addition to the lack of an operator's manual, you have another, possibly even more basic, problem. Evolution, which led to the exquisitely designed body you live in, does not care about you. Once you are born, you are on your own. If you have lots of children that survive, your genetic code will survive and prosper, but once you have passed child-bearing age, evolution has no further use for the rest of you at all, and your body gradually breaks down and dies. So not only do you need an operator's manual, but you also need to understand how you were made in the first place in order to combat this inevitable decline.

Molecularly based, personalized medicine will give you a rather intimidating operator's manual. It will contain information you may not want to know but really need to be aware of to maintain your health and avoid illness. When used in combination with our ever-improving ability to engineer biological systems, it will provide knowledge that could lead to an ability to fix yourself—your personal repair manual—by manipulating yourself at the cellular and molecular level. It will be by far the most valuable thing you will ever own.

How will we bring your personal operator's manual into reality? The first step is to make an inventory of the molecules that you are made of. The sum total of all this molecular information can be called the "molecular you." The second step is to store all this molecular information in digital form. The resulting dataset comprises the "digital you." The digital version of you will be an impressive amount of data, but not that much use to you unless you can use it to answer your questions about yourself. So the final step on the way to achieving your personal operator's manual will be to devise computerized methods to query your digital self to get definitive answers to important questions you may have.

What questions will your personal manual be able to answer? As we shall see, when fully operational, it will answer more questions than you might think possible. If you don't feel well, you will be able to ask it what is wrong with you and what the best treatment may be. You will be able to find out what drug will most effectively treat whatever disorder you have, and whether you will experience harmful side effects. You will get answers concerning what diet may be best for you and what foods you should avoid. You will be able to find out whether the medicine you're taking or the lifestyle change you've made is effective. It will tell you of your risks of diseases, and you'll get early warnings that a disease is forming in some part of your body well before it becomes life threatening.

The initial versions of your digital self will contain four categories of molecular information, and you can expect more categories to be added over time. First will be your genome: the molecular information that will be measured and stored will be the sequence of your genome, which contains the blueprint of your physical being. Your genome can be taken from almost any cell in your body, as they all contain the same sequence of DNA. Second will be your proteome. Initial measures of your proteome will likely involve determining the levels of 100 or more proteins in your blood, which should be sufficient to get an immediate snapshot of your health. Third will be your metabolome; measurement of 100 or more metabolites in your blood will yield clues as to how your body is dealing with your diet and can also diagnose disease. Finally, we will have to get a measure of your microbiome, or the bacteria and other micro-organisms that live in and on your body. Here, the detection of a few hundred bacteria in your feces will provide vital diagnostic and therapeutic information, particularly for the origin and treatment of immune disorders.

To understand the type of information the digital version of you will provide, and the insight it will give into how to fix whatever is wrong with you, you need to understand a bit about the biology of your body, the processes that go on inside you that make you the fascinating organism that you are. Let's start with your cells—those little bits of you that Leeuwenhoek was the first to observe. You have a lot of cells in your body, approximately 30,000 billion of them, and each of those cells is on average 10 micrometers, or 10 millionths of a meter in diameter. To understand how small a micrometer is, the thickness of the lines forming the letters you're looking at as you read this book is about 100 micrometers. That means ten cells could fit into a line wide enough to be part of a letter big enough for you to read. But the journey towards smallness doesn't end there. Each cell in your body contains a lot of even smaller bits and pieces. Some of these are a thousand times smaller than a cell.

To describe how big these components are, we have to use the nanometer as a measure. There are a thousand nanometers in a micrometer. Luckily, we don't have to go any smaller than that or we'd have to use quantum mechanics to understand ourselves. Each cell contains a nucleus that is approximately 100 nanometers in diameter. And the nucleus contains your genome, your deoxyribonucleic acid, or DNA—the genetic material that codes for the proteins that make the cells that make up your body—wrapped up in twenty-three pairs of bundles called chromosomes. DNA is made of four molecules—guanine (G), cytosine (C), adenine (A), and thymine (T)—known as "bases," which are joined together in long strands. Each of these strands is associated with another "complementary" strand to make up the iconic double-helix structure that Watson and Crick first identified. The complementary strand has a sequence of bases that is complementary to the sequence on the first strand: all the Gs are opposite (paired with) Cs, and all the As are paired with Ts. And vice-versa.

Approximately 99.9 percent of the 3 billion base pairs in your genome are the same as in any other member of the human race. All your differences—the features that make you unique—are encoded by only 0.1 percent of your DNA. But 0.1 percent of your genome corresponds to 3 million base pairs, so there is the potential for a lot of genetic differences. Included in these differences are some sixty brand new mutations—changes in the sequence of bases in your DNA—that have never existed in any person ever before. You really are a mutant. All these genetic differences determine not only differences in eye and hair color between you and anybody else, but also whether you have a higher risk of lung cancer or a lower risk of Alzheimer's disease or a greater chance of a heart attack. The ways that you differ genetically from everybody else also allow the forces of natural selection to work. If you prosper and have lots of children that survive, your genetic code will be conserved and passed down to future generations.

In our exploration of your biology and how molecular-level information such as the sequence of your genome can be incredibly useful, let's start from the beginning, from when your mother and father had (hopefully) a mind-blowing sexual encounter that led to one of your father's sperm cells getting together with one of your mother's eggs to produce a fertilized egg—otherwise known as a totipotent stem cell—from which all the other cells in your body have been made. The sum total of all the DNA in this totipotent stem cell, half of which came from your mother and half from your father, is your genome. The sequence of your genome is fixed: it doesn't change in your lifetime. This DNA supplied all the information needed for the totipotent stem cell to divide time and time again to ultimately form your heart, arms, legs, and every other part of your body. If we could understand all the instructions encoded in your genome, we could predict a lot of things about you: what you would look like at various ages, what reasoning abilities you were going to have—and what diseases you might be susceptible to. Your genome codes for how tall you are, what color eyes you have, how well coordinated you are, the color of your skin—all the physical characteristics you have—whereas your environment has determined what languages you've learned, what religion you might or might not believe in, and which football team is clearly the best in the world as far as you're concerned.

The proteins that your genome codes for enable you to think or move or see or smell. If you had a lethal dose of radiation, which would destroy your DNA, you would not die immediately, but you would be a dead man—or woman—walking. That's because you wouldn't be able to make new proteins to replace old ones as they are degraded; all the proteins in your body are turned over on a regular basis. The sequence of bases in your DNA code for proteins using twenty amino acids that can be put together in any order. It takes a sequence of three bases to code for a particular amino acid, so if a protein is composed of 1,000 amino acids, it requires a gene consisting of a stretch of 3,000 bases of DNA to code for it. In order to make the protein that the gene codes for, the sequence of bases on the gene in the genome is first copied into another stretch of nucleic acids called ribonucleic acid (RNA; which is very similar to DNA) that then contains the code for just this one gene. This "messenger" RNA (mRNA) is then translated into a protein.

The process of forming a protein from a gene is called gene expression. Gene expression and how well the protein produced will work depend on many factors. For instance, gene expression depends on which variant of a gene you've inherited from your parents. These variants can be dominant or recessive, and you need only one copy of a dominant variant—for example, the one that codes for wet earwax—for that trait to be expressed. In contrast, you need two copies of a recessive variant—the one that codes for dry earwax, say, to see that trait expressed.

Lots of things can go wrong with gene expression. If one of the DNA bases in the gene that is expressed is wrong or is omitted, the resulting protein will have a different amino-acid composition and may be defective, leading to genetic diseases such as familial hypercholesterolemia, Huntington's disease, or sickle-cell anemia. The story surrounding the severe form of familial hypercholesterolemia, in which two recessive variants are present, is a great example of how a genetic analysis can lead to basic understanding of a disease and the development of appropriate medicines. Individuals afflicted with severe familial hypercholesterolemia inherit defective genes from both parents that code for a protein called low-density lipoprotein receptor (LDL-R). The cells of these people are unable to accumulate low-density lipoproteins (LDL, commonly referred to as "bad" cholesterol), which transport cholesterol from your liver to peripheral tissues such as muscle and heart. As a result, LDL levels in the blood build to extremely high levels, resulting in cholesterol deposits forming atherosclerotic plaques within the arteries, which then restrict blood flow and cause heart attacks. For people with familial hypercholesterolemia, these heart attacks can occur early in life—during the teenage or young adult years. In families suffering from this condition, there are tales of fathers play-wrestling with their teenage sons, and both father and son dropping dead of heart attacks as a result of the sudden exertion.

In the 1970s, after high cholesterol levels in the blood were identified as the cause of atherosclerosis and high rates of heart attacks, researchers immediately focused on finding ways to inhibit the production of cholesterol in the body to reduce atherosclerosis, which was then the major cause of death in the Western world. This research resulted in the discovery of statins, which interfere with the production of cholesterol in the body. Despite the side effects that statins can have for some people, they have been instrumental in reducing the incidence of heart disease in the Western world to the extent that cancer is now the dominant killer.

Aside from differences in DNA sequence, there are other ways in which protein production can be affected. One common way in which you may differ from the person next to you is in the number of copies of a particular gene you have in your genome. These genetic differences, known as copy number variants (CNVs), can cause changes in the number of proteins made. If you have more copies of a gene that makes proteins that metabolize certain drugs, you will have a different response to those drugs than a "normal" person might. This idiosyncrasy will be revealed when your genome is sequenced. CNVs have also played an important role in evolution. Chimpanzees, for example, make only two copies of a protein known as amylase, which is present in saliva and plays a role in digesting starches, such as those found in potatoes and wheat. Humans, however, can have as many as fifteen copies of amylase—presumably an adaptation that assisted in our transition to a diet that included starchy foods.

A protein that has the wrong amino-acid composition, whether as a result of a faulty gene or errors in either transcription from the genome or translation of the mRNA, probably won't fold into a functional shape. In addition, misfolded proteins are typically not water soluble. An example is the denatured proteins that form the skin on the surface of boiled milk. Misfolded, insoluble proteins in your body can build up as harmful deposits called amyloid plaques and are associated with more than twenty serious human diseases, particularly neurological diseases such as Alzheimer's, Parkinson's, and Huntington's. Amyloid plaques also play a role in prion diseases such as mad cow disease or its inherited human variant, Creutzfeldt-Jakob disease. Once you know which protein is present in the amyloid plaques, you can then design therapies to specifically inhibit production of the protein being deposited, or ways to dissolve the plaque itself.

Only about 2 percent of your genome consists of the 20,000 genes that code for the proteins that make up your body. For a time, it was thought that the "noncoding" regions represented genetic material acquired during human evolution that was no longer needed. Some called these regions "junk DNA."[1] Whoever came up with that phrase should have known better. Evolutionary forces certainly do not favor wasting energy, and it takes a lot of energy to make the enormous amounts of DNA present in the genome in each cell in your body. It turns out that at least some of the noncoding DNA in your genome codes for RNA sequences that do not make proteins but instead regulate gene expression by a process called RNA interference, or RNAi. The RNAi sequences, called microRNA (miRNA) do this by binding to specific mRNA molecules that have a complementary sequence to them. This process causes the mRNA to be degraded and prevents it from making a protein.

MicroRNAs play extensive roles in regulating gene expression in your body, particularly during generation of your organs in embryo, as well as during tissue regeneration and aging. MicroRNAs also play important roles in the growth of cancer cells, and the detection of specific miRNAs in your blood can be diagnostic for the presence of cancer in your body.

All of your cells contain the same genomic DNA, so how do all of the specialized cell types in your body arise? This phenomena is the subject of epigenetics, which concerns how gene expression is regulated so that in specialized cells, only part of the DNA in your genome is translated into proteins. The whole process of differentiation—cells dividing time and time again to form the different organs that you're made of—relies on a highly orchestrated process of genes turning on and off until the subset of proteins that a cell makes are appropriate to its function. For example, muscle cells make lots of long string-like proteins called actin and myosin. Signals transmitted from your brain can cause these proteins to contract, giving rise to muscle movement. In your eyes, large amounts of a protein called rhodopsin are made. Rhodopsin changes its structure when it absorbs light of certain frequencies, and eye cells use this change in structure to transmit a signal to the brain so that you can see. Cell differentiation occurs in a precise fashion. You certainly don't want teeth to form in your muscles or an eyeball to form in your liver.

There are two main ways that a cell can modulate gene expression via epigenetics. There is an on-off switch called methylation, which involves chemically modifying genomic DNA to prevent a gene from being expressed. Alternatively, gene expression can be regulated by controlling how tightly the DNA containing the gene is wound up in the chromosome it is associated with.

Scientists are increasingly able to reverse the differentiation process of a cell to cause it to revert to the stem cells from which the tissue was made.[2] This finding has huge implications for personalized therapeutics and arises from research that has been progressing steadily for more than forty years. In the 1960s, scientists discovered that when the nucleus of a frog skin cell was injected into a frog egg cell whose nucleus had been removed, the recipient egg could produce a normal tadpole. This result means that all the epigenetic controls on the fully differentiated, non-embryonic skin-cell genomic DNA were removed when placed in the environment of the frog egg, indicating that the chemical modifications of the DNA and how tightly it was coiled are reversible. What was also novel and scary was that the new tadpole matured into a new frog that was genetically identical to the frog from which the donor nucleus was derived.[3] This process is called cloning, a graphic example of what was once science fiction coming to life.

Approximately twenty species, ranging from mouse to mule, to horse, to water buffalo, have now been cloned. The first mammal to be cloned was Dolly the sheep.[4] She was cloned in 1996 using cells taken from a donor sheep's udder. As with the frog in the example above, the nucleus was removed from the donor cells and placed in a sheep egg cell from which the nucleus had been removed. The reconstituted egg cell was then placed in the uterus of a host sheep, and Dolly was delivered approximately five months later. She was named Dolly after Dolly Parton because she'd been cloned from udder cells. Who says scientists don't have a sense of humor?

There is little doubt that any human, including you, could be cloned using technology now available. But from a personalized medicine point of view—ethical questions aside—what use would this be to you? It would take years for your clone to be big enough to provide donor organs such as a replacement heart. Apart from the fact that you may not be able to wait that long, by that time your clone may not be too amenable to giving his or her body parts away. It is here that stem cells come to the rescue, at least potentially. You began as a totipotent stem cell that divided to form other cells that, in turn, eventually formed all the other differentiated cells that make up your skin, heart, brain, and so on. All these tissues are renewed regularly: your skin is replaced every two or three weeks, your blood every four months, your skeleton every ten years, and your heart every twenty years. This renewal is orchestrated by "adult" stem cells—that is, cells that are capable of dividing to renew the tissues in which they reside.

So now we have a somewhat less ethically challenged potential solution to renewing failing organs. If you want to renew your heart cells, you need to stimulate, or replace, the adult stem cells that make heart tissue. The same is true for your kidney or any other cells or organs in your body. As a result, stem cells are the subject of intense research, and new findings come daily. Scientists are now working on ways of making stem cells from any tissue by reversing the epigenetic process that leads to the fully differentiated cells, thereby producing "induced pluripotent stem cells (IPSCS)." These IPSCS can then be led back down the differentiation pathway to produce any tissue you may want. For example, skin cells can potentially be reprogrammed to become heart cells. From a personalized medicine standpoint, if, say, you want to see what effect drugs to treat atrial fibrillation will have on your heart as opposed to anyone else's, you should, in the not too distant future, be able to scrape a few cells off the inside of your cheek and get them reprogrammed into cardiac cells that are genetically identical to the ones in your heart. You could then treat them with drugs and drug combinations to determine which ones will work best for you and have the least chance of causing adverse drug reactions.

The future of stem cells as therapeutics is remarkable, given their potential ability to renew any part of your body. One issue is that as you age, the number of adult stem cells in your tissues decreases and their ability to differentiate into functional cells declines. Thus, even though your skin replaces itself every two weeks or so, the new skin produced is not quite as good as the old skin, leading to the thinner, wrinkled skin that older people don't like very much. If we could find a way of stimulating production of adult stem cells in your body, or reprogram them so that they differentiate more accurately, then they could replace your skin with younger skin, your heart with a younger heart, and your bones with younger bones.

While this may seem impossible, do not underestimate the power of the technologies that Newton and Darwin unleashed on the world. Already there are indications that stem cells can be reprogrammed in the tissues where they are found. In an experiment that has connotations of Dracula, researchers at the Harvard Stem Cell Institute connected the circulation of a young mouse to that of an old mouse whose heart was showing signs of hypertrophy, or enlargement, which comes with age and is a precursor to heart failure.[5] Within four weeks of sharing the younger mouse's blood supply, the heart of the older mouse started to become smaller and "younger." A protein, GDF11, which is found in large amounts in young mice but which declines with age, was identified as a possible signal. Sure enough, injection of this protein into older mice produced the same signs of reversed aging in the heart.

So, where are we as we delve down into the molecular you? So far, we have covered how your genome leads to your proteome and the ways that the cell you started from can give rise to all the other cells in your body. But there's a lot more to you than that. There's the old saying "You are what you eat," and in a literal sense, that's true. The proteins, carbohydrates, fats, minerals, and vitamins that you eat all go into making you what you are. A large proportion are either incorporated into proteins in your body or used for energy to power your body. The way that the proteins, carbohydrates, and fats that you eat are used or "metabolized" gives rise to an enormous number of molecules in your body. These molecules are commonly referred to as metabolites.

Consider what happens to proteins, such as those in meat, cheese, or eggs, after you've chewed and swallowed them. They travel to your stomach, where they are bathed in strong acid and are partially decomposed into their constituent amino acids, and then they move into your intestines, where the breakdown is completed. The amino acids that made up the proteins are then transported across the lining of your intestines to enter the bloodstream, where they are taken up by the cells in your body and made into proteins required for cell function. All these amino acids and amino-acid fragments in your blood are metabolites, and the sum total of all the metabolites in your body is your metabolome. If you have defects in your ability to metabolize certain foods, or if you suffer from metabolic diseases such as diabetes, those conditions will be reflected in your metabolome.

You are probably beginning to think, "My God, does this process never end? Do I have to know about every molecule and cell in my body?" Luckily, not really. But if you want to know what data your individualized operator's manual will use to tell you things you really need to know, and also how that information will suggest ways to fix any problems you have, you should stick with the program for just a little longer. There's one more category of things that you're composed of that just has to be included in the molecular description of you: your microbiome—all the bugs that live in and on your body.

Your body is a symbiosis of your human cells with hundreds of trillions of other organisms (microbes) that live inside you and on you. For every one of your cells containing your DNA, you also have ten bacterial cells, and they, along with yeasts, viruses, and parasites, make up your microbiome, which contributes to your state of health in ways we are just beginning to understand. There are more than 10,000 species of bacteria in your body, and these populations differ substantially between individuals. There's a good chance that there are species of bacteria and fungi living inside your ear or in your colon that have not been characterized yet, because many of these organisms have not been grown outside your body. The particular environment in your body that allows them to thrive can be difficult to reproduce.

Bacteria in your microbiome can have a very direct effect on your health. For example, your microbiome possesses most of the gene processing power in your body and can metabolize certain prescription drugs. Thus the makeup of your microbiome can influence the effect drugs have on you. Your microbiome can affect your health in other interesting ways: for example, a *New Yorker* article in 2012 described a man in Pittsburgh who had been suffering for years from a chronic infection in his left ear.[6] His doctors had tried everything, including several types of antibiotics, as well as antifungal drops. Then one day he turned up in the clinic with his ear completely cured of any infection. It turned out that he had taken some of the wax out of his good ear and put it into his bad ear. A few days later, he was fine. Presumably, the bacteria in his good ear had replaced the bacteria that were causing the chronic infection in his bad ear.

A recent review in *Nature* has pointed out the importance of mammals passing through their mother's vagina, which is colonized by an enormous number of types of bacteria.[7] Babies born by Cesarean section do not necessarily pick up these bacteria and may have an incomplete microbiome, which in turn can influence how the baby's immune system develops. In 2012, approximately 30 percent of all children born in North America were born by C-section, and the incidence of allergies and asthma is far higher among those children than it is for vaginal-birth babies.

And it doesn't stop there. It has been some time since it was discovered that the bacterium called *Helicobacter pylori* plays a causative role in the formation of stomach ulcers, leading to the treatment of stomach ulcers by using antibiotics. But why is *H. pylori* there in the first place, and does it play any positive role? The answer would appear to be yes: there is strong evidence that destroying *H. pylori* can alter metabolism in ways that increase the risk of obesity. In people whose stomachs are infected with *H. pylori*, appetite-stimulating hormones are much less detectable after a meal. But in people whose stomachs are not infected, the levels of the hormone remain high, so the message to stop eating doesn't make it to the brain.[8] Research has shown that mice fed antibiotics at dosages similar to those used to treat children with ear infections gained considerable weight compared to mice that did not receive the antibiotic.[9] This, perhaps, is not surprising: most antibiotics consumed in North America are used as dietary supplements to promote faster growth in poultry, cows, and pigs.

We have had a preoccupation with killing bugs since Louis Pasteur showed that infections and illnesses could be caused by microscopic germs entering the body and since Alexander Fleming developed the wonder drug penicillin, which revolutionized our treatment of infectious disease by killing infectious bacteria. However, we may be overdoing it. Perturbing your microbiome by taking antibiotics is not without its dangers. As many as 40 percent of children treated with a broad-spectrum antibiotic will develop a condition called pediatric antibiotic-associated diarrhea due to the havoc that these drugs cause in the bacteria colonizing the intestines.[10] About 10 percent of people carry a dangerous bacterium called *Clostridium difficile*. The bacterium is normally held in check by other residents of the gut. But when those companion bacteria are destroyed by antibiotics, *C. difficile* can erupt, causing severe diarrhea and deadly inflammation in the colon. The infection causes hundreds of thousands of illnesses and 14,000 deaths in America each year. Nearly every *C. difficile* infection occurs as a result of antibiotic treatment.[11]

Conversely, restoring your microbiome to a healthy state by using some rather unusual approaches can dramatically improve your health. For example, fecal transplants replace "bad" bacteria in the gut—those that are associated with diseases such as inflammatory bowel disease—with "good" bacteria taken from healthy donors. The donor's fecal material is placed in the patient's intestines, usually during a colonoscopy. Results from initial clinical trials have been remarkable. In one study to treat inflammatory bowel diseases such as Crohn's disease and ulcerative colitis, sixty patients who were treated using a fecal transplant achieved a 95 percent cure rate. Other trials have reported success rates of more than 80 percent.[12] This is important: nearly a million Americans suffer from inflammatory bowel disease with major effects on their quality of life. Luckily, it is fairly easy to persuade donors for fecal transplants to provide the necessary material, although the recipients may feel less enthusiastic.

The microbiome in your stomach and intestines break down food that your own proteins can't, and in the process, they create vital molecules such as vitamin B and vitamin K. And healthy microbiota in the gut and on the skin, not to mention in the ears, eyes, and respiratory and reproductive systems, can be allies against infections by harmful bacteria. Striking the right microbial balance is key: for example, the vagina is home to yeasts and bacteria that usually keep each other in check. A subtle change to the vaginal environment can cause one population to flourish over another, resulting in a yeast infection.

So the molecular version of you has to include your personal microbiome. You will have to get over any squeamishness you may have about the bugs that live symbiotically with you; they are a vital part of your being. You are a tightly coordinated system consisting of billions of micromachines and nanomachines, all of which have to run smoothly individually and act together to produce the living, breathing you.

If the thought of fecal transplants and borrowed earwax to rescue your microbiome seems a little weird or possibly abhorrent to you, you're not the only one. It points to a possible problem in Western society: in our quest for cleanliness, we may have gone overboard. Many immunological and autoimmune disorders are much less common in the third world than they are in the Western world. Almost 10 percent of youth in North America suffer from asthma, but in rural Africa it is much less prevalent. This situation may be related to a need to keep your immune system healthy by challenging it appropriately.

Realizing how complicated your immune system is and getting a little dirty may be an important component of your personalized medicine protocol. For example, certain immune cells contain components called toll-like receptors (TLRs) that help to fend off infectious agents. There are more than ten TLRs present in immune cells in the skin and other places susceptible to infection, and TLRs are quite specific with regard to the type of bug that they are programmed to react to and destroy. TLR3, TLR8, and TLR9 recognize RNA from viruses. Most others are specific for proteins found in bacteria. What is clear is that inappropriate activation of these receptors leads to autoimmune problems. Artificial activation of TLR4, for example, which is programmed to respond to certain bacterial infections, gives rise to asthmatic symptoms.

Given the fact that your immune system has evolved to protect you against bacterial and other infections, and that you contain such an enormous population of bacteria and other microbes, it should come as no surprise that your microbiome can have major effects on the function of your immune system. Your microbiome and immune system are clearly barely tolerant of each other, yet they are dependent on each other. Scientists recently demonstrated that the immune systems in genetically identical, same-sex mice responded quite differently to the same stimuli. This effect was eventually traced to different microbiome compositions in the individual mice. So disorders of your immune system, which range from asthma to arthritis, to inflammatory bowel disease, can potentially originate from, or be exacerbated by, an imbalanced microbiome.

The very presence of organisms that the immune system was evolved to fight may be necessary for proper immune function. The lack of stimulation of our immune system in early life and the development of immunological problems later on has led to the "hygiene hypothesis": that clean upbringings, relatively free of parasites and infectious agents, do not lead to development of a healthy immune system and can cause it instead to become hyperactive. A hyperactive immune system is not what you want: it can result in everything from allergies to disorders in which your immune system attacks your own tissues, such as occurs in multiple sclerosis or lupus.

Keeping your immune system occupied in fighting the battles it was designed to fight might just reduce the chances of it becoming oversensitive and starting to reject parts of you. People who are infected with hookworms seem to suffer fewer autoimmune-related diseases, including asthma and hay fever. This observation has led to a fairly radical treatment for autoimmune disorders known as Helminthic therapy. This sounds innocuous enough until you realize that it involves infecting yourself with parasitic worms that your immune system evolved to fight many eons ago. Helminthic therapy has been proposed as a treatment for a variety of autoimmune diseases: inflammatory bowel disease, multiple sclerosis (a nasty autoimmune disease affecting 300,000 North Americans, in which the body attacks the insulation surrounding its own neurons), asthma, dermatitis, and food allergies.[13]

Although maintaining your microbiome in a healthy state and in balance with your immune system appears to be a good idea, there is certainly good reason not to go all the way with getting dirty again. The health gains made by the development and use of antibiotics and vaccines are enormous. However, eating a little dirt, avoiding antibiotics when you can, and getting a few infections, especially when you're young, may not be a bad thing either. While we are still a long way from a detailed understanding of the relationship between your microbiome and your health, the outline is becoming clear. We have evolved an immune system to deal with bugs and parasites of all sorts, resulting in a curious symbiosis and a delicate balance. If your microbiome is perturbed, you will be too.

The catch phrase for an old detective TV series called *Dragnet* was "Just the facts, ma'am, just the facts"; and in this chapter, we have covered a lot of facts regarding the things that make up the molecular you. And your genome, your proteome, your metabolome, and your microbiome are just the start. There are other "omes" that have not been mentioned and more yet to be discovered. Hidden in this treasure trove of molecular information are facts that provide the clues vital to the detective work of finding out what is right or wrong with you; whether you are in the early stages of disease and whether the therapy you are undergoing is working. So now we have to find ways of measuring all these molecules to get a description of you at a molecular level, put it into digital form, and then figure out what it means. That's the topic of the next chapter.

4

THE
DIGITAL
YOU

BY NOW, YOU might be asking, "If personalized medicine is so important, where is it? My doctor has never mentioned it. I read this abstract stuff in the paper or in magazines saying new genetic tests will bring us to a cure for cancer in five years or whatever, but people have been saying stuff like that for twenty years. As far as I can see, medicine hasn't really changed that much in my lifetime. It still seems pretty hit or miss." The unfortunate thing is, you're absolutely right.

But this time it's different.

What makes personalized medicine possible now is described by that overused term convergence. A multitude of technologies have now begun to converge to make personalized medicine possible. The technologies that originated with Newton and Darwin now provide us with the ability to sequence your genome from, say, one of your skin cells in a couple of hours, measure a few hundred proteins or metabolites from a drop of your blood to characterize your proteome and metabolome, or describe the microbiome you never wanted to know you had by analyzing fecal matter taken from toilet paper you have just used. There's the computer technology originated by Babbage and Turing and enabled by the nanotechnology envisioned by Feynman, all of which gives us the enormous data storage and processing power that we need to deal with the massive data cloud consisting of your genome, your proteome, your metabolome, and your microbiome; the sum total of which describes you more completely than anything ever has before. Then there's the technology originated by Maxwell that led to the electronic age, the Internet, social media, and all the remote-sensing devices that are now available. All of these technologies are converging to measure you at the molecular level, store these data digitally, analyze this "digital you" to determine your state of health and disease and then suggest the best way to keep you in a healthy state or treat any illness diagnosed.

The concept of the digital you is very important, though you may find it unsettling that such detailed information about you should be rendered in such an accessible form. But that ability is just another expression of the digital revolution, otherwise known as the information age, which in two short generations has transformed almost everything in our civilization. Except medicine. We used to have typewriters; now we have computers. We used to write letters; now we email. We used to go to the library if we wanted to find something out; now we use Google. We used to have travel agents; now we have Expedia. We used to have phones that weren't all that smart and that stayed in one place; now we have portable phones that can do more than we can comprehend. We used to have records and record players and more recently compact discs, and they too are going the way of the dodo as smartphones and cloud services become music central. There are many other industries in transition. We still have books that are made of paper, but Amazon and Kindle have other intentions. We still have cars that you actually have to drive, but Google will change that soon. The list is endless, but the technology is the same. Everything is being reduced to digital form so that it can be readily stored, transmitted, analyzed, and utilized.

Consider a song. One hundred years ago, if you wanted to hear someone sing a song, you had to take out the horse and buggy or fire up the Model T and go to the theater to hear it. Or you could have bought some rather scratchy recordings that sounded vaguely like the original artist when played on a phonograph, but the effect certainly was not the same. Things improved as vinyl records became available after the Second World War but then changed completely in the 1980s, when compact discs replaced them. So what happened? We moved from analogue to digital. Records and their precursors relied on picking up the sound vibrations from the air and imprinting those vibrations as little ridges in grooves on the wax or plastic surface of a record. If the record was then spun at the right speed, and a needle was placed in the grooves of the record to rub over the ridges, it would vibrate, and you heard the song. That was analogue recording. Digital recording onto a compact disc is completely different. Here, the sound vibrations are converted into a stream of numbers representing the frequency and intensity of sound over time. When placed in a CD player, these numbers are converted back into sounds by reversing the recording process. Now, of course, we are forgetting about the CD and streaming the numbers from the Internet directly to your computer or iPhone to reconstruct the song. Similarly, when we are creating the digital you, we convert your molecular information into numbers that can be used to recreate you—or at least a pretty good imitation of you. It won't quite be you, but it will hum a few bars.

What bars will it hum? Well, initially, it too will be a little scratchy, but the main thing is that you will be able to start asking your digital self some important questions. Your personalized operator's manual will start to come to life. For example, once you have your genome in a digitized format, you'll be able to ask it whether you will have a bad reaction to a drug that your doctor prescribes, whether that drug will make you cough, or whether it will work on you at all. You'll be able to ask it about your risk of inherited diseases. You may soon be able to ask it whether you have any chance of being that elite athlete you always wanted to be or whether a career as a rocket scientist is in the cards. More seriously, if you get cancer, you will be able to have your cancer-cell genome sequenced and ask which mutated genes are present and which drugs may best be used to treat them. The convergence of social media and patient-to-patient organizations could well lead you to post your cancer genome on the Internet so that you can find out what other people with similar cancer genetic profiles have done and how well their therapies have worked for them. This represents a rather interesting transition of power, one in which patients, as opposed to doctors or scientists, get to decide on what information gets shared with whom.

So far, so good. What else will the digital you enable you to do? A lot more. As you start to monitor your proteome, say, in the form of the proteins in a particular bodily fluid such as your blood, you'll get a lot more data that you can add to your digital self. You'll have to do this regularly, maybe every two or three months, in order to get data showing that you're trending in one direction or another, as your proteome can change substantially depending on your health. If you are trending towards other diseases such as arthritis or diabetes, you will see increases in inflammatory proteins or retinol-binding protein respectively. Seeing these "biomarker" proteins move in the wrong direction may be enough to get you off the couch occasionally. Eventually your proteome will provide early warning of everything from heart failure to kidney failure, to viral infections, lung disease, stroke, heart attacks, cancer— you name it. And when stored in your digital self and looked at over time, you'll be able to see whether you're moving in the right or the wrong direction, and whether the efforts you're making to avoid full-blown disease are working or not. You will be able to experiment with your digital self to see whether your diet, lifestyle change, or exercise program is doing what you want it to.

Your metabolome and your microbiome will also be part of the digital you. Your microbiome may be off-kilter because you have overused antibiotics, your diet is wrong for you, or you inherited an unhealthy variety of bacteria from your mother. You may well want to complement all this information with other data, such as your blood pressure, electrocardiogram, heart rate, and sleeping patterns, as gathered by the recording devices that you wear. Eventually, when we can find ways of measuring it, you will want to store your brain connectome (the connections between neurons in your brain) to get a handle on your mental health and why you feel so irrationally happy, even though your digital you says you shouldn't. Or vice-versa. So the questions now become how do we gather the data we want, how do we store it, and how do we analyze it so that you can get answers to your questions about that most important person: you.

Let's start by sequencing your genome. The DNA-sequencing methods developed by Sanger have now been supplanted by much faster, next-generation sequencing techniques in which the genomic DNA is first broken down into thousands of short fragments. The sequence of each of these fragments is then determined simultaneously using millions of reactions all going on at the same time. The sequences of the DNA fragments are then fed into a database and analyzed by genome-assembly software that relies on finding fragments that contain regions with the same DNA sequence, to reconstruct the sequence of the entire genome. But technology isn't stopping there: new approaches are on the horizon that can sequence DNA through electronic techniques rather than the chemical techniques originated by Sanger. These methods could decrease the time it takes to sequence human genomes to a couple of hours, using a device only slightly bigger than a USB memory stick. In this device, the DNA to be sequenced is fed as long strands through a nanopore—a hole with a diameter of a few nanometers—and the electrical resistance as the bases pass through the hole is measured. Each base has a slightly different size or charge, giving a distinct resistance signature for each base and thus allowing the sequence to be determined.[1]

All this sequencing stuff may sound like science fiction, but think of this: when you were an embryo in your mother's womb, the process of sequencing your genomic DNA and making a new copy in a dividing cell took about five hours. Three billion base pairs were read during that time, and three billion new base pairs made, corresponding to a rate of 160,000 bases per second, all with an error rate of less than one in every 10 million bases that were made.[2] Talk about nanotechnology in action! We don't have to invent any of this, just reverse engineer it. So genome sequencing is certainly going to get even faster, and cheaper, than it is today.

How about proteomics? How are we measuring different proteins, what tissues are we taking the proteins from, and how are the data related to health and disease? Most effort is going into using the blood as a window into what is happening inside us. Your blood bathes every organ in your body, and proteins specific to each of your organs leach out into the blood as it passes through. It has been estimated that we could measure the health of a particular organ by measuring a subset of only twenty or so proteins in the blood that originate from that organ. The problem is that there are many thousands of proteins in the blood and they differ in concentrations by more than nine orders of magnitude.[3] In other words, some proteins are present at concentrations that are more than a billion times higher than other proteins, and this makes the less-prevalent proteins difficult to detect and quantify.

One technique used to measure your proteome is mass spectrometry. Each protein in your blood has a unique molecular weight, and mass spectrometers are very good at detecting the molecular weights of molecules in a sample, from which the identity of the protein the sample contains can be determined. Other techniques use very specific tags such as antibodies or smaller molecules that bind to particular blood proteins very tightly but don't bind to any others. By measuring the amounts of a given molecular tag that is associated with a blood sample, for example, the species and amounts of a given protein in your blood can be determined. Although it is difficult to predict which technique will be the winner, it's clear that we now have the ability to measure many hundreds, if not a thousand, proteins in a blood sample within a few hours and at costs of less than $1,000. Like genomic analyses, proteomic analyses of your blood are going to get faster and cheaper and, in the near future, will no doubt cost less than $100 for measurement of a hundred or more proteins.

At present, blood proteins are analyzed one by one in specialized laboratories, and the results reported to your doctor a week or so later. But the day is fast approaching when a much more complete version of your proteomic profile will be available to you directly for uploading into your digital self. There are a number of ways this could be done. Christoph Borchers of the University of Victoria, for example, has developed mass spectrometry techniques that allow dried blood proteins to be reliably analyzed.[4] To obtain your blood protein profile by this approach, you would simply smear a pinprick of blood on a piece of blotting paper and FedEx it to the laboratory, getting the results back by email to be downloaded into your digital self a couple of days later. Eventually, it is possible that a small, disposable chip will be developed to perform similar functions in real time. Analysis of the proteomic data will reveal immediately useful information, ranging from levels of bad or good cholesterol (no more cheesecake!) to whether the chemotherapy you are taking to treat your cancer is working, whether your cancer has returned, whether you are trending towards a heart attack, whether that hit on the head caused a concussion—in short, a complete snapshot of your health and disease status.

The technique used to measure your microbiome could be the same genome-sequencing technology used to decipher your genomic DNA, but this time samples from your ear, nose, or feces, which contain high levels of bacteria and other microbes, will be analyzed. Rapid genome sequencing of the microbes will detect the presence of particular strains of bacteria and other microbes that coexist with you by detecting their characteristic genetic signatures. The populations detected will depend on where the sample is taken from, as bacterial populations vary substantially based on whether they are taken from your mouth, ear, skin, or stool. Similarly, measurement of your metabolome will depend on whether samples are taken from your urine, blood, saliva, or fecal matter. Here again, the technique will probably be mass spectrometry. Investment in companies that make mass spectrometers would seem to be a good bet as the practice of personalized medicine becomes more prevalent: mass spectrometry has become the go-to technique for the rapid detection of hundreds of different molecules present in biological samples. You are likely already familiar with mass spectrometers: simple versions are used at airports to detect chemicals that indicate the presence of explosives.

Once all this information has been collected, it needs to be stored and analyzed. The problem of storage will probably be easily solved, although some people may tell you otherwise. There will be a lot of data. But all we have to do is wait for a little while, and technology will deal with it—at least, that's the lesson of recent history. The cost of data storage used to be astronomical. In 1956, you would have had to pay $10 million for one gigabyte (a billion bytes) of storage. In 1981, the cost of a gigabyte was $300,000. By the year 2000, it had dropped to $10. In 2010, the price of storing a gigabyte of data dropped to just 10¢.[5] Prices have dropped because technology improved and storage devices can be created at much lower costs. The sizes of the devices that can store the data are also much smaller.

Even so, some people will point out that we're talking about a lot—and here we mean a *lot*—of data. Storing your genome of roughly 3 billion base pairs requires about 800 megabytes of storage. Genes are often sequenced many times to ensure accuracy, so it's common to save approximately 100 gigabytes, or 100,000 megabytes, of information for a single human genome.[6] That amount of data can definitely be costly to store, but there are always ways around problems. For starters, you could store just the differences between your genome and a common reference genome. This tactic reduces things by 99.9 percent. Or you could store a few cells in the refrigerator and re-sequence the genome as needed. At a sequencing cost of $100 or less, this method may well be cheaper than storing the data electronically.

So, you say, "That's good so far, very impressive. I can see how we'll generate all this information and store it, but you still haven't told me how I'm going to use this damn data to prevent or cure my disease or make myself feel better." Ah, yes—slight problem there. That's where the bottleneck is, and any readers who want a well-paid, highly secure occupation for the next twenty years should become experts in bioinformatics, particularly as it pertains to interpreting the large datasets surrounding genomic, proteomic, and other "omic" information. To illustrate some of the difficulties, let's look at cancer treatment. Each cancer cell usually has between twenty and eighty mutations that distinguish it from a normal cell. The question then becomes, which mutated genes are the driver mutations—the mutations that cause the cancer to grow? The cancer bioinformatics community is now tackling problems like this one with some success. However, the fact that a person's cancer may have different mutations depending on which tumor in their body is tested or from where in any given tumor the sample is taken indicates the scale of the problem. Before appropriate therapy can be designed for a particular cancer patient, multiple sequencing of different cancer cells taken from different biopsies from that patient would need to be done.

Nonetheless, you can start to see why personalized medicine is increasingly possible. You can now get some pretty detailed molecular-level information about yourself. And you can store it digitally, either in the cloud or on your own hard drive if you don't like sharing your personal bytes. You can also see how the data you collect about yourself may be useful for detecting genetic diseases and finding new treatments for diseases such as cancer: if we can determine causative genes, we can then try to inhibit them. But personalized medicine is much more useful than that—a fact that will become clear as the digital you is compared with the digital versions of thousands of other people. You're probably familiar with the concept of big data in various contexts, such as the collection of closed-circuit camera surveillance data in a major city. We are getting increasingly adept at mining big data for the information we want. Within days of the London bombings in 2005, facial-recognition software had, from the tapes of hundreds of closed-circuit TVs, identified the bombers. One can only imagine how fast that could be done today. Similar analyses of the big data that will soon be surrounding you, with similar data clouds derived from other people, will reveal enormously interesting information.

So how does comparison of your data with data from other individuals help identify the causes of your disorders and result in a therapy meant just for you? One example concerns the relation between genotype (your genome) and phenotype (your personal traits). Comparison of genotype with phenotype over thousands or millions of individuals will reveal in exquisite detail how various genes contribute to every aspect of you, from the color of your hair to a tendency to lisp to athletic potential. If we analyze a subset of people taking a particular drug, we can start to correlate who'll have symptoms such as dizziness, nausea, fatigue, or other nasty side effects according to their genetic makeup. The correlation between the genotype of people with a particular disease and their environment will start to bring to light the subtle relationship between environment and individual susceptibility to disease.

For people with a particular disease, using social media to compare their digital self with that of many others suffering from the same disorder will have major impact. By correlating the severity of disease and the effectiveness of various therapies with genomic and other "omic" data, we can expect the development of improved, individualized treatments. The impact of social media and the Internet on health is already profound: more than 80 percent of Internet users now use "Dr. Google" to research health-related issues. Virtual communities focused on health and disease are thriving. One such community, PatientsLikeMe, was originally founded to connect people suffering from amyotrophic lateral sclerosis (ALS) with each other but now includes people with hundreds of other conditions, including multiple sclerosis, HIV, and fibromyalgia, and as of early 2014, has more than 220,000 members,[7] providing a forum for patients to share their stories and report on how well the treatments they undergo work for them. The effectiveness of these sites for determining the best therapies will be dramatically amplified when patients start sharing their digital selves with each other.

Even without sharing personal digital data, some of these patient networks already drive new ways to treat disease. The CureTogether network[8] was founded to help people with chronic pain and allows its members to anonymously rate the various treatments they've tried, resulting in what can be characterized as a virtual clinical trial. For instance, members with vestibulodynia, a chronic-pain condition affecting the vulva, were invited to self-report the effectiveness of various treatments over a three-year period. When the pooled data were analyzed, it was found that conventional treatments actually made the condition worse, whereas other therapies were surprisingly helpful. CureTogether now has patient-reported reviews of treatments for arthritis, Crohn's disease, and bipolar disorder, among other conditions. CureTogether was recently acquired by 23andMe, a direct-to-consumer genomic sequencing and analysis company, which will gather genetic information on patients to see how this data relates to effectiveness of treatment and the toxicities associated with various drug therapies.

Patient networks can also enable research efforts to develop new drugs to treat diseases that have no cure. Again, these efforts will gain considerable focus and momentum when patients begin sharing their genomic, proteomic, and other personal data with each other. These networks already have some notable successes; for example, PXE International was founded by Patrick and Sharon Terry in 1995 after their two children were diagnosed with pseudoxanthoma elasticum (PXE), a rare genetic disorder that can cause blindness. PXE International founded a tissue bank to collect samples from PXE patients for genetic analysis to try to find the gene causing PXE.[9] In 1999, using this tissue bank, researchers determined the gene responsible, and a diagnostic test for PXE was developed in 2007. If you know the causative gene for a condition, the search for a treatment is much more straightforward. Many researchers are now engaged in finding a treatment for PXE.

Patient groups and social media also allow other virtual clinical trials to be performed. Knowing that patients suffering from a side effect will try to find information about it online, Russ Altman and colleagues at Stanford University found that patients on the antidepressant Paxil who were also taking the cholesterol-lowering Pravachol (pravastatin) were more likely to search for symptoms of hyperglycemia, or high blood-sugar levels, which include dehydration, blurry vision, or frequent urination. "Historically, it's been really hard to detect synergistic effects of drug combinations that aren't necessarily side effects of any of the drugs alone,"[10] Russ Altman commented. "I believe patients are telling us lots of things about drugs, and we need to figure out ways to listen." This information regarding the interaction of Paxil and Pravachol is important, particularly for people who are already diabetic, as it turned out that their blood-sugar levels were raised substantially if they were taking both of these drugs. Such interactions could potentially be discovered very directly by mining shared digital databanks of patient groups concerned with depression or high blood-cholesterol levels.

So there will be techniques to measure a lot of things about you to construct a digital version of yourself, methods for analyzing that data to relate it to your health, and ways of sharing that data with others to arrive at improved diagnoses and treatments. But it doesn't stop there. All this information is going to be combined with data obtained by technology allowing remote sensing of your physical status. These analyses will provide information about vital signs such as heart rate, respiration, blood pressure, and temperature, in addition to more specialized data. Monitors for blood-glucose levels in diabetics are a particular priority: nearly 10 percent of the population of the United States has diabetes, costing the health-care system an estimated $245 billion every year.[11] Diabetes contributes to the deaths of more than 200,000 people a year and can reduce life span by up to ten years. Much of the damage due to diabetes could be prevented by keeping blood-glucose levels within a narrow range, and many companies are developing sensors to measure glucose levels that report back to an insulin pump, which will administer precisely the right amount of insulin. This process has to be fail-safe, however, as too much insulin can lower blood sugar to levels that result in coma and death, which is the terror of parents of infants with type 1 diabetes.

Many other mobile health devices are in the planning or testing stages. There are already apps for your phone that allow you to perform an electrocardiogram to ascertain the health of your heart. If you're concerned about an irregular rhythm, the graph can be emailed to your doctor. Implantable cardioverter defibrillators, which give the heart a shock when they detect an arrhythmia, are in testing phases. Cardiac bandages to monitor heart function twenty-four hours a day, seven days a week, are now available that transmit directly to your computer. Sensors are under development that can be embedded in a small vein to detect circulating cells that have been sloughed off from weakened blood-vessel walls as much as a week before a heart attack. This research is really important, since approximately half of all heart attacks are fatal, causing nearly 600,000 deaths per year in the U.S. alone.[12] It would be good to have early warning of these events well before you drop dead. Similar embedded devices are in the works that will aid in cancer detection (by detecting cancer cells derived from a primary tumor) or in detection of everything from lupus to celiac disease.

So if you think that you already have enough apps for your smartphone, you are sadly mistaken. The number of apps that will be available to monitor your health will soon constitute a dominant proportion of the market. Aside from receiving messages from sensors on and in your body that will allow you to monitor your health minute by minute (it is hard to imagine the joy this will give a serious hypochondriac or the agony it will cause their doctors), your smartphone will be able to access your digital you to upload new data and to download other data to analyze as needed. You'll certainly be able to access your genomic data at the doctor's office to help him or her decide which drug would be best for you and which you should avoid.

So the digital version of you—which is the sum of your genomic, proteomic, metabolomic, microbiomic, and potentially other omic data, combined with a digital record of your vital signs over time as detected by remote sensing—is on the way. This data will be informative, to say the least—particularly when you compare your digital self with the digital versions of others in your situation. The biggest single gap that remains is interpretation of this data. But as you can see from the progress being made with big data, it will become very precise, very soon.

So, you ask, when can I give this digital version of me a test run? When can I get my hands on my very own operator's manual? The next chapter will show that in many ways, your digital self and operator instructions to get diagnoses based on molecular-level information can be a reality right now. All those questions you're scared to know the answers to will soon be answered. If you want them to be.

5

SIGNS
OF THE
REVOLUTION

THE TIPPING POINT, where medical practice will suddenly adopt the principles of personalized medicine, will be reached within the next five years. You will experience a memorable personal tipping point when you first get your genome sequenced, your microbiome analyzed, your metabolome assayed, and your proteome measured and then sit down with your doctor or wellness coach to discuss the implications of this very definitive data that is all about you. The data will be so precise and all-encompassing that it will show not only what may be wrong with you but also what you ate for breakfast yesterday and what type of dog you own. The impact of this information on you and the way you live your life will be greater than any other technological advance you have ever experienced. Remember when you started using Google and suddenly had access to all the information in the world and couldn't imagine how you operated before? Or, for those who are old enough, remember the feeling you had when you started using email and suddenly had immediate communication with all parts of the world, for free? Or, for those of you who are really old, the first time you realized that having your own computer could actually be useful? Or, for those of you who, like the author, are positively ancient, the time you picked up your first hand-held calculator that could multiply and divide and take square roots? Well the personalized medicine revolution will trump them all.

The harbingers of the revolution are all around us.

Early versions of the digital version of you are starting to appear, although progress has been slow because of the enormous institutional, technical, and societal issues involved. The deeply conservative instincts of the medical profession have not helped either. The first manifestation of the digital you is (or will be) your electronic medical record (EMR) sometimes known as your electronic health record (EHR). The first attempts to introduce EMRs date back to the late 1960s; in the 1970s, the Department of Veterans Affairs had a working Computerized Patient Record System that established the ability of EMRs to reduce medical errors. Problems ranging from lack of standards, security concerns, and aversion to change prevented general adoption of EMRs until, with some frustration, President Obama pushed the Health Information Technology for Economic and Clinical Health Act into law in 2009. The legislation mandated a transition to EMRs for physicians and hospitals that treat patients covered by government insurance.

Still, it is surprising that in the U.S. in 2012 (the latest year for which records are available), only 72 percent of physicians used any form of electronic health record, ranging from just 54 percent in New Jersey to 89 percent in Massachusetts. In 2009, only 48 percent of physicians used EMRs. And right now, EMRs are not all that complicated. They consist of a digital store of your complete medical history, including medications and allergies, immunization status, laboratory test results, radiology images, vital signs, and personal statistics like age and weight. The lack of EMRs has meant untold duplication, errors due to incomprehensible handwriting, lack of knowledge about pre-existing conditions, and ongoing patient frustration with doctors who refuse to enter the digital age that the rest of us embraced twenty years ago. How many times have you been referred to a doctor, only to be asked the same questions all over again or be required to do a test that you've already done, simply because the doctor has no access to an electronic version of your medical history?

Some of the reasons for delay, it has to be admitted, are not the fault of the medical profession. Privacy is an enormous concern. Your EMR, because it is in electronic form, is susceptible to the same sort of hacking as any other personal data stored on your computer or by your credit card company or by your bank. Clearly you don't want an insurer or employer to get hold of your medical record without your authorization. But if your bank can achieve a secure online system for you to conduct your financial transactions, why can't one be created for your medical information? Regardless, the digitization dam that's been holding back universal EMRs has clearly burst, and we are finally entering the digital age of medicine.

Assuming you have one, can you get hold of your own electronic medical record? You should be able to—after all, it's all about you. But ownership can be complicated, and doctors who have purchased an EMR system may feel that information in it about you belongs to them. Often, a strange distinction exists: the doctor or hospital owns your medical record, but you own the data in your medical record. In any event, if your medical record is digitized, you should be able to get hold of a digital copy.

The next step will be to add your genomic, proteomic, microbiomic, and all the other data to your EMR to achieve a more complete digital version of yourself. Early signs of development of such personalized data clouds and their utility are being seen for a small number of individuals who have access to the sophisticated resources currently required in order to study themselves in detail at the molecular level. One example is Michael Snyder, a geneticist at Stanford University. He learned that he was at high risk for developing type 2 diabetes as a result of a genetic analysis.[1] "I was not aware of any type-2 diabetes in my family and had no significant risk factors," Snyder said, "but I learned through genomic sequencing that I have a genetic predisposition to the condition." He decided to study his molecular self using the resources of his laboratory to gather and interpret the data. Over a fourteen-month period, Snyder had his blood drawn twenty times for a proteomic and metabolomic analysis to construct what his research team called his "integrative personal omics profile," or iPOP. During those fourteen months, Snyder contracted two viral infections, and during the second infection, his glucose levels spiked. Snyder was subsequently diagnosed with type 2 diabetes, and in response, he altered his diet and ramped up his exercise routine. After six months, his glucose levels returned to normal without any drug treatment. Knowing that he was predisposed to diabetes allowed him to take immediate action when he saw changes in his blood-glucose levels, bringing the disease to a halt. "This is the first time that anyone has used such detailed information to proactively manage their own health," said Snyder. He added, "Right now, this type of analysis is very expensive. But we have to expect that, like whole-genome sequencing, it will get much cheaper. And we also have to consider the savings to society from preventing disease."

Individuals like Michael Snyder are pointing the way to how medicine of the future will be practiced. It will be much more proactive than reactive; detecting disease at the earliest stages before it becomes too late. It is obvious that not many of us will have access to the resources that Snyder has to either gather the molecular-level data required or to interpret it. However, there are many companies springing up to perform the genomic, proteomic, metabolomic, and microbiomic analyses required. There are now more than twenty companies and institutes worldwide that will sequence your genome for you, including companies such as Illumina in the U.S. and institutes such as the Beijing Genomics Institute (BGI) in China. BGI, which had more than 4,000 employees in 2011 and is presumably considerably larger now, was a key player in the 1,000 genomes project to sequence 1,000 people from a variety of ethnic origins to gain insight into human genetic variation. This data was published in the journal *Nature* in 2012. Companies are being formed on an almost daily basis to conduct proteomic, metabolomic, and microbiomic characterizations as the technology required for high-throughput analyses comes on line.

Interpretation of the resulting datasets will probably be the rate-limiting factor in extending the benefits of these molecular-level examinations to the general population. Much of this interpretation will first be performed by panels of experts in particular diseases, who will analyze the digital records of hundreds or thousands of patients to discover what combination of omic data provides the most accurate diagnostics or suggests the most appropriate therapies for individual patients. It is possible that machine-learning techniques, such as those used by Amazon to suggest books for you based on your purchasing history, will also be employed to detect patterns in the data. Computer algorithms will then be written that will allow these findings to be applied to everybody else.

You or your doctor will use these "expert system" algorithms to analyze your own particular digital data cloud to diagnose disease and to decide on therapy. This new process has major implications. Expert diagnostic and prognostic systems will be continually refined as data from people around the world with similar omic profiles and diseases are analyzed, and such systems will certainly be able to prescribe more reliable, personalized medical advice than your doctor can currently provide. You will still be better off if you have a doctor, but he or she will be of a different sort than the one you have now.

Doctors of the future not only will sit down with you and examine the physical you, but will also have to analyze your digital self with you, bringing to your attention not only the signals of health and disease, but also the latest methods of interpretation, pointing out trends in your biological data that are moving in the wrong direction and helping you find ways to reverse them. Your doctor will have to change from being your disease manager to being your health coach, working with you as part of a team to keep you in an optimal state of health. This kind of relationship is different from the one most of us have with our doctors at the moment.

The first signs of this changing relationship are evident, and not all physicians are happy about it. Many of us are becoming our own doctors: armed with information gleaned from the Internet, we march into the doctor's office with diagnoses of our own conditions. Eighty percent of us use the Internet the instant we feel something is wrong. This phenomenon is leading to terms such as cyberchondria: sufferers obsessively search the 'net for any symptom they may have, invariably finding that they are suffering from a particularly aggressive form of an incurable disease. But Internet research does serve a useful and—for many—essential purpose.

Many of us do not have doctors we can call on, and Dr. Google is our only recourse. For people who do, does anybody have a doctor who has truly joined the digital age? One you can send emails to and set up appointments with electronically? Does anybody have a doctor who has instant access in his or her office to the latest X-ray scans done when you visited the emergency room at a local hospital because of an intestinal complaint? Does anyone have a doctor who scans the latest scientific literature and calls you up when some recent finding may be important for you to know? Not very many of us can answer yes to even the first two questions, which makes doctor's visits sometimes frustrating and Dr. Google very inviting; and nobody has a doctor who is up to date with the scientific literature and who can analyze your digital data to determine what is relevant to you. So right now, if you want to take advantage of the benefits of personalized medicine, you are going to have to start to assemble your digital self yourself as best you can and use your doctor as a sounding board to help interpret what you find. Some people may complain about having to do this, but it is really very empowering. Acquiring your own digital data and using it to answer questions you have about yourself is the first step in demystifying your body in health and disease and constitutes the initial stages of the personalized medicine revolution: you are finally getting the information you need for your very own operator's manual and using it to take care of your own health.

The forces driving this transition are profound. Physicians will say you should always see a doctor before self-medicating, and so you should. It has been estimated that a simple Dr. Google search to correlate your symptoms with a disease results in a correct self-diagnosis 60 percent of the time.[2] Using this information to determine which drug you should take is therefore not a good idea, as 40 percent of the time you'd be wrong. But doctors are often wrong too. It has been estimated that in the U.S., up to 15 percent of doctors' diagnoses of diseases leading to death were proven wrong on autopsy.[3] Diagnosis of your disorder is absolutely key to successful treatment. It is unlikely that you will be cured of pneumonia when the problem is lung cancer.

And here's where the digital you that includes genomic, proteomic, and other molecular data is going to have enormous impact, because when you ask your molecular self what the problem is, your chance of getting the correct answer is going to increase dramatically from what you can achieve with Dr. Google—or your doctor, for that matter. Your searches on the Internet will then take on a different form: you will not be asking what is the matter with you so much as asking what the best treatment is. For example, you'll be correlating your data with that of others with similar disorders via social media to see what works best. And you'll be bringing potential therapeutic options in addition to diagnostic information to your doctor, and conferring with him or her about the best way to treat the disease you have or the disorder you're trending towards.

The reason that diagnoses made by questioning the digital you will become so accurate is that the molecular-level information contained there is starting to provide many readily measured molecular biomarkers—in the form of genetic features or levels of particular proteins, for example—that give precise information about your risk of disease or your actual disease. Genetic biomarkers have long been used to diagnose inherited diseases, of which there are multitudes. One example concerns lipid-storage diseases such as Gaucher's disease, which is caused by a mutation in a protein called lysosomal glucocerebrosidase, which breaks down a class of relatively insoluble compounds known as sphingolipids. Gaucher's disease can be definitively diagnosed by detecting mutations in the gene coding for this protein. The consequences of Gaucher's disease are severe: the most aggressive form causes death by age two due to brain damage. These lipid-storage diseases are relatively rare, with an incidence of between 1 in 40,000 to 1 in 120,000 live births, and affect a few thousand people worldwide.[4] However, they are examples of genetic ailments that can be detected by a simple genetic biomarker. Prenatal screens for these biomarkers often result in a decision to abort.

An area known as pharmacogenomics, which concerns the relation between your genotype and the effects that drugs will have on you, provides another example of how early precursors to the complete digital you are influencing medical practice. Taking the wrong drug can have terrible consequences if you have the wrong genetic makeup for dealing with that drug. In addition, it would be good to know if the prescribed drug will actually work for you. The danger is compounded by the drug culture we live in. Fifty percent of North Americans take one prescribed drug or another, and people over sixty-five average five or more drugs, which leads to a high potential for adverse drug reactions.

The irony is that for many drugs, we already know the genetic markers that predict bad side effects. More than 120 drugs approved by the Federal Drug Administration (FDA) have known genetic biomarkers to guide whether a particular person should or should not take that drug.[5] These biomarkers are often stated on the package insert that accompanies the drug when you pick it up from the pharmacist. This information is, of course, currently completely useless, because neither you nor your doctor know what your genetic profile is and consequently whether you will react well or badly to any drug he or she prescribes. Drug prescription is therefore a trial-and-error process, and a rather dangerous one. The application of pharmacogenomics—correlating your genetic makeup to the way your body will deal with a particular drug—has the potential to fix all that. All you will have to do is ask your digital self what effect that drug will have on you.

Pharmacogenomics has been used to guide whether or not a drug should be prescribed for a particular individual for some time. But these tests are usually used one by one in a hospital setting to discover whether or not a particular drug will work. For instance, the anticancer drug Herceptin is used to treat breast cancer. If your cancer cells do not make the protein that Herceptin binds to, Herceptin will do nothing for you; therefore, a simple genetic test is often done to help doctors decide whether or not to use it.

The problem is that we need these tests to be generally available for more commonly used drugs, including drugs sold over the counter. Tylenol, or acetaminophen, is among the most widely used pain relievers and is considered a very safe drug. But for people with a mutation in a gene called CD44, Tylenol can cause acute liver injury; even the recommended dosages can be life threatening.[6] For other drugs, our genes determine the dose we should get. Warfarin is a blood thinner prescribed to heart attack and stroke patients to prevent blood clots. People who have a mutation in a gene called *VKORC1*—which corresponds to roughly 37 percent of Caucasians and 14 percent of people of African descent—metabolize Warfarin poorly and so should receive a smaller dose of the drug to minimize adverse effects.[7] Ninety percent of commonly prescribed drugs are broken down in your liver by proteins belonging to the cytochrome P450 (CYP) family.[8] The dose an individual receives should be adjusted depending on whether a person over-expresses or under-expresses the proteins that break down the drug; otherwise, the drug may not work or may produce unacceptable toxicity.

The need to make these genetic tests available to all of us to protect us from adverse drug reactions is obvious—especially given the multitude of drugs being prescribed for us. And it's beginning to happen. In Indiana, for example, David Flockhart is introducing a simple genetic test to guide prescription practices in a hospital outpatient setting for approximately fifty commonly prescribed drugs, with the aim of improving outcomes and preventing adverse drug reactions.[9] Similarly, Martin Dawes is leading efforts in British Columbia to introduce a genetic test to guide prescription practices by family doctors for more than 100 drugs.[10] This testing targets patients who are over sixty-five and who are taking ten or more drugs—a population that is at high risk for adverse drug reactions. Remarkably, this innovation marks the first time in the world that family doctors, who write 85 percent of drug prescriptions in North America, will have access to genetic information to help them make more informed decisions—despite the fact that in many cases, the genetic information to influence drug prescription has been available for twenty years or more.

A central focus of the work of Flockhart and Dawes is the development of clinical decision support systems (CDSS) to assist physicians in interpreting the genetic data. Although all physicians know that genetic differences can influence a patient's response to a drug, very few have received formal training in pharmacogenomics. The CDSS will be computer-based and will first be generated by an expert panel consisting of physicians with extensive experience in pharmacogenomics and genetic counseling. Once the panel reaches consensus regarding recommended prescription practices for a patient with a given set of genetic biomarkers, a computer algorithm will be written that will reach the same decisions as the expert panel. This algorithm will be programmed into the patient's EMR so that when a doctor types in a drug prescription for a patient, a pop-up will appear to indicate whether that drug is suited to that patient and what an appropriate dose would be. The assistance given by the CDSS is the thin edge of the wedge. Such support systems will become more sophisticated and more predictive as more data, including whole-genome sequences or other proteome and microbiome data, are added to the digital version of you.

The need for pharmacogenomic tests to guide individualized administration of anticancer drugs is even more acute and is only slowly being addressed. Here, your digital self in the form of your genome can be used to determine whether or not you'll have a bad side effect from a chemotherapy drug. A Canadian trial group is playing a leading role here to prevent adverse drug reactions in children. The group, called the Genotype-Specific Approaches to Therapies in Childhood (GATC), is led by Michael Hayden and Bruce Carleton and is focused on cisplatin-induced deafness and doxorubicin-induced cardiotoxicity (heart toxicity).[11] Cisplatin is an extremely important and effective drug for the treatment of cancer. More than one million new patients are dosed with cisplatin every year for treatment of liver, ovarian, brain, lung, bladder, and head and neck cancers. However, cisplatin is also a very nasty drug. Among other side effects, it causes permanent hearing loss in 10 percent to 38 percent of patients. The situation is even worse for children under fourteen: nearly 40 percent will develop severe hearing loss.

Why do some children develop severe hearing loss while others don't? Is it related to their genetic makeup? Hayden and Carleton are addressing those questions. They recruited more than 160 children and compared the genotype of children who went deaf as a result of treatment with cisplatin with the genotype of children who did not. They found that for children with mutations in a gene associated with hearing called COMT (catechol-O-methyltransferase), there was a 90 percent chance of deafness if they were treated with cisplatin.[12] Some children who did not have that mutation still went deaf when treated with cisplatin. Now the hunt is on for other genes involved in hearing that might also be affected by cisplatin, which will improve the sensitivity of the test.

Well, you may say, that is all very well, but is there a drug that could be substituted for cisplatin if the child tested positive for potential hearing loss, and wouldn't you be putting the child's life in jeopardy if you didn't use cisplatin? This is true, but the genetic test spurs research into drugs that protect against the toxic effects of cisplatin. Other research is aimed at developing ways to deliver cisplatin more specifically to the tumor while avoiding tissues that play a role in hearing. The presence of the genetic test as a "companion diagnostic" provides an incentive for developing such drugs. Companies that make these drugs will be able to identify the patients who will benefit and will be able to charge a premium for their product.

Genetic testing for the risk of a toxic side effect such as hearing loss can have unexpected emotional consequences. A pediatric physician tells a story of a patient of his, a three-year-old girl, who had brain cancer. Her prognosis was bad: the doctor estimated she had perhaps six months to live, possibly nine months if chemotherapy were used. The parents asked if she could be tested for susceptibility to hearing loss before they agreed to chemotherapy that included cisplatin. The doctor asked, "Why? You'll gain a bit more time with your child if we treat her, whether or not she tests positive." The father responded, "Doctor, you don't understand. My daughter has just begun to talk; in fact, she can speak two languages [the parents came from different ethnic backgrounds]. We want to be able to talk with her as long as we can."

Doxorubicin is another horrible cancer drug that is widely used to treat blood cancers, breast cancer, and most childhood cancers. Nearly a million people receive this drug every year in North America. It is highly effective: the improvement in childhood cancer survival rates from approximately 30 percent in the 1960s to greater than 80 percent today can be attributed in part to the use of doxorubicin. But it is still a horrible drug. Heart function can be significantly compromised in 10 percent to 30 percent of patients; in severe cases, heart failure can occur, resulting in a mortality rate of more than 60 percent. Approximately 20 percent of children receiving doxorubicin will have reduced heart function for life or will require a heart transplant. But the response of patients to doxorubicin is highly variable. Some patients can tolerate three times the normal dose, while others suffer heart damage at any dose. Again, by comparing the genetic profiles of people who can tolerate high doses of doxorubicin with those who cannot, researchers are beginning to uncover a biomarker to guide whether an individual should receive a low dose—or any dose at all—as part of a chemotherapy regime. The particular biomarker in this case is a mutation in a protein that pumps drugs such as doxorubicin out of cells. The test can predict, with 75 percent accuracy,[13] those who will suffer cardiotoxicity. Luckily, in this case, there is a potential substitute for those at risk: a formulation of doxorubicin packaged into small vesicles that has similar potency but has much-reduced cardiotoxic potential.

Biomarkers are being developed and validated for many other anticancer drugs to identify those at unacceptable risk. Examples include vincristine and drugs based on Taxol, which can produce peripheral nerve damage leading to numbness or pain in your hands and feet. But drugs that are very toxic, such as many anticancer drugs, are not the only ones with risks. Many commonly used drugs have major risks too. For example, there is a clear need to identify whether you rapidly metabolize painkillers such as codeine. Codeine works as a painkiller because it is metabolized in your body to produce morphine by a protein in your liver called CYP2D6. Some people have more than one copy of this gene or have other mutations that result in very rapid conversion of codeine to morphine.[14] So if you are a new mother who is a fast metabolizer, breastfeeding your child and using codeine to manage postpartum pain can lead to potentially lethal levels of morphine in your infant's bloodstream. You definitely need to know this information beforehand.

The identification of mutations in your genome is increasingly enabling the development of individualized therapies. A major example concerns monoclonal antibodies. Antibodies are proteins produced by your immune system to recognize invaders such as bacteria or viruses. Antibodies bind to specific molecules (termed antigens) on the surface of target cells such as bacteria, cancer cells, or cells infected by a virus and tag the cell for destruction by other components of the immune system. In the mid-1970s, César Milstein and colleagues at Cambridge University found ways of producing large amounts of monoclonal antibodies (MAbs) that could recognize almost any desired antigen on a cell surface.[15] This ability has led to the development of MAbs that recognize personalized, patient-specific antigens. The best known example is Herceptin, a MAb that binds to the HER-2 protein, which is over-expressed in approximately 25 percent of early-stage breast cancers and can lead to improved survival for patients suffering from metastatic breast cancer.[16] In this case, a genetic test is first performed to determine whether the patient's tumor is over-expressing the HER-2 protein, as Herceptin will have no benefit if it doesn't.

Other drugs are appearing that target specific disease-causing proteins made by defective genes that have been identified through genetic analyses. These molecularly targeted drugs very specifically inhibit the function of a particular protein associated with a disease. For instance, about 4 percent of patients with non-small-cell lung cancer have a mutation that drives cancer growth due to a protein that is the product of two genes fused together. A drug called Xalkori inhibits the defective gene product and can shrink or stabilize the tumors in most patients carrying the causative gene. Richard Heimler, a father of two and an active member of the Lung Cancer Alliance, was diagnosed with non-small-cell lung cancer at age forty-four. He writes[17]

> I had pneumonectomy [lung removal] surgery of my right lung in 2004. Two years later, I was diagnosed with a small malignant brain tumor that was removed surgically. This was followed with six months of chemotherapy. A year later, I was diagnosed with a small malignant tumor under my ribs and it was successfully removed. A year later, I was diagnosed with another small brain tumor and had gamma knife radiation to successful [sic] destroy the tumor. A year later, I was diagnosed with multiple small tumors on my left lung and immediately began chemotherapy.

After testing positive for the particular mutation Xalkori targets, Heimler was treated with the drug in an experimental trial. Today, he reports that his tumors no longer show up on CT scans, a testament to the potency of personalized therapies. Xalkori received FDA approval in late 2012.[18]

Kalydeco is another targeted drug used to treat a monogenic disease—that is, a disease caused by only one defective gene. Cystic fibrosis (CF) is a monogenic disease arising from defects in the CFTR gene that codes for the CFTR protein that transports chloride ions across cell membranes. Patients with CF have thick, sticky mucus in the lungs that causes chronic lung infections; other symptoms include scarring of the pancreas, impaired digestion, and infertility. As recently as the 1980s, people with CF didn't live much longer than fourteen years, but today they have a life expectancy of approximately thirty-five years primarily because of improvements in managing the disease, such as ways of dislodging the mucus in the lungs.[19] Kalydeco, however, is aimed at curing the disease rather than managing it. The drug binds to a version of a defective CFTR protein that is found in 3 percent to 5 percent of people with CF and improves its ability to function.[20] Alex Parker of Victoria, Australia, was diagnosed with CF when she was six months old and lived with the condition for twenty-three years before a genetic analysis showed that she carried the particular mutation that Kalydeco could treat. Parker describes CF as producing the congestion and lethargy of a bad cold, along with bloating and a stomachache:[21]

> You wake up every morning struggling to breathe. You feel nauseous after you eat. You force yourself to exercise in hope that it might just move the mucus from your lungs. Then one day they give you two little blue

pills a day and all your suffering almost instantly stops. Your dreams start to become a reality and you start living a normal, energetic and fun-filled life. This is what happened to me. This is what happened to me the moment I started on Kalydeco.

Another testament to treatment based on a highly personalized approach, for sure.

Genetic biomarkers are also leading to dramatic measures to prevent disease. The BRCA1 gene is expressed in breast tissue and in the ovaries, and codes for a protein that either helps repair damaged (mutated) DNA or triggers a suicide process to destroy the cell if repair is not possible. A mutation in the BRCA1 gene can lead to a defective repair or cell suicide protein, allowing the cells to proliferate unchecked. Women who carry that mutation have about a 60 percent chance of developing breast cancer in their lifetime (versus 12 percent in the general population), and a 40 percent chance of developing ovarian cancer.[22]

Mutations in the BRCA1 gene therefore provide an important biomarker for the risk of developing breast cancer. Knowing whether or not you have that biomarker can have considerable impact, as illustrated by the case of the actress Angelina Jolie. Her mother died from breast cancer at age fifty-six. Jolie had her genome analyzed at age thirty-eight and found that she was positive for the BRCA1 mutation. According to Jolie, doctors told her that her risk of developing breast cancer with her particular mutation was 87 percent. In 2013, she acted preemptively, undergoing a double mastectomy. She wrote, "Cancer is a word that strikes fear into people's hearts, producing a deep sense of powerlessness. But today it is possible to find out through a blood test whether you are highly susceptible to breast and ovarian cancer, and then take action." She continued, "The decision to have a mastectomy was not easy. But it is one I am very happy that I made. My chances of developing breast cancer have dropped from 87 percent to under 5 percent. I can tell my children that they don't need to fear they will lose me to breast cancer."[23]

Genetic analyses can also be used to develop personalized therapies aimed at infectious diseases such as HIV/AIDS. As is well known, viruses mutate rapidly, and the strain that one patient is infected with may well differ from the strain infecting another patient. Julio Montaner, director of the British Columbia Centre for Excellence in HIV/AIDS, is using genetic analyses to detect the particular genetic profile of the virus a patient is infected with. As he says, "This technology will be invaluable to the lives of our patients. We will be able to quickly treat patients by delivering personalized medicine based on their unique strain of the virus. This will help us save time and money while also significantly decreasing the number of new HIV and AIDS cases."[24] For Montaner, this represents the next step in his long battle against HIV/AIDS. He was a major contributor to the introduction of anti-HIV triple drug therapies in the 1990s that effectively changed HIV/AIDS from a lethal disease to a chronic condition.

Genetic biomarkers for hereditary diseases also help to focus efforts to treat diseases where preventive efforts are not possible. In 1993, researchers identified a link between a gene called *ApoE*, which codes for a protein involved in transporting cholesterol in your blood and in your brain, and late-onset Alzheimer's disease. *ApoE* has three variants known as *ApoE2*, *ApoE3*, and *ApoE4*. Individuals who carry two copies of the *ApoE4* gene have twenty times the risk of developing Alzheimer's disease compared with the general population.[25] This finding has focused research on the relationship between *ApoE4* and Alzheimer's disease, including determining whether or not *ApoE* has a role in dissolving the distinctive amyloid plaques associated with Alzheimer's disease.

The discovery of biomarkers such as the *ApoE4* gene also poses a dilemma for those who may be at high risk for currently incurable diseases such as Alzheimer's or Huntington's disease. The question is, if there is no cure, do you want to know that you're going to get it? Overall, anecdotal evidence suggests about half the population will adopt a passive approach and either will not want to be tested for inherited diseases or, if they are, will want to have information given to them only for actionable disorders—disorders for which there is a treatment. The other half will want to know the data in its entirety and act on it to try to reduce their risks.

And, in the end, it is important to know what your risks are, because there are always things that you can do, some of which are not intuitively obvious. Researchers at the University of British Columbia in Vancouver recently performed a study on women aged seventy to eighty with mild cognitive impairment.[26] These women were assigned to one of three groups: weight training, aerobic training, or balance-and-tone training. In each program, participants exercised two times a week for six months. At the end of the study, those who had participated in weight training fared best: they outperformed the other groups on tests measuring attention, memory, and higher-order brain functions like conflict resolution.

So weight lifting might help prevent or delay dementia. Who'd have thought? When you think about it, though, maybe it makes sense. When you're exercising, particularly when you're lifting a heavy weight, you're not just exercising the muscle that is lifting the weight; you are also exercising the nerve that is sending the message to the muscle to lift the weight. These nerves are hard-wired into your brain, and the more you strain your muscles, the harder your nerves fire to stimulate the muscle. Nerves consist of bundles of neurons, the same cell types that are also involved in higher brain processes such as perception and consciousness. In the same way that exercise has been shown to stimulate production of stem cells in muscle, it is possible that by exercising your nerves, you induce more neuron stem cells in your brain. Which is presumably a good thing for cognitive function.

Other good things can come from knowing about a genetic problem you might have, even if there is no treatment. As detailed in Elaine Westwick's blog in 2011,[27] Angela Francesco's mother, and her grandmother, had Huntington's disease, a degenerative condition affecting muscle coordination and cognition, inexorably leading to death. Huntington's is caused by a mutation of the Huntington gene—the HTT gene—and unlike the BRCA or ApoE genes, where having the mutation only increases your risk for disease, the HTT mutation guarantees it. Francesco hadn't wanted to know her own status—until she made marriage plans. She got tested for the Huntington's genetic biomarker, and the news was not good: "When we walked out of the clinic, I was devastated. I just could not imagine how life would continue. But it did. I was back at work the next day, we started planning our future, a big holiday, our wedding, our house together, our plans for children..." Her desire to have a child free of Huntington's drove her and her husband to use in vitro fertilization using a donor egg, and she became pregnant. On her blog, Francesco wrote, "Someone has given us an unbelievable gift, and with that we have stopped a fatal disease (in our family) for generations to come."

Genomic biomarkers are being used not only to predict adverse reactions to drugs but also to guide therapy. The major focus of personalized medicine as it is practiced today is identifying genetic biomarkers found in cancerous cells and using this information to guide cancer therapy. Massive efforts are underway to shift from the current system, in which patients are treated according to where their cancer originates (breast, lung, prostate, pancreas, etc.), to a system in which the treatment is based, at least in part, on the genetic makeup of their cancer. This shift is enabled by the availability of ever-cheaper sequencing capabilities, but there are many challenges. Identifying the so-called driver mutations that are actually helping the cancer cell grow is a particular problem. These are the ones you want to interfere with. And then there's the issue of finding drugs that inhibit expression of the driver genes or interfere with the function of the proteins they produce.

The scale of the efforts that are being made to improve cancer therapy using genetically based personalized approaches is truly impressive. The MD Anderson Cancer Center in Houston is conducting a $3 billion "moonshot" program to cure breast, leukemia, lung, and prostate cancer using protocols based on gene-sequencing technology.[28] Genomics England has announced a program to sequence the genomes of up to 100,000 cancer patients and the genomes of their cancers.[29] The Ontario Institute for Cancer Research has instituted a billion-dollar program to "cure cancer in our lifetime" using personalized medicine approaches with an emphasis on cancer-genome sequencing. There is not a major cancer center in Europe or North America that does not have a large-scale initiative with similar intentions. Is it working? Stories are beginning to emerge that give rise to optimism.

The first example of how genomic data can influence cancer treatment was reported in the journal *Genome Biology* in 2010 by researchers at the BC Cancer Agency in Vancouver and concerned a patient who presented with a cancer on his tongue.[30] The first stage of treatment was to surgically remove the tumor, followed by irradiation to kill any cancer cells that were missed. The irradiation didn't work or was too late; subsequently, the patient developed lung cancer as a result of metastases that had traveled to his lung. Biopsies were then taken of the tumor tissue in the lung, and these were subjected to genome sequencing. It was found that a gene called receptor tyrosine kinase (*RET*), which is known to promote cancer growth, was expressed thirty-five times more in the tumor tissue than in normal tissues. A drug called sunitinib was identified that inhibits function of the *RET* protein; when this was administered, the lung tumors shrank significantly, and the disease remained stable for five months. After that, however, the tumors started to grow again. Genome sequencing of the tumors revealed that new mutations had appeared. Unfortunately, no drugs could be identified to disable the proteins made by these defective genes, and the patient died. Nonetheless, without the genetic analysis, sunitinib would not have been used to treat this patient, and the initial response would not have been observed, illustrating the importance of genetic information for identifying the drugs that will work on any particular cancer.

The story of Lukas Wartman is another example. As described in a *New York Times* article published in 2012,[31] Wartman developed acute lymphoblastic leukemia (ALL), a devastating disease that has a five-year survival rate of 40 percent. For individuals who relapse after initial chemotherapy, as was the case for Wartman, the survival rate drops to 10 percent.

Analysis of Wartman's DNA and RNA by researchers at Washington University indicated that his leukemic cells were making large amounts of a protein called FLT3, and this protein could be a driver of cell division. Interestingly, sunitinib also inhibits FLT3. When this drug was administered to Wartman, his cancer promptly went into remission, allowing Wartman to undergo a potentially curative stem cell transplant. The genetic information was vital because sunitinib is not usually used to treat ALL. Without the genetic analysis, Wartman's doctors would not have thought of using it. So there is reason to hope that one day you will have cancer drugs that actually work on the type of cancer you have, as opposed to the current situation in which there is only a 25 percent chance they will be effective.

For diseases other than cancer and inherited diseases, biomarkers based on genetic data only provide information on your risk of disease but do not tell you whether you actually have that disease. However, biomarkers based on your protein profiles in body fluids such as blood, saliva, or urine will tell you what disorder you actually have. We have had blood tests to detect proteins that are biomarkers for disease for many years, but most of these measure single proteins (or metabolites) such as C-reactive protein to diagnose inflammation, alkaline phosphatase to ascertain liver damage, creatinine to detect kidney damage, glucose to determine sugar levels, or troponin 1 to detect damage from a heart attack. Your blood, however, contains a tremendous amount of additional information that we haven't yet tapped.

Cancers also secrete proteins into your blood in the same way that proteins from your heart, liver, lungs, and kidneys are secreted into the circulation, providing potential blood tests for cancer. For example, lung cancer is the leading cause of cancer death (3 million cases every year in the U.S.), and the lung nodules that may be cancerous are usually visualized by CT scans as lesions of various sizes. Small lesions less than 0.9 centimeters in diameter are treated by "watchful waiting" to see if they will grow—growth being a sign of malignancy. Large lesions bigger than 2 centimeters in diameter are treated by surgery, leaving approximately 600,000 people, whose nodules measure 0.9 to 2 centimeters, in a "dilemma zone," where diagnoses of cancer are attempted by using positron emission tomography (PET) scans or biopsies. Biopsies are invasive and can be dangerous to your health, both procedures are very costly, and the combined results are often not definitive. A Seattle-based company called Integrated Diagnostics has developed a blood test that measures the levels of 13 proteins in the blood (selected from an initial panel of 400) and can tell whether a lung nodule is benign with 90 percent accuracy, thereby accounting for approximately 70 percent of nodules in the dilemma zone.[32] The test clearly offers peace of mind for a considerable number of patients, and in addition, it has the potential to save the U.S. health-care system approximately $3.5 billion annually by preventing unnecessary PET scans and biopsies. Similar molecular-level blood tests can be expected to become available for many forms of cancer and will become more accurate as time goes on.

A precise knowledge of the proteins associated with disease is also giving rise to entirely new classes of drugs based on gene therapy. For those who are not familiar with how new drugs are developed, the usual process is haphazard, slow, and extremely expensive. Typically, a protein is identified that may be involved in some disease process, such as a protein that drives cancer growth. Then attempts are made to find "small molecules" that can stop that protein from functioning. All the drugs that are familiar to you, that you take every day to cure a headache or arthritic pain or an infection, such as aspirin or ibuprofen or penicillin, are molecules that are small enough to be able to get inside cells to reach the proteins they interact with.

Finding the right small molecule for a new target protein can involve screening hundreds of thousands of small molecules to find one that interacts with the protein and inhibits its function. Then an interminable amount of time is spent using chemistry to try to make the molecule better—more potent and more amenable to administration either orally or by injection. Following that, detailed animal studies are required to show that the molecule actually works to cure the target disease and is not so toxic that it kills the animals. These studies are followed by hugely expensive and time-consuming clinical trials—first to find a safe dose in people (Phase I), then to find if the drug can cure the target disease in people (Phase II), and then to compare it to the best available therapy currently used to treat the disease (Phase III). Only then is there a possibility that the drug will be approved by regulatory agencies such as the FDA. This process takes on average fifteen years and can cost a billion dollars if the cost of drugs that fail to make the grade are included. And at the end of it, you have a drug that goes everywhere in the body, not just where you need it, and that can be guaranteed to have a nasty side effect on some portion of the population in some region of their bodies.

There must be a better way to develop new drugs that work for you, and there are reasons for optimism. This is due to improved molecular-level understanding of the disease and underlying biology. For example, the genetic disease called familial hypercholesterolemia leads to high levels of low-density lipoprotein (LDL) in the blood, the so-called "bad" cholesterol. LDL contains a protein called ApoB100, leading to the possibility that if we could inhibit production of ApoB100 in a targeted way, we could reduce LDL levels. Once you have decided what your target protein is, you immediately know the sequence of the gene in the genome that codes for that protein, because the sequence of amino acids in the protein is determined by the sequence of bases in the gene. In turn, knowing the gene sequence allows for a precise way to develop new drugs based on DNA or RNA that inhibit production of the target protein. If you introduce a short (approximately twenty base pairs is usual) piece of DNA (an oligomer) into a cell, it will bind specifically to a region of the genomic DNA with a sequence complementary to the oligomer and prevent the gene that contains that sequence from being expressed. Therefore, the protein the gene codes for will no longer be made. This process is often referred to as "gene silencing." Complementary means that the C, T, A, G on the oligomer line up with their complementary bases G, A, T, C on the genomic DNA. The short pieces of DNA, known as antisense molecules, can be developed quickly compared to small-molecule drugs and can potentially be used to treat a wide range of diseases. Kynamro, the first systemic antisense drug to gain FDA approval in January 2013,[33] inhibits production of ApoB100 and significantly reduces LDL levels in the blood. Clinical trials are in progress for other antisense treatments for disorders ranging from inflammatory diseases to blood clotting disorders, to Duchenne's muscular dystrophy, a rare genetic musculoskeletal disease.

Short sequences of RNA that bind to mRNA coding for the target protein can be used in a similar fashion. The advantage of the RNA approach is that it is catalytic: the presence of one piece of RNA can lead to the destruction of many mRNAs that

contain a complementary sequence. The RNA molecules used
to bind to the mRNA and cause its destruction are called short
interfering RNA (siRNA) and again can be made quickly once
you know the protein that you wish to "silence." siRNA can
potentially be used to treat all the diseases that antisense drugs
can, but with greater potency. The Ebola virus, for example, is
a contagious hemorrhagic virus that can lead to bleeding inter-
nally and through the nose, mouth, and other bodily orifices.
It kills approximately 70 percent of people infected. The Ebola
virus, like other viruses, is taken up into cells in your body,
where it takes over cellular machinery to make more copies of
itself. These new copies of the virus then go on to infect other
cells. A collaboration between a Vancouver-based company,
Tekmira Pharmaceuticals, and the U.S. Department of Defense
has shown that intravenous delivery of siRNA that silences the
genes Ebola requires to replicate can result in 100 percent
cures for animals infected with the virus.[34]

The antisense or siRNA approach has the potential for another
benefit: the development of personalized drugs. For instance,
as cancer progresses, many mutations can creep into the genome
of the cancer cells, with the result that each person's cancer
becomes a rare disease, requiring individualized treatment. In
some cases, drugs to inhibit the causal proteins will already
exist; but in many cases, drugs to affect these proteins will not
be available. However, siRNA molecules, that will very effectively
silence the offending proteins if they can be delivered to the
tumor cells, can be made within a week or so. Thus one can
envisage a rapid interplay between identification of new target
proteins as the tumor produces new mutations, and the development of new siRNA medicines to control and reverse the
tumor growth that results. It is likely that such medicines will
be tested in humanized mouse "avatars," in which your tumor

is grown and the effects of the siRNA medicine are monitored to see if it is effective before it is administered to you.

An area of explosive growth of personalized therapies for cancer involves finding ways to activate the immune system to fight cancer. That such an approach is possible stems from an observation by a physician named William Coley in the 1890s. Coley noted a patient who had a terminal form of cancer who contracted a severe bacterial infection. After the patient recovered from the infection, his cancer regressed, indicating that the infection somehow activated the patient's immune system to fight the cancer as well as the infection. In the 1950s Lewis Thomas and Frank Macfarlane Burnet suggested that the immune system could eradicate tumors by recognizing specific molecules on the surface of the tumor cells, and that cancers that progress somehow evade this immune surveillance.[35] These observations have stimulated considerable research, now coming to fruition, on how cancer cells evade detection and elimination by the immune system.

Most of this progress is due to an improved understanding of how the immune system works. Briefly, the key players are dendritic cells (DCs), T cells, and natural killer (NK) cells. DCs can be thought of as the generals of the immune system: they direct the production of "soldiers" in the form of T cells and NK cells, which are targeted to kill infected cells or cancer cells. However, to cause the targeted T cells and NK cells to be made, the DCs must first identify the infected cell or the cancer cell and then go through a maturation process. If the cancer cell is able to avoid detection or prevent the DCs from maturing, then the cancer will continue to grow. To bypass this problem, scientists are developing ways to take T cells or NK cells from the patient, engineer them so that they recognize the cancer cells, and then infuse them back into the patient. A very personalized approach!

The T cell method is showing remarkable results. First T cells are isolated from a patient's blood, and then a virus is used to insert a gene coding for a receptor on the surface of the T cell that recognizes cancer cells. These genetically modified T cells are then mass produced and infused back into the patient. As reported at the American Society of Hematology meeting in December 2013, incredible results have been achieved in initial trials in children suffering from leukemia caused by uncontrolled growth of B cells, the cells that produce antibodies.[36] B cells have a protein on their surface known as CD19. When T cells were made that express a receptor for CD19, and then given to the patients, nineteen of twenty-two children experienced complete responses. Some of these children had gone through more than ten previous therapies without success. "Our results demonstrate the potential of this treatment for patients who truly have no other therapeutic option," Dr. Stephan Grupp of the University of Pennsylvania said. "In the relatively short time that we've observed these patients, we have reason to believe that this treatment could become a viable therapy for their relapsed, treatment-resistant disease." Similar spectacular results have been observed in adults who showed complete responses in fourteen of sixteen cases. In some patients, up to seven pounds of tumor were eliminated in just a few weeks.

As with any therapy, there are downsides. A kidney problem known as tumor lysis syndrome can result from an overload of dead and dying tumor cells. Elevated levels of immunostimulatory molecules in the circulation can also cause problems but these can be controlled through the use of immunosuppressive drugs. A major concern is how this exquisitely personalized therapy, which requires sophisticated facilities for T cell isolation and genetic engineering, can be extended to thousands of patients. There is also the question of whether or not this approach can be translated into the treatment of solid tumors, which often have more effective tactics to avoid detection by the immune system. However, the point has been made: appropriate stimulation of the immune system can cure cancer.

The advent of the personalized medicine revolution has been accompanied by many ethical and societal issues. An early example is Louise Brown, who was conceived by in vitro fertilization in 1978: the world's first "test-tube" baby. Although her birth was a major medical achievement that offered infertile couples hope for their own biological children, it also raised a host of ethical concerns. The issues, which ranged from the appropriateness of surrogate mothers to the legal status of fertilized eggs, have still not been resolved and are set to become even more complicated. In 2013, the U.K. became the first country in the world to announce plans allowing "three-parent children."[37] The process by which a three-parent child could come into being potentially addresses diseases such as Kearns–Sayre syndrome, a condition characterized by weakness or paralysis of eye muscles and by abnormalities in heart function. Kearns-Sayre syndrome is caused by mutations in the DNA in the mitochondria—the power plants of the cell. Mitochondria—and therefore their DNA—are passed down from mother to child, through the egg, not through the nuclear DNA, which is a combination of the DNA from the mother and father. The idea of three-parent children is that an embryo's nuclear DNA—inherited from its mother and father—would be implanted in a donor egg with functional mitochondria. The child would have his or her parents' genetic material but would be spared the devastating effects of the defective mitochondria.

Other ethical issues concern the general availability of genetic information. Researchers need both healthy and unhealthy research participants to help answer the many important questions about the correlation between genotype and phenotype. Dan Roden, head of Vanderbilt University's personalized medicine program, has pointed out that "large numbers of patients, of diverse ancestries, are required to develop evidence to 'personalize' medicine."[38] In other words, to understand most genetic disorders, researchers have to sequence the DNA of hundreds of people with those disorders and then compare their DNA with that of thousands of people who do not have the disorder to get a statistically significant result that lets them determine the location and sequence of the faulty gene or genes. So do we have a moral duty to make our genes available for research?

Questions arise such as whether or not patients undergoing genetic testing should be told about incidental findings—like a potentially harmful mutation that researchers stumble across while looking for something else, or the fact that a patient's father isn't who he or she thinks he is. How much involvement should your family have in your decision to provide genetic information, given that information about your genes could also offer hints about theirs? Should researchers be allowed to use leftover samples from other studies for experimental purposes? The concerns are legion.

The issues being dealt with by legal, regulatory, and public policy groups as they try to deal with the consequences of molecular-level information about disease are another sign of the inroads molecular medicine is making. For example, can genes be patented? The *BRCA1* and *BRCA2* mutations that signify a high risk of breast cancer were patented by a company called Myriad Genetics, and as a result, the company had a stranglehold on the market. In a landmark case, Myriad's patents were challenged, and the case ended up in the Supreme Court in 2013. The judges handed down a unanimous decision that "a naturally occurring DNA segment is a product of nature and not patent eligible merely because it has been isolated."[39] This decision certainly favors progress: if patents were involved in the testing for each of the approximately 1,800 disease-associated genes discovered so far, the costs for testing for all of them would be out of reach for most people and for their insurers.

Regulatory agencies such as the FDA don't quite know what to do with biomarker tests that are, or are going to be, exceedingly accurate and that are sold directly to the consumer. Right now, the process for getting a biomarker test approved by the FDA as a diagnostic for a particular disease costs approximately $24 million USD. There are literally hundreds, if not thousands, of new diagnostics based on genomic, proteomic, and other molecular-level information that are making their way through clinical testing. Not all companies will want to go to the time and expense of achieving FDA certification, particularly if the market size for a specialized test does not warrant the expense. Such a test may be sold in regions such as the European Union, where the approval process is cheaper and faster. Alternatively companies could avoid making any precise diagnostic claims for their test but recommend you see your doctor if there is a problem. It won't take much detective work, however, to find out what they imply.

An early example concerns the experience of 23andMe, a company that, until recently, for $100, would provide you with a genetic profile indicating your risk for various diseases if you provided them with a vial of your saliva. In late 2013, the FDA issued a strong warning to 23andMe, which markets directly to consumers, saying:[40]

Some of the uses for which 23andMe's personal genome service is intended are particularly concerning, such as assessments for BRCA-related genetic risk and drug responses because of the potential health consequences that could result from false positive or false negative assessments for high-risk indications such as these. Assessments for drug responses carry the risks that patients relying on such tests may begin to self-manage their treatments through dose changes or even abandon certain therapies depending on the outcome of the assessment. For example, false genotype results for your warfarin drug response test could have significant unreasonable risk of illness, injury, or death to the patient due to thrombosis or bleeding events that occur from treatment with a drug at a dose that does not provide the appropriately calibrated anticoagulant effect.

In response to the FDA warning, 23andMe has stopped issuing health reports to new customers, offering only ancestry reports and raw genetic data. But we certainly haven't seen the end of the story. The calls from consumers and patients for diagnostic tests based on genetic, proteomic, metabolomic, microbiomic, and other biological data are becoming incredibly intense as these tests become ever more available and more accurate. There are now many companies that will give you not only genomic data but proteomic, metabolomic, and microbiomic information derived from a sample of your blood or fecal material that has considerable diagnostic content. You will want this information to help you diagnose disease or, as we shall see, to maintain wellness. How these pressures are handled will test the limits of the power of regulatory bodies around the world.

Regulatory bodies face other pressures resulting from an individualized approach to medicine. Personalized approaches are not very compatible with current drug testing and approval processes. A drug deemed unsafe in a classic clinical trial may, in fact, be safe—and effective—for patients with a particular genetic profile. Similarly, a drug considered ineffective for a majority of the population could be extremely effective for a small group of people with a particular genetic defect. Development of the beta-blocker drug bucindolol (Gencaro) was halted when a 2001 study showed that it didn't improve survival in patients with heart failure. But after the discovery that patients with two genetic variants that regulate heart function respond well to Gencaro, interest in the drug was rekindled, and new clinical trials—focused on those who have the genetic variants—are under way.[41] By coupling drug trials with genetic testing, researchers are able to more easily determine who will benefit from a drug and who will suffer adverse effects.

Regulatory issues also arise as we understand more about the biology of complicated diseases such as cancer. Molecular-level characterizations of these diseases reveal differences between the disease one person has as compared to another. As a result, more and more supposedly common diseases are becoming rare diseases. For example, advanced lung cancer can have eighty or more mutations; and a particular pattern of these mutations may be observed in only one patient. It is difficult to run a randomized, controlled trial, which regulatory agencies usually require for drug approval, when you have only one patient in it. The approach being developed here involves so-called n-of-1 clinical trials, in which the trial consists of the case study of a single person. Talk about personalized medicine! In n-of-1 trials, the sole participant would receive both the active drug and the placebo, and the randomization would be in the order of administration of test drugs. Although n-of-1 trials have been dismissed as providing merely anecdotal evidence, Nicholas Schork and his team at Scripps Health have made a compelling argument that "the ultimate goal of an n-of-1 trial is to determine the optimal or best intervention for an individual patient using objective data-driven criteria" and hence is "compatible with the ultimate end point of clinical practice: the care of individual patients."[42] For example, there are four major classes of antihypertensive drugs, and some physicians have used crossover rotations of these drugs to see which ones work best in individual patients, to the considerable benefit of the patient.

Societal issues arising from the practice of personalized medicine are proving to be just as contentious as the ethical concerns, if not more so. Prenatal genetic screening to identify children with Down's syndrome or Tay-Sachs disease or a myriad of other inherited genetic diseases is changing our societies in basic ways because most of these children are aborted. The introduction of a simple prenatal blood test to detect whether a child has Down's syndrome has resulted in a remarkable increase in abortions—more than 90 percent of such children are aborted in Europe, and only slightly less in North America,[43] leading to the possibility that in a generation or two, Down's syndrome may disappear, even though women are having children at a later age, which increases the chances of children being born with Down's syndrome. In addition, blood tests can now reveal many other things about an unborn child, including the sex. As a result, societies that do not value women are beginning to develop disruptive gender imbalances: for example, China will have nearly 40 million more men than women in 2020.[44] History suggests that such imbalances can be very destabilizing to societies.

This chapter has covered a lot of ground, and the message is clear. The impact of personalized, molecularly based medicine is already profound and increasing rapidly. The first versions of the digital you are being developed that include genetic information in addition to standard clinical data, and this information is being used to detect, diagnose, and guide treatment for genetic diseases ranging from inherited disorders to cancer, as well as to determine which drugs you should take and which you should avoid. Similarly, the digital version of you will soon be augmented by proteomic analyses of your blood to detect any disease you may have or may be trending towards, or whether the drugs you are taking or the lifestyle changes you are making are actually working. Drugs are being developed that are very specifically targeted to a particular disease you may have. And society is beginning to wrestle with the advent of technologies that tell you, with increasing accuracy, all about yourself. The groundwork for personalized medicine is in place and, for those in the vanguard, the revolution has begun.

PERSONALIZED MEDICINE IN THE NEXT TEN YEARS

WHAT MAJOR ADVANCES can we expect in the next ten years? As Yogi Berra said in his unique way, "Predictions are difficult, particularly about the future." But some things are clear. Personalized medicine is here to stay. It is going to spread as people acquire and share their digital data; it is going to become more accurate as big data analyses and technological advances lead to further improvements in our understanding of disease; it is going to be expanded into maintaining health in addition to identifying and treating disease; it is going to democratize medical care in the sense that very sophisticated diagnostics will become generally available to consumers; it is going to lead to enormous new industries aimed at maintaining wellness and treating potential rather than actual disease; it is going to completely disrupt current medical practices; and it is going to pose considerable ethical and social dilemmas. Many of these changes will arise from four areas where research activity is particularly intense: advances in gene therapy, improved understanding of brain function, investigations into the biology of aging, and the use of molecular-level medicine to maintain wellness.

Personalized medicine and gene therapy go hand in hand. The idea behind gene therapy is that if we can detect the genetic basis of a disease, that disease can be treated by inserting new genes into your genome in place of defective ones. The reasoning is straightforward: if a gene in your genome contains a mutation, leading to a protein that doesn't work properly, why not insert a functional copy of the gene into the genome? Putting this idea into practice has been somewhat difficult, however. For obvious reasons, your body has evolved elaborate defense mechanisms to prevent any invader from injecting its DNA or RNA into your genome.

Given that evolution has produced viruses that can insert their genome into the genome of target cells as part of the infective process, scientists have made great efforts to use viruses to replace defective genes in cells with functional versions. First attempts used modified viruses, containing the therapeutic gene, which could not be infective (that is, the virus could not replicate itself). However, the virus inserted the new gene into the genome of the target cell at random locations. This development proved risky because random insertion of DNA into your genome can potentially perturb expression of other genes and lead to new problems. Something like this process seems to have happened in gene-therapy trials in the early 2000s to treat children suffering from an immune disorder called X-linked severe combined immunodeficiency (X-SCID). X-SCID is often referred to as "bubble boy" disease because children suffering from this disease are extremely susceptible to infection, sometimes requiring a sterile chamber environment to avoid bacteria or viruses. Sadly, some of the children who received gene therapy for X-SCID to replace the defective gene developed leukemia a few years later. Researchers believe the random insertion of the gene activated an oncogene—a gene that can cause cancer.[1]

Another problem is that your immune system is programmed to recognize invading viruses and eliminate them from your body and also to kill cells that become infected by a virus. These immune reactions can be so intense that they are sometimes lethal. As discussed in a *New York Times* article published in 1999, Jesse Gelsinger suffered from ornithine transcarbamylase (OTC) deficiency, a rare genetic disorder that results in a buildup of ammonia due to incomplete breakdown of proteins.[2] In Jesse's case, this was controlled with a low-protein diet and drugs— thirty-two pills a day. In a quest to correct his OTC deficiency, Jesse was injected with a modified cold virus that contained the gene for OTC. The subsequent immune response was so strong that Jesse suffered multiple organ failure and died four days later. That was a black day not only for Jesse but also for gene therapy. Further development was halted for almost ten years.

These and other failures have led to some cynicism about the future of gene therapy for treating hereditary diseases such as Gaucher's or Huntington's, or diseases such as cancer. Claims that effective gene therapies are just around the corner and will provide a new method of curing hitherto incurable diseases are often dismissed as hyperbole. When an early version of the human genome sequence was announced in June 2000, Bill Clinton stated, "Genome science will revolutionize the diagnosis, prevention and treatment of most, if not all, human diseases. In coming years, doctors increasingly will be able to cure diseases like Alzheimer's, Parkinson's, diabetes and cancer by attacking their genetic roots... In fact, it is now conceivable that our children's children will know the term *cancer* only as a constellation of stars."[3] It hasn't quite turned out that way— yet. But there are signs of progress.

So what's changing now? The first gene-therapy drug was approved for human use by the European Medicines Agency in 2012: Glybera,[4] a drug to treat lipoprotein lipase (LPL) deficiency, a very rare (one in a million) inherited disease that can lead to severe pancreatitis. The delivery vehicle used is a virus that does not induce a strong immune response, known as adeno-associated virus (AAV), which is injected into the thigh muscle. The treatment has been shown to reduce lipid levels in the blood and prevent attacks of pancreatitis for up to two years. This success has led to other AAV-based gene therapies that are in development, including treatments for hemophilia, retinal degeneration, Parkinson's disease, and muscular dystrophy. Viruses are also proving useful for introducing genes into immune cells to enhance recognition of tumor cells, as discussed in the previous chapter.

As detailed in chapter 5, a form of gene therapy using antisense or siRNA oligonucleotides (short pieces of DNA or RNA, usually about twenty bases long) to silence target genes associated with disease is also increasingly successful. Isis Pharmaceuticals, a biotechnology company based in California, received FDA approval for Kynamro—a drug to treat high cholesterol by inhibiting production of a protein required to make LDL.[5] In addition, Alnylam Pharmaceuticals, a biotechnology company based in Boston, is developing a siRNA drug called patisiran which entered Phase III clinical trials in late 2013.[6] Patisiran silences a gene called transthyretin (TTR); mutations in the TTR gene cause defective TTR proteins to be made that can form insoluble amyloid plaques of denatured protein in heart and nerve tissue, causing heart failure and a progressive loss of sensation in the hands and feet. The only current treatment is a liver transplant. It is anticipated that the lower levels of TTR protein in the blood induced by patisiran will lead to reduced deposition of amyloid plaques, perhaps causing previously formed plaques to dissolve. There are many other DNA- or

RNA-based drugs in clinical development, and there is good reason to believe that they are going to be very effective.

So the future of gene therapy is increasingly bright. A particularly exciting development is that technology for manipulating your DNA is evolving rapidly. Nanosurgery on your DNA to correct defects may soon be an option. So-called CRISPR (clustered regularly interspersed short palindromic repeats) technology can be used to cut out the DNA of defective genes and insert the correct sequence. As Feng Zhang, a professor at MIT says, "We can go into the native genome, the natural DNA in the cell, and then make a modification in the genome to correct deleterious mutations."[7] This is incredible. Already this technique has been used to cure mice of genetic defects leading to cataracts and to insert DNA into the genome of stem cells to correct the cystic fibrosis gene. Other researchers are using the technique to delete a gene known as *PCSK9*, which can dramatically lower cholesterol levels, potentially providing a "vaccine" against heart disease.[8] So gene therapy is experiencing a remarkable renaissance, and many personalized, precise, and safe gene medicines are marching their way towards everyday clinical use.

Personalized medicine and your brain: that's a big one. Let's start with dementia, forgetting who you are. It doesn't get more personal than that. Dementia is a disease of old age, and its incidence doubles roughly every five years after the age of sixty-five. The prevalence of dementia in late old age is extreme, rising from 12 percent at age eighty to 22 percent for men and 30 percent for women at age ninety.[9] So you might want to live for a long time, but you'd better hope there's a cure for Alzheimer's disease and other disorders that cause cognitive impairment by the time you pass eighty. (Hopefully, something better than weight lifting.) You'll also need to save a lot of money: in the U.S. in 2010, the cost for care of demented people was in the range of $200 billion, taking into account the cost of assisted living.[10] This is not cheap: twenty-four-hour care can easily cost $100,000 a year. Your children may love you, but if they are paying, they may think wistfully of the days, possibly mythological, when the Inuit could ship their infirm elders out to sea on the nearest ice floe.

How about personalized medicine and your mental health? According to the National Alliance on Mental Illness, nearly one in two people in the U.S. will suffer from depression, anxiety disorders,[11] or another mental health problem at some point in their life, and about one in seventeen currently has a serious mental illness. Costs due to mental illness run in excess of $100 billion per year in lost productivity; in addition, schools have to offer special education, the court system is saturated with people who have mental disorders, and mental health problems culminating in suicide are a leading cause of death in younger people.

And then we have all the other problems that are brain related: Huntington's, Parkinson's, epilepsy, schizophrenia, autism, meningitis, stroke, concussion, brain tumors—the list goes on and on. And we are really not very good at treating any of these conditions. So is personalized medicine going to do anything about it? This is a tough question to answer. So far, personalized medicine for the brain is limited to attempts to tailor antidepressants and other drugs used to treat mental problems to avoid adverse drug reactions. Overall the field is fundamentally limited by a lack of understanding of how the brain works. So the question becomes, are we going to see improvements in our understanding of how the brain operates over the next decade, which can then be expected to lead to individualized solutions? The answer to that is, "Probably."

The central problem here is relating the biology of the brain to behavior. Activity in various parts of the brain can be observed in response to various stimuli using techniques such as functional magnetic resonance imaging (fMRI). However, despite many advances, the spatial resolution is still relatively poor. Each pixel of the fMRI image corresponds to at least 100,000 neurons; the firing of individual neurons cannot be detected. But it is crucial to detect these individual events. The thoughts you have are likely due to "emergent behavior" resulting from the simultaneous firing of thousands of neurons in your head. The term emergent behavior, in this case, refers to behavior that cannot be predicted by analysis of any one neuron; it is many neurons interacting together that enable your brain to think, act, and dream. The potential for emergent behavior in the brain is huge. There are approximately 11 billion neurons in your brain, and each of these has on average 7,000 connections with other neurons. Neurons are connected to each other by synapses that transmit electrical signals from one neuron to the next, so there are approximately 100 trillion individual synapses that can be firing at any one time. In the language of omics, this is called your connectome. It is a daunting task to map the connectome and correlate thousands, tens of thousands, or even greater numbers of synapses firing at once with your ability to remember, feel, see, and talk.

But there are many wild and wonderful new technologies that are attempting to do just that. Currently in development are nano-size sensors to detect electrical impulses when implanted deep in the brain, techniques to image the brain according to the voltage across the neural membrane (which corresponds to nerve firing), as well as optogenetics—inserting genes into neurons that respond to light by causing ions to flow across neural membranes, thus turning neurons on or off.

The information-processing demands are huge. As Rafael Yuste and George Church indicate in an article in *Scientific American* in 2014,[12] imaging the activity of all the neurons in a mouse brain could generate 300 petabytes of data in an hour. Compare this to storing your genome, a mere 800 gigabytes— about 400,000 times less data. Moving to the human brain will require considerably more data generation, storage, and analysis. But just as it was impossible for Watson and Crick to imagine sequencing the whole human genome in 1954, it would be unwise for us to say this kind of imaging can't happen within the next ten years.

So we can see the day coming when, thanks to one imaging technique or another, rudimentary maps of the brain activity associated with our moods, behavior, and actions will be achieved. It is not hard to envision that this will lead to some very personalized therapies, be they for depression, addiction, schizophrenia, or a host of other disorders, by simply interfering with the activity pattern associated with extremes of mood and behavior. Equally, of course, it could go the other way, with customers paying to be induced into a constant state of orgasm or other forms of ecstatic pleasure. Whether or not such therapies or indulgences will be available in ten years is certainly arguable, but it is likely that we will start to see the outlines of how to get there.

What about aging and personalized medicine? A focus on the elderly and treating aging as a potentially preventable disease makes sense in a lot of ways: the elderly consume a disproportionate share of the health-care budget, in large part because of chronic conditions such as dementia, arthritis, diabetes, and cardiovascular disease, to say nothing of more acute diseases such as cancer. The costs are huge: people aged sixty-five and over made up around 13 percent of the

U.S. population in 2002, but they consumed 36 percent of total U.S. personal health-care expenses.[13] In Canada, the current number is closer to 44 percent.[14] These costs are only going to increase as baby boomers cross the sixty-five-year-old threshold. Some estimates suggest a doubling in costs for the elderly by 2030. Whatever the numbers, the situation is clearly not sustainable.

You are probably not used to thinking that aging could be seen as a disease, and for that matter, neither is the FDA. It doesn't acknowledge aging to be a treatable condition. And promoting that concept, with its connotations of seeking immortality, certainly puts you in some fairly flaky company. But research aimed at understanding and treating aging processes has gained respectability and has generated some credible approaches.

The telomere story, for example, is becoming increasingly persuasive. In the early 1960s, Leonard Hayflick, a professor at Stanford University, discovered that when human fetal cells were cultivated in a medium that contained all the essential ingredients to keep cells happy, they divided approximately fifty times, then stopped and entered a period of senescence. Senescence means that the cells became "old" and either committed suicide by a process called apoptosis or remained alive but exhibited different gene-expression profiles from their precursors, indicating altered, presumably reduced, functional capabilities. In the 1970s, it was discovered that the ends of the DNA strands in chromosomes contain regular repeats of DNA sequences, dubbed telomeres, and that when a cell divides, it does not completely replace these DNA repeats; in other words, the telomere gets shorter every time a cell divides. This finding was finally used to explain the "Hayflick limit": if the telomeres become short enough, then the cells can no longer divide.

As a result, the study of telomeres has become a central feature of aging research because it suggests that the reason you get old and die is because your telomeres get shorter as you get older, resulting in more senescent cells that don't function very well. And there seems to be some truth in that. Senescent cells accumulate with increased age in species ranging from mice to humans. Suppressing senescent cells in mice has been shown to improve their health. You may have heard of the disorder known as progeria. Children suffering from this condition undergo premature aging and die, essentially of old age, in their early teens. These children have a mutation in a gene that results in rapid cell senescence.

Shorter telomeres in humans are associated with many age-related diseases including cancer, cardiovascular disease, and dementia. But would immortality be possible if you maintain telomere length? It's not out of the question. In studies that led to a Nobel Prize in 2009, a protein called telomerase was identified that can lengthen the telomere to let cells keep on dividing. This discovery was followed by characterization of a type of worm that is, to all intents and purposes, immortal.[15] As Dr. Aziz Aboobaker of the University of Nottingham explains, "Planarian worms appear to [be able to] regenerate indefinitely by growing new muscles, skin, guts and even entire brains over and over again." So what is going on? As Aboobaker states, "Usually when stem cells divide—to heal wounds, or during reproduction or for growth—they start to show signs of aging. Our aging skin is perhaps the most visible example of this effect. Planarian worms and their stem cells are some-how able to avoid the aging process and to keep their cells dividing." The Nottingham team identified a planarian version of the gene coding for telomerase and found that at least one species of Planarian worms dramatically increase the activity of the gene that codes for telomerase when they regenerate, allowing stem cells to maintain their telomeres as they divide to replace missing tissues.

While all cells contain the gene for telomerase, it is expressed at low levels (or not at all) in most cells. It is expressed in a subset of blood cells called peripheral blood mononuclear cells (PBMC), and its activity can be measured using a relatively simple blood test; alternatively, telomere length can also be measured in various tissues. Efforts have been made to find drugs that activate telomerase, and indeed small-molecule activators of telomerase have been identified and shown in early studies to improve the apparent health status of mice. Interestingly, statins to inhibit cholesterol synthesis seem to have a telomerase-activating effect. There is evidence that growth hormones, such as human growth hormone, also activate telomerase. Meditation and adherence to the Mediterranean diet have also been associated with lengthening telomeres. A big factor is exercise, as there is growing evidence that it plays a direct role in activating telomerase—in other words, in keeping you younger.

The observation that exercise results in longer telomeres could explain the remarkable benefits of exercise in almost every area of human health. Exercise is an amazing drug; it reduces the risk of colon cancer by at least 25 percent, breast cancer by 20 percent to 40 percent, lung cancer (in smokers) by 35 percent, and skin cancer (in mice) by over 60 percent.[16] A statement from the American Heart Association in 2003 says, "Habitual physical activity prevents the development of coronary artery disease and reduces symptoms in patients with established cardiovascular disease."[17] There is also evidence that exercise reduces the risk of other chronic diseases, including type 2 diabetes, osteoporosis, obesity, and depression. It reduces blood pressure. In fact, what doesn't exercise do? It seems it keeps your telomeres long as well, which may explain some of its "magic bullet" qualities. In an article published in 2008, Tim Spector and associates at King's College London examined the effects of exercise in 2,400 sets of identical twins, and the findings were unambiguous:[18]

> People who did a moderate amount of exercise—about 100 minutes a week of an activity such as tennis, swimming or running—had telomeres that on average looked like those of someone about five or six years younger than those who did the least—about 16 minutes a week. Those who did the most—doing about three hours a week of moderate to vigorous activity—had telomeres that appeared to be about nine years younger than those who did the least. As the amount of exercise increased, the telomere length increased.

A potential downside associated with telomerase activation is that approximately 90 percent of tumor cells exhibit telomerase activity, which is consistent with their ability to divide indefinitely, so increasing cancer risk could be a concern— although it is clear that exercise does not increase cancer risk; rather, the reverse. In any event, it is likely that we will soon discover ways to prevent the accumulation of the senescent cells that makes us old. This advance could well happen within ten years. After all, the fundamental miracle is that you were born and grew to be what you are; correcting defects that appear is really just a matter of understanding the biology at the molecular level and using this understanding to reengineer tissues as they age. In the meantime, it might be a good idea to hit the gym.

Other biomarker tests that correlate with aging are also appearing. One type of epigenetic modification occurs when chemical tags known as methyl groups are attached to specific regions of genomic DNA: production of proteins from genes in those regions is inhibited. Steve Horvath of the University of California examined the relationship between DNA methylation and aging in brain, breast, skin, colon, kidney, liver, lung, and heart tissue taken from people ranging in age from newborns to 101 years old. He found 353 DNA sites where methyl groups increased or decreased with age and developed a predictive algorithm based on this data. As reported in *Genome Biology* in 2013, he found that the computed age based on DNA methylation closely predicted the age of numerous tissues to within just a few years.[19] In embryonic and induced pluripotent stem cells, the DNA methylation age proved to be near zero. Horvath says, "My goal in inventing this age-predictive tool is to help scientists improve their understanding of what speeds up and slows down the human aging process."[20] Horvath plans to examine whether DNA methylation is only a marker of aging or itself affects aging.

The onslaught on aging is gathering momentum. The observation noted in chapter 3 that the blood of young mice led to rejuvenation of the hearts of older mice has now been confirmed and extended to other organs. In three separate studies published in *Science* and *Nature* in early 2014, scientists reported that they reversed aging in the muscles and brains of old mice by running the blood of young mice—or the protein GDF11—through their veins.[21] Researchers at Harvard found that treated mice could run longer on a treadmill and had more branching blood vessels in their brains than untreated mice. GDF11 is also found in human blood. Will the observations in mice extend to people? We will certainly find out in the next ten years.

Craig Venter of genome-sequencing fame has also joined the anti-aging bandwagon, raising more than $70 million in early 2014 to start a company called Human Longevity, Inc. "Our goal is to make 100-years-old the new 60," said Peter Diamandis, CEO.[22] The company aims to scan the DNA of as many as 100,000 people a year to create a massive database that will be complemented by microbiomic, proteomic, and metabolomic data. Correlation of this data with age and presence or absence of disease is anticipated to lead to new tests and therapies that can help extend healthy human life.

Google is entering the longevity arena by forming a company called Calico.[23] Rumors have it that an objective of Calico is to extend the life of people born in the last twenty years by as much as a hundred years. Google, of course, is going to have the advantage of huge data-mining capabilities. As an early investor in 23andMe, it also has access to extensive genomic data for analysis. Other companies with similar aims are springing up with increasing frequency, backed by enormous amounts of money from private investors. As Steven Edwards, a policy analyst at the American Association for the Advancement of Science, states, "For better or worse, the practice of science in the 21st century is becoming shaped less by national priorities or by peer-review groups and more by the particular preferences of individuals with huge amounts of money."[24] And their impact seems likely to grow, given the relative decline in publicly funded research and the enormous wealth of these private individuals. A *New York Times* analysis shows that the forty or so richest science donors who have signed a pledge to give most of their fortunes to charity have assets surpassing a quarter-trillion dollars. It is not irrational to suggest that a large proportion of this money will be invested in efforts to extend the human life span, particularly the life span of the wealthy individual.

What do the next ten years hold in terms of personalized medicine and preventive care to maintain wellness? This area is set for explosive growth. Americans spend over $30 billion a year on natural health products that have no proven value,[25] and somewhat more on "functional foods" (such as probiotic yogurt) that may have benefits, but you often don't know for sure. You can imagine what consumers would spend if they knew that the food and food supplements they purchased were actually doing some good. More importantly, it would be good to know which drugs will work for you and be compatible with you. Adverse drug reactions result in approximately 10 million hospital visits per year in the U.S. and cost nearly $200 billion. Some programs just starting now will address all these issues and much, much more. One of the first is being organized by Leroy Hood of the Institute for Systems Biology in Seattle.[26] Hood is a pioneer and an extremely effective proselytizer for personalized medicine, and his study may well become a premier example of preventive medicine in the future.

If you want to know everything you can about yourself, Hood's study is for you. Participants will be extensively examined both at the molecular level and at macroscopic levels using the latest methods made possible through omic and remote-sensing technology. Their genomes will be sequenced and analyzed to identify genetic risk factors for disease and for drug compatibility. Their physical activity, heart rate, and sleep patterns will be continually monitored to ascertain health status. And every three months, microbial species in the colon, metabolites such as blood glucose (a biomarker for diabetes) and creatinine (a biomarker for kidney function), and about 100 proteins that will indicate the health of your liver, lungs, brain, and heart will be analyzed and monitored for transitions from health to disease.

Eventually, Hood plans to enroll 100,000 people, generate personal big-data clouds for all these individuals and follow them for thirty or more years. It's a measure of Hood's drive and passion, not to mention optimism, that at age seventy-five he is embarking on a study that could take thirty years to reach maturity. Transitions to common diseases such as cardiovascular diseases, cancer, and neurological diseases will occur among the test participants over this period, and by analyzing this data, Hood hopes to develop predictive models to delineate early biomarkers for disease, allowing early intervention before the disease becomes life threatening, as well as ways of detecting the resolution of disease as the participant's biomarkers return to normal. These biomarkers should also allow you to rapidly determine whether the therapy you are using to treat whatever disease you may have is, in fact, working.

All this data and subsequent analysis will lead to actionable possibilities. As Hood writes, "An actionable possibility is a feature for an individual that, if corrected, could improve wellness or avoid disease. A friend was told that he had early onset osteoporosis in his mid-30s—a disease that potentially could confine him to a wheel chair for the rest of his life. After genetic analysis, he discovered that he had a defective ability to absorb calcium. He took 20 times the normal amount of calcium for several years and returned his bone structure to normal and after about 12 years continues to remain normal on this regimen. Thus this genetic defect is actionable in that it can be corrected by taking more calcium."

Another example Hood gives concerns a physicist who began to lose interest in his work and had difficulty concentrating. As the problem continued for a considerable time, he underwent blood screening. It turned out that he was severely deficient in iron. Within days after replacement therapy, he returned to normal and resumed his former life with his typical enthusiasm. Hood believes that we have 300 to 500 of these actionable genetic variants and that many of them arise from nutritional deficiencies that can be readily corrected.

At present, the practice of medicine, particularly in hospitals, is focused on treating disease rather than preventing it. Public-health medicine and primary-care efforts by general practitioners do emphasize preventive care but mainly through encouraging exercise and healthy diets, as well as smoking cessation. This blunderbuss approach is in stark contrast to the precise, individualized information gained and used in Hood's project. The combined data generated by Hood's and other wellness initiatives will be of enormous value, as it will establish a database that can be mined to create new biomarker tests of health and disease and offer new information about the effects of environment and diet on our physical and mental states, and will also create completely new industries aimed at maintaining health and extending life. For example, data providing evidence that you're trending towards disease will lead to new therapies aimed at correcting these trends rather than treating the disease itself.

What else can we expect over the next ten years? One thing is certain: we are going to make new biological discoveries that will upset present notions about how our cells and our bodies work. The functional roles of the 98 percent of your genome that does not code for genes are an area of intense research, and it appears that a large proportion of the noncoding region of the genome plays regulatory roles for gene expression. Furthermore, approximately 90 percent of disease-associated mutations are in noncoding regions, and finding out how those mutations influence disease is likely to lead to new treatment modalities.

Other surprises are in store as we identify new biomarkers associated with disease or wellness. As discussed previously, diagnostics that use genomic, proteomic, and other data are well on their way to being of practical use. Recent studies show that the small bits of RNA called microRNA (miRNA) in body fluids such as blood can also have important diagnostic uses, such as early detection of cancer. For example, pancreatic cancer is difficult to detect until it is too late. Nicolai Schultz of the Herlev Hospital in Copenhagen has identified a panel of miRNAs in the blood that appear to be diagnostic for the presence of pancreatic cancer.[27] As Schultz states, "The test could diagnose more patients with pancreatic cancer, some of them at an early stage, and thus have a potential to increase the number of patients that can be operated on and possibly cured." Other studies suggest that miRNA screens could be used to detect ovarian cancer—another cancer that is often detected too late for effective therapy.

The potential utility of miRNA diagnostics is not limited to cancer. Eckart Meese and Andreas Keller at Saarland University have shown that by measuring the levels of twelve types of miRNA in the blood, they could predict, with 93 percent accuracy, whether or not an individual had Alzheimer's disease.[28] "At this point of our research, we are only at the beginning of a biological understanding of the miRNA pattern identified," they said in an interview. "Our results make us confident that miRNA signatures can likely play a role in the future diagnosis of Alzheimer's disease." Because Alzheimer's disease starts years before cognitive decline begins, a test for the early stages of the disease could allow early intervention, before irreparable damage is done. It is also possible that such tests could be useful to assay whether Alzheimer therapeutics are actually working by determining whether the miRNA levels revert to a normal profile.

We can expect other new types of diagnostics as well. There are stories of dogs alerting their owners to diseases such as lung cancer and breast cancer. These animals may have an ability to detect volatile organic compounds (VOCs), which can be diagnostic for cancer. Considerable work is being done to ascertain the utility of VOCs as biomarkers of disease. Peter Mazzone and his team at the Cleveland Clinic have developed a breath test for lung cancer.[29] Mazzone's test, the colorimetric sensor assay, consists of an array of pigments that change color when they come in contact with certain VOCs, and it is sensitive enough to distinguish between different types of lung cancer, including non-small cell cancer, adenocarcinoma, and squamous cell carcinoma.

New approaches to disease detection will come from unlikely sources. Pancreatic cancer, which killed Apple founder Steve Jobs, has a five-year survival rate of only 15 percent, in part because we are unable to detect early-stage disease. Fourteen-year-old Jack Andraka developed a low-cost paper strip–based test for mesothelin, a pancreatic cancer biomarker.[30] The test uses carbon nanotubes—tiny cylinders made with carbon sheets an atom thick—coated with an antibody that binds to the mesothelin. When this protein latches on to the nanotube, it changes the separation between the carbon nanotubes in a way that also changes their electrical conductivity. His invention won him the $75,000 Gordon E. Moore Award, the grand prize of the Intel International Science and Engineering Fair in 2012, when he was fifteen.

New molecular-level diagnostics for infectious disease will also appear. For example, antibiotic resistance is a major health threat, with 23,000 Americans dying from resistant strains of infections each year. A key contributor to resistance is the over-use of antibiotics, particularly to treat viral infections, which antibiotics cannot affect. Because it can be hard to tell the difference between a viral and a bacterial infection, physicians often write prescriptions for antibiotics, just in case. In many countries, patients buy them over the counter, just to make sure. At Duke University, Geoffrey Ginsburg and his team have detected different gene-expression profiles in response to viral infections as opposed to bacterial infections.[31] Ginsburg's test boasts a 90 percent accuracy rate in identifying a viral respiratory infection and can return results within twelve hours, compared with the days that traditional test results take.

Other new advances, especially for treating cancer, are likely as we achieve greater understanding and control of the immune system. As detailed in chapter 5, great advances are being made by manipulating the immune system to treat blood cancers such as leukemias, and it is likely that in the next decade, similar methods will be developed to treat solid cancers such as lung and breast cancer. Creating these treatments will require the development of ways to defeat the ability of these cancer cells to suppress the immune system, but efforts are under way to do just that. At Stanford University, Irving Weissman and his team have developed an antibody that prompts the immune system to recognize and attack cancer cells.[32] The ability of cancer cells to avoid recognition by the immune system comes partly from a protein called CD47, which sends a "don't eat me" signal to macrophages—the white blood cells that destroy pathogenic invaders. By blocking CD47, Weissman's antibody allows the macrophages to attack the cancer cells and in turn mobilize the body's entire immune response against the cancer. What's exciting about Weissman's work is that CD47 isn't specific to any particular cancer: "What we've shown is that CD47 isn't just important on leukemias and lymphomas," says Weissman. "It's on every single human primary tumor that we tested."

Surprises are definitely going to come as we understand more about the brain and how it functions. In 2013, Michael McConnell at the Salk Institute for Biological Studies discovered that our neurons vary to a striking degree: as many as 40 percent of neurons exhibit large chunks of deleted or duplicated DNA (known as copy number variants, or CNVs) as compared to a "standard" neuron.[33] As McConnell told *ScienceDaily*, "The thing about neurons is that, unlike skin cells, they don't turn over, and they interact with each other. They form these big complex circuits, where one cell that has CNVs that make it different can potentially have network-wide influence in a brain." Spontaneous CNVs have been linked with schizophrenia and autism, so developing an understanding of how CNVs form could clarify origins of mental health disorders.

As you may already have come to appreciate, technology never ends, and we are going to get additional surprises as new technologies come online. Three-dimensional (3D) printing, now in its infancy, is going to have a profound impact. Its applications couldn't be more personalized. In March 2013, a man in the northeastern U.S. had 75 percent of his skull replaced by a 3D-printed polymer implant, designed with the help of CT scans.[34] Using an inkjet-type device, Keith Martin and his team at the University of Cambridge have successfully layered living retinal cells.[35] Said Martin, "This is the first time that cells from the adult central nervous system have been successfully printed. We've demonstrated that you can take cells from the retina and you can effectively separate them out. We can print those cells out in any pattern we like, and we've shown that those cells can survive and thrive." Although this research is still in its early stages, it points to the potential for sculpted tissues customized to the patient. Martin suggests that these techniques will lead to eventual cures for macular degeneration and glaucoma, the two leading causes of blindness in developed countries. It is not hard to imagine the combination of 3D printing techniques and stem cell technology leading to an ability to grow organs outside your body, for subsequent implantation.

Advances in stem cell technology will also lead to new drugs. For example, Gabsang Lee of the Johns Hopkins Institute for Cell Engineering extracted skin cells from an individual suffering from Riley-Day syndrome, a rare genetic disorder affecting sensory nerves.[36] People with Riley-Day have frequent vomiting crises, problems with speech and movement, difficulty swallowing, inappropriate perception of heat, pain, and taste, unstable blood pressure, and gastrointestinal problems. Using the induced pluripotent stem cell approach, Lee and his team coaxed those skin cells into becoming neurons. They were then able to screen thousands of drugs to see which ones would make the neurons express higher levels of the genes that were not produced in adequate amounts. "Because we could study the nerve cells directly, we could for the first time see exactly what was going wrong in this disease," said Lee. They ultimately identified a compound that shows promise for stopping or reversing Riley-Day syndrome.

Personalized approaches to health care are also going to be extended to more tailored treatment of the very young and the very old. As noted by the Institute of Medicine, "The majority of drugs prescribed for children—50 to 75 percent—have not been tested in pediatric populations."[37] In essence, we treat children as if they are little adults, usually changing dose levels according to their weight. Adults and children have "profound anatomical, physiological, and developmental differences," which translate into differences in how they metabolize drugs—meaning that results from drug trials on adults may not apply to children at all.

Variability is a huge problem for the elderly. John Sloan, a physician who cares for geriatric patients, writes that "the fragile elderly are different from one another in all sorts of ways."[38] He cited kidney function as an example:

> As you get older, particularly when you get really old, two things happen. One, kidney function gets worse. So an average eighty-year-old patient will definitely have worse kidney function than she did when she was twenty. But thing number two is that the older you get, the wider the range of kidney function gets. Kidney function becomes heterogeneous. Result: blood levels of kidney-filtered drugs are heterogeneous. One elderly person has kidney function close to that of a normal forty-year-old; another one has awful, barely functioning kidneys. Give a kidney-filtered drug at its textbook dose to the first one, everything is cool. Give it to the second one, the blood level is through the roof and side effects have her flat on her back.

For the fragile elderly, this variability can extend to many organs, making prescribing the right dosage of a drug a huge challenge. As a result, many patients are overmedicated, and serious adverse drug reactions can be dismissed as just another consequence of aging. Compounding the problem is that these patients are usually on several drugs at once, and they can interact with each other to produce new problems. Accurate biomarkers to monitor the therapeutic effects of drugs in this population are desperately needed to achieve the right doses of the right drugs and avoid adverse drug interactions.

At the beginning of this chapter, the democratization of medicine was mentioned as a probable event resulting from molecularly based medicine over the next ten years. But what does this mean? It means that through the availability of inexpensive, accurate, molecular-level diagnostic tests, consumers will be able to get much more definitive information regarding their own health, which will allow them to become much more actively involved in managing it. Patients will no longer be passive recipients of diagnosis and treatment by the medical profession. Health care is moving from hospitals and clinics to the home, into the hands of you, the consumer, as personalized medicine technologies improve self-monitoring and your understanding of your body in health and disease. There are risks and many regulatory issues, but one thing is certain: the democratization and demystification of health care is starting to happen.

There is one large—and unanswered—question in all these conjectures about what may happen over the coming decade: Will all this information make any difference on a population-wide level? Will individuals change their behavior when they can get accurate, predictive information about their health status? This is not an idle question: current evidence suggests that many of us won't. We all know we should follow a balanced diet low in saturated fats and get more exercise, and smokers have all been told the health risks of cigarettes, but most of us indulge in behaviors that we know are harmful to our health. As health-care editor Paul Cerrato wrote in a commentary for *InformationWeek*,[39] "Most people want to see a doctor only when something breaks down, and then they expect a pill or procedure to make things right, just as they expect their car mechanic to fix their cars. Health care for most Americans is about having someone else 'make it better,' not about personal responsibility." Google's attempt to launch a personal health-record product, Google Health, was shut down after a few years of low uptake, with the company announcing on its blog, "There has been adoption among certain groups of users like tech-savvy patients and their caregivers, and more recently fitness and wellness enthusiasts. But we haven't found a way to translate that limited usage into widespread adoption in the daily health routines of millions of people."[40] It is entirely possible that a similar situation will evolve for personalized medicine, in which an elite few who actually use the information available gain considerable benefits but the majority do not. It will be interesting to see how this scenario evolves.

So within the next ten years, personalized medicine will be available to you and will be front and center in the medical scene. It will surely create unrealistic expectations and will be the subject of many portentous editorials saying that the hype far exceeds reality. It will place enormous strains on the medical system as patients become increasingly empowered by real information that they will want acted upon immediately and as doctors try to adjust to a new environment where many of their present skills become outmoded. It may well cause a large number of healthy people to become sick as they try to correct trivial problems they detect. It will cause enormous growth in the health-maintenance industry, which will become the biggest industry of all time. And it will increasingly cater to the desire to change ourselves in ways that make us smarter or better looking or younger. Human evolution won't be practiced in the Darwinian sense anymore: we'll do it to ourselves.

7

THE GENIE
IS OUT OF
THE BOTTLE

SO, WHERE ARE WE? In the previous six chapters, you have seen how the development and application of modern science over the last 400 years have led to an understanding of everything from planetary motion to the innermost workings of the cells in your body. You have learned about many of the bits and pieces that you're made of, what they do, and how you can measure them, resulting in the "molecular you." We have seen how the advent of the digital age allows us to store all this information electronically, and how analysis of the "digital you" embodied by this massive data cloud can identify biomarkers that provide an incredibly accurate picture of your state of health and disease. Remote-sensing devices can now analyze every breath you take and every beat of your heart and alert you well before you pass your best before, or rest in peace, date. Through social media, you will soon be able to share these intimate details with sympathetic listeners suffering from disorders just like yours, compare your digital selves to find the most effective therapies that should work for you, and locate where these are available. Taken together, these advances are driving massive changes in the practice of medicine as we know it today.

But that's only the beginning of the potential disruptions molecular medicine may cause.

Let's explore the near future first. Chapter 6 described what might happen during the next ten years, and it seems pretty exciting. Ten years from now, cancer will be managed much better than it is today. Detection of causative "driver" genes in your cancer genome should allow for a personalized cocktail of drugs to be administered to you to cure or control the particular cancer you have. Blood tests to detect pre-cancerous conditions and very early manifestations of cancer should be routine, allowing for effective treatment before cancers metastasize to other parts of the body. Increasingly sophisticated imaging techniques will detect the extent of your cancers more readily, leading to more complete removal of cancer cells during surgery. Today's anticancer drugs will be augmented by "smart" nanomedicines that are specifically designed to kill cancer cells and avoid healthy tissue. Perhaps most importantly, we will have ways to turn your immune system on so that it recognizes and destroys many forms of cancer. In short, a remarkably powerful array of weapons are coming online to contain and cure cancer.

How about cardiovascular disease, the other major killer in Western society, leading to heart attacks and strokes and accounting for nearly 50 percent of all deaths? Again, in the near future, we should see major advances to the point that most manifestations of heart disease will be treatable. Heart failure, the end-stage of heart disease, could be treatable, although that treatment will rely on advances in methods for rejuvenating aged hearts trending towards failure, such as ways to make heart stem cells "younger." These advances might include the human analogue of the GDF11 protein. We should have much more sophisticated techniques to predict and prevent strokes: simple blood tests to give warning signals of such events so that appropriate action can be taken. However, treatment of brain damage after it has occurred as a result of a stroke may not be that much better unless we can develop new ways to remove dead brain tissue and stimulate new neuron growth to replace dead cells.

Focused attacks based on molecular-level understanding of genetic diseases such as cystic fibrosis, Huntington's disease, or Alzheimer's disease should soon result in improved treatments. As molecular-level understanding increases, rapid advances become possible; when you know what is causing the problem, the path to a solution is much clearer.

The rapid advances in accurate diagnostics that can be anticipated in the near future, and their availability to you, will challenge the medical establishment's role as the gatekeeper of medical advances, because knowledge and power will be passed to you, the consumer. For example, the current fifteen-year wait time for a new medical advance to reach the doctor's office—to reach you—will not be tenable when you know with certainty what disorder you have, and have done your research as to which therapy is most appropriate to you and where it is available.

Let's look at a future scenario: You wake up one day feeling ill. You're very tired and somewhat nauseous. On most days when you feel like this, you open up your smartphone and find a pop-up suggesting that you drink a bit less alcohol and get more sleep. But today your smartphone suggests you run a blood analysis, because the onboard sensors on your smartwatch or bracelet have detected that things aren't right: perhaps your temperature has risen or your heart is beating a little faster. You pull out a disposable needle and prick your finger, just like diabetics do routinely, and daub a drop of blood on a disposable sensor that you plug into your smartphone. Instantly, a thousand proteins and metabolites in your blood are measured and compared against your normal levels. Meanwhile, your smartwatch and other onboard sensors are relaying your blood pressure, temperature, heart rate, body weight, respiration, and other data to be uploaded to the latest version of your digital data cloud—your digital you. Through your voice-activated personal data assistant (a.k.a. a super smartphone—Siri will work better by then), you ask your digital self, "What's wrong with me, and what should I do?" Armed with the data, your digital self answers, "We are coming down with a type of flu that has a 98 percent probability of being the same as a local strain that has been recently detected in other people in our vicinity." It works out the most appropriate individualized therapy for you, finding drugs that will work for you and that won't induce some nasty side effect. It then notifies the nearest pharmacy to prepare your individualized therapy. You pick it up, and by the next day, you're feeling your usual self again.

A second scenario: You are walking at what is usually a comfortable pace but suddenly become breathless. You sit down but can't seem to catch your breath. In this case, your onboard monitoring systems are picking up warning signs—abnormal heart rhythm, low blood oxygen, and other signs pointing to heart failure. The information is relayed to emergency services, and your smartphone informs you that an ambulance is on its way, arriving soon enough so that emergency care, such as oxygen, can be given. On arrival at the emergency room, you find that the appropriate drugs for your condition have already been prepared for you, using input from your digital you to decide which drugs will work for you, which dosage to use, and which drugs to avoid. If conditions such as atrial fibrillation have set in, blood-clot–dissolving agents will be administered before more serious problems, such as stroke, can occur.

A third scenario: Perhaps you develop type 1 diabetes. Cells are taken from your skin or some other source, and the differentiation process that caused those cells to become skin cells is reversed, yielding stem cells capable of becoming any cell in your body. They are then induced to become beta cells capable of producing insulin in response to high blood-glucose levels. These beta cells are grown in tissue culture to the required amounts and then injected intravenously into your body, where they seed in your liver and other locations, sense the glucose levels in your circulation, release insulin as needed, and resolve your diabetes. Or you find that you're trending to type 2 diabetes; you feel fine, but your onboard sensors have noted warning signs that your blood-sugar levels are rising. You receive increasingly insistent messages—a pop-up every time you open your computer or use your smartphone—that you must alter your lifestyle. You will be told to get off the subway one stop earlier or not to go back to the buffet table. You will eventually succumb to these intrusions as increasingly dire warnings flash up indicating the number of years of your life that are in jeopardy and the limbs you may lose as the diabetes progresses.

Personalized medicine heralds the start of an age of maintaining health, as opposed to treating sickness, and personalized medicine will become the major industry of the future, particularly as the health-maintenance industry increasingly engages in an anti-aging agenda. We see many signs of this now. Thirty years ago, fitness centers were almost unknown; today, if a hotel doesn't have good workout facilities, guests are irate. The health and anti-aging centers of the near future will be something to behold. There will be detailed genomic, pro-teomic, metabolomic, microbiomic, and vital-sign analyses to begin with, followed by daily exercise routines and diets devised specifically for you. Motivation will be provided by very precise molecular measurements that will show definitively when you make even minor progress. From standing desks at work to regular visits to a health center, very few of us will spend less than an hour a day maintaining our health. Prehab instead of rehab will be normal rather than unusual. Who would look askance at somebody in rehab for two hours a day to recover from the effects of a stroke? Far better to spend an hour a day in prehab and avoid the stroke in the first place.

What else does the near future hold? Certainly, personalized medicine will be creating havoc within the medical profession. The role of doctors in making diagnoses will be increasingly supplanted by computer analyses of the digital you. Accurate diagnoses combined with advanced imaging techniques and analyses of genomic and other data in the digital you will mean that safe and effective treatments will be readily identified. Thus the role of doctors will be in transition, as it has been for some time. Fifty years ago, doctors cared for people who were really unwell: 80 percent of their job was looking after the dying or seriously ill. Today, the treatment of chronic disease has become the norm. Care of type-2 diabetes, high blood pressure, arthri-tis, and cancer survivors takes up the majority of time. As these chronic disorders become increasingly controlled through a molecularly based, personalized approach, and as diagnosis and treatment are largely decided by analysis of the digital you, only complex and severe problems will need the doctor. So what will doctors be doing?

Two scenarios are possible. Those who do not have access to a doctor—or advanced health care—will find the playing field dramatically leveled. Relatively inexpensive omic data—potentially in the range of $100 for a complete analysis—and free online analyses available through the Internet will enable patients around the world to access state-of-the-art diagnostic resources. This information, combined with Internet searches and social media such as PatientsLikeMe, CureTogether, and other disease-specific websites, will also make it possible for you to discover what the most appropriate treatment is and where it is available. You'll be able to do some cost-comparison shopping as well as check references from satisfied (or unsatisfied) customers. Having decided on the best, most cost-effective therapy, you will then make an appointment and travel arrangements to get treated.

An alternative scenario—and one that people with adequate health plans and access to doctors will tend to move to: You will still have a doctor, but you will rely on him or her to prevent you getting ill, rather than to treat you after you become unwell. Your doctor will likely be associated with a health-maintenance center that you belong to, and it is likely you will pay your doctor according to his or her success in keeping you well. Your doctor will help keep you well by assisting you not only with the latest ways of gathering important personal data but also by helping you analyze and interpret your digital self and by advising you on the most appropriate course of action. You will probably fire your doctor if you get sick too often. This is a novel concept—paying doctors only for effective treatments and recommendations. Takes one back to the halcyon days of ancient Mesopotamia: according to Hammurabi's code of laws, physicians who performed surgery were held responsible for errors or failures. If a freeman died as a result of surgery, the physician could have his fingers cut off. If a slave died as a result of surgery, the physician had to replace the slave with one of equal value. In any event, we may not need so many doctors with the training they presently have. The expert systems that interpret our personal data cloud will bear a lot of the load. But doctors who play the role of health coach will be very much in demand to manage and optimize our health in the same way that we now use financial professionals to manage and grow our investments or lawyers to manage and solve our legal problems.

But let's move on to the really interesting bit: what's in the cards for personalized medicine over the longer term—say, fifty years from now? Here we realize that the genie is certainly out of the bottle: a molecular-level understanding of ourselves has many consequences, and not all of them are unambiguously wonderful.

Right now, the efforts humankind has made to understand and cure our various ailments are starting to show signs of working. As Winston Churchill said after Britain won its first battle in the Second World War: "This is not the end, this is not even the beginning of the end, but it is, perhaps, the end of the beginning."

So what is the end? This question is difficult to answer because the sky is the limit. We are only now coming to appreciate the incredible power that the focused application of science and technology can have on our individual selves. Only slightly more than 400 years after the initial attacks on magical thinking by Galileo and Newton, we are starting to come to grips with what we're made of, how it's put together, and how it can be fixed. Progress is accelerating wildly. Approximately 90 percent of scientists who ever lived are alive today. A large proportion of them are working to bring better health to all. Until 1900, human knowledge doubled approximately every century. By the end of the Second World War, knowledge was doubling every twenty-five years. Today, nanotechnology knowledge is doubling every two years, clinical knowledge every eighteen months, and total human knowledge every thirteen months. IBM is projecting the doubling of knowledge as the Internet is built out to be as short as every twelve hours. Knowledge drives technology drives change, and we are hurtling blindly into future change at an ever-increasing rate.

So if you think the rate of change now is way too fast, fasten your seatbelts. The rate of change is going to get a lot faster, particularly in medicine. The changes enabled by new knowledge will be aided and abetted by the fact that when it comes right down to it, we all want to escape from the natural order of things. The signs are all around us. If your hip or knee wears out, replace it. If your heart slows down, put in a pacemaker. If you can't hear, get a hearing aid. If you can't get an erection, use Viagra. Now it's about to get much better—or worse, depending on your point of view. It is starting, obviously enough, with diagnosis and treatment of disease, and there is no way you can argue that this is anything other than good. Clearly, your cancer should be identified and treated in a way that actually affects the cancer and does not harm the rest of you. Clearly, it is ridiculous that after an operation to remove a cancer, you have to wait for three months or six months to see whether the disease is returning: you should have a simple blood test to map your progress on a weekly or daily basis. Clearly, you should not wait until a disease is advanced before you treat it; you should know well ahead that you are trending towards disease and take appropriate action. Clearly, you shouldn't take a drug that doesn't work to treat your disease; you should use only drugs that work on you and don't harm you. It is all so clear, but there are many concerns.

Chief among these concerns is the probability that the rate of increase of knowledge and the associated rate of improvement in technology is a double-edged sword. On one hand, as applied to your health, the potential benefits are legion. On the other hand, as Donald Rumsfeld would put it, there are many unknown unknowns that could surprise us. Stanislaw Ulam, in a tribute to the great mathematician and physicist John von Neumann more than fifty years ago,[1] recollected a conversation "centered on the ever accelerating progress of technology and changes in the mode of human life which gives the appearance of approaching some essential singularity in the history of the race beyond which human affairs, as we know them, could not continue." Many serious thinkers today have similar concerns. Raymond Kurzweil, who is a director of engineering at Google, who received the National Medal of Technology and Innovation in 1999 (America's highest honor in technology), and whom PBS named as one of the sixteen revolutionaries who made America,[2] published a book in 2005 entitled *The Singularity Is Near: When Humans Transcend Biology*, predicting a "technological singularity" before 2050.[3] This singularity is defined as a point where progress is so rapid it outstrips humans' ability to comprehend it. Once that singularity has been reached, Kurzweil predicts machine intelligence that is much more powerful than human intelligence. What this would mean for the world, and our place in it, is not at all clear.

The global consequences of rapid technological change such as those suggested by Kurzweil are arguable, and some would dismiss them as science fiction. However, what is not arguable is that as a result of dramatically improving technologies, much more definitive information is becoming available about how we are made, what is wrong with each of us, and what will work for each of us, and that information in turn is opening the door to using new understanding of biology to cure our diseases, correct our defects, and extend our lives. It can be expected that these efforts will become increasingly intensive and that the rush towards personalized medicine in the near future will be an expression of this. There is an enormous demand for these services because we feel that we are captives of so many things we cannot fix or control. We are captives of disease, pain, and disability—particularly as we get older. We are captives of our bodies—robust or not, attractive or ugly. We are captives of life itself; as Jim Morrison, lead singer for the Doors, put it: "No one gets out of here alive."

Thus the endgame of personalized medicine will be an ability to not only fix diseases we may have but also extend our lives and "improve" ourselves. The list of improvements we may want is endless: to make ourselves more intelligent, more attractive, more athletic, younger—the wish list can be pretty extensive. Whether this power will come in 50 years or 100 years can be debated, but what cannot be ignored is that in less than 500 years, a blink of an eye in evolutionary time, we have come to the rapidly expanding understanding of life that we have today. It would be delusionary to deny the potential for extending our life spans and fixing our imperfections. As our wishes come true, fundamental drivers in our civilization will be perturbed. The fact that we are going to die in the not too distant future drives a lot of our behavior; it drives a search to understand why we're here, why we do what we do, and where we're going, particularly after we die. This search has not been particularly fruitful, so we invent constructs such as nationality and culture and religion and invest these with a significance and importance that is not entirely rational yet makes sense of our lives and provides a set of rules to live by.

The probable reality is that we are exquisitely evolved survival machines, whose objective is survival of the species, and nothing more. Every attribute we have can be fitted into that framework. And in the Darwinian scheme of things, once we have procreated and raised our young, evolution has no further use for us, and that's when we age and die. But our search for meaning in life will change significantly if we are able to eliminate pain and suffering and extend life indefinitely: we still won't understand what the hell is going on, but it won't be as pressing an issue if pain and death are not around the next corner. Eat, drink, and be merry, for tomorrow you may not die.

Personalized medicine that leads to dramatically extended life spans is an amazing, and sobering, prospect, and it is here that the darker side of the genie we have let out of the bottle begins to emerge. From the individual point of view, of course, this promise is wonderful. We may no longer be subject to the impersonal cruelty of Darwinian pressures, no longer have to die within some predetermined timeframe, and no longer have to endure the pain of terminal disease. The prospect of genetic surgery suggests the advent of designer bodies: If we are able to replace old stem cells with new ones that are younger, why not change the genetic code so that your eyes will gradually change to that piercing blue that you've always wanted? Why not code for that larger penis, or those longer legs, or neurons that work a little better? But we had better be careful, because we are changing the natural order of things and there will be repercussions.

From an environmental point of view, of course, the ability to extend life significantly, say to 150 years or more, would be an unmitigated disaster. Technology has already dramatically extended our life spans over the last 200 years, from 40 years in 1800 to 80 years in 2012. The fact that there are so many of us is at the heart of all environmental problems, and increased life spans certainly won't help. Even more of a problem will be the lack of renewal and the frustration of younger generations when parents and grandparents don't die off. And what of super-rich captains of industry or dictators who just won't go away? Another 100 years of Donald Trump or Robert Mugabe? Or prolongation of ancient credos that keep women subjugated and old wounds festering, never healed by the renewal process inherent in death? There is little doubt that revolution will be in the air.

So the future will be interesting. For the readers of this book, if you want to enhance your health, the way is clear. First, exercise, eat healthful food, and don't smoke. You should pay attention to this advice: it applies to all of us. Second, the molecular-level information you need to find out your own risks, diagnose your particular ailments, and discover the best treatments just for you is coming online. You should pay attention to this opportunity: it may save your life. Third, we are merrily changing the natural order of things to ensure survival of the individual as opposed to the species, with not a clue as to the consequences. You should pay attention to this phenomenon: it could lead to the end of the human race as we know it. You can't stop our mad dash into the future, but you really do need to know what is happening. Personalized molecularly based medicine is driving the major revolution of your time.

We are all pioneers in a brave new world.

ACKNOWLEDGMENTS

I HAVE MANY people to thank who helped me to write this book.

First and foremost is Nancy Flight, love of my life, who after hearing me talk on the benefits of personalized medicine recognized a potential book and found a way to get me to write it. Without her this book would not have happened. I thank her for that, for her incisive advice and encouragement and so much more. Next, I thank my collaborators on the Personalized Medicine Initiative: Mike Burgess, Martin Dawes, Rob Fraser, David Huntsman, Bruce McManus, and Jim Russell. It has been a remarkable privilege and education working with such consummate professionals and, even better, an enormous amount of fun as we scheme to change the medical system. I also thank my children, Jane Cullis and Jeffrey Cullis, for their pointed, intelligent, and gratefully received criticisms. Lastly, I thank my editors: Iva Cheung, who helped enormously in the initial stages of putting this manuscript together, and Catherine Plear, who was of tremendous help in transforming my fevered jottings into a manuscript that is much more readable.

With all this help, I should have produced a much better book. Any errors, omissions, or terminological inexactitudes are, of course, purely my fault. I do hope, however, that the central theme of this book—that personalized medicine is and will be the major revolution of our time—is clear. We do live in exciting times.

SOURCES

CHAPTER 1

1. Kanu Chatterjee et al., "Doxorubicin Cardiomyopathy," *Cardiology* 115, no. 2 (January 2010): 155–62.

2. Chuenjid Kongkaew, Peter R. Noyce, and Darren M. Ashcroft, "Hospital Admissions Associated with Adverse Drug Reactions: A Systematic Review of Prospective Observational Studies," *The Annals of Pharmacotherapy* 42 (2008): 1017–25.

3. Robin McKie, "Growing Lifespan Shows No Sign of Slowing, but Don't Expect Immortality," *The Observer*, March 6, 2011, http://www.theguardian.com/society/2011/mar/06/lifespan-mortality-health-diabetes.

4. Qiuping Gu, Charles F. Dillon, and Vicki L. Burt, "Prescription Drug Use Continues to Increase: U.S. Prescription Drug Data for 2007–2008," *NCHS Data Briefs*, no. 42 (2010), http://www.cdc.gov/nchs/data/databriefs/db42.htm.

5. Jason Lazarou, Bruce H. Pomeranz, and Paul N. Corey, "Incidence of Adverse Drug Reactions in Hospitalized Patients," *Journal of the American Medical Association* 279, no. 15 (April 15, 1998): 1200.

6. Lorna Hazell and Saad A.W. Shakir, "Under-Reporting of Adverse Drug Reactions: A Systematic Review," *Drug Safety: An International Journal of Medical Toxicology and Drug Experience* 29, no. 5 (January 2006): 385–96.

7. Brian B. Spear, Margo Heath-Chiozzi, and Jeffrey Huff, "Clinical Application of Pharmacogenetics," *Trends in Molecular Medicine* 7, no. 5 (May 5, 2001): 201–4.

8. Cleveland Clinic, "Health and Prevention: Statin Medications and Heart Disease," *Cleveland Clinic,* http://my.clevelandclinic.org/ heart/prevention/risk-factors/cholesterol/statin-medications-heart -disease.aspx.

9. Huabing Zhang et al., "Discontinuation of Statins in Routine Care Settings: A Cohort Study," *Annals of Internal Medicine* 158, no. 7 (April 2, 2013): 526–34.

10. Lara M. Mangravite et al., "A Statin-Dependent QTL for GATM Expression Is Associated with Statin-Induced Myopathy," *Nature* 502, no. 7471 (October 17, 2013): 377–80.

11. Siddhartha Mukherjee, *The Emperor of All Maladies: A Biography of Cancer* (New York, NY: Scribner, 2011), pp. 35–37.

12. Y. Li, R.B. Womer, and J.H. Silber, "Predicting Cisplatin Ototoxicity in Children: The Influence of Age and the Cumulative Dose," *European Journal of Cancer* 40, no. 16 (November 2004): 2445–51.

13. Matthew Herper, "The Truly Staggering Cost of Inventing New Drugs," *Forbes*, February 10, 2012, http://www.forbes.com/sites/matthewherper/2012/02/10/the-truly-staggering-cost-of-inventing-new-drugs/.

CHAPTER 2

1. Stephen Bent, "Herbal Medicine in the United States: Review of Efficacy, Safety, and Regulation: Grand Rounds at University of California, San Francisco Medical Center," *Journal of General Internal Medicine* 23, no. 6 (June 2008): 854–59.

2. "Charles Darwin's Health," *Wikipedia,* accessed September 12, 2014, http://en.wikipedia.org/wiki/Charles_Darwin's_health.

3. J.B. Durand, A.B. Abchee, and R. Roberts, "Molecular and Clinical Aspects of Inherited Cardiomyopathies," *Annals of Medicine* 27, no. 3 (June 1995): 311–17, http://www.ncbi.nlm.nih.gov/pubmed/7546620; Shiro Kamakura, "Epidemiology of Brugada Syndrome in Japan and Rest of the World," *Journal of Arrhythmia* 29, no. 2 (April 1, 2013): 52–55; B.J. Maron et al., "Prevalence of Hypertrophic Cardiomyopathy in a General Population of Young Adults: Echocardiographic Analysis of 4111 Subjects in the CARDIA Study," *Circulation* 92, no. 4 (August 15, 1995): 785–89; Carlo Napolitano, Silvia G. Priori, and Raffaella Bloise, "Catecholaminergic Polymorphic Ventricular Tachycardia," in *GeneReviews,* ed. Roberta A. Pagon (Seattle, WA: University of Washington, 2014); Peter J. Schwartz et al., "Prevalence of the Congenital Long-QT Syndrome," *Circulation* 120, no. 18 (November 3, 2009): 1761–67.

4. Robert F. Service, "A $1000 Genome by 2013?," *Science News,* July 2011, http://news.sciencemag.org/math/2011/07/1000-genome-2013.

CHAPTER 3

1. Alok Jha, "Breakthrough Study Overturns Theory of 'Junk DNA' in Genome," *The Guardian*, September 5, 2012, http://www.theguardian.com/science/2012/sep/05/genes-genome-junk-dna-encode.

2. Jonah Riddell et al., "Reprogramming Committed Murine Blood Cells to Induced Hematopoietic Stem Cells with Defined Factors," *Cell* 157, no. 3 (April 24, 2014): 549–64.

3. J.B. Gurdon and V. Uehlinger, "'Fertile' Intestine Nuclei," *Nature* 210, no. 5042 (June 18, 1966): 1240–41, http://www.ncbi.nlm.nih.gov/pubmed/5967799.

4. K.H. Campbell et al., "Sheep Cloned by Nuclear Transfer from a Cultured Cell Line," *Nature* 380, no. 6569 (March 7, 1996): 64–66.

5. Francesco S. Loffredo et al., "Growth Differentiation Factor 11 Is a Circulating Factor That Reverses Age-Related Cardiac Hypertrophy," *Cell* 153, no. 4 (May 9, 2013): 828–39.

6. Michael Specter, "Germs Are Us," *The New Yorker*, October 22, 2012, http://www.newyorker.com/magazine/2012/10/22/germs-are-us.

7. Ilseung Cho and Martin J. Blaser, "The Human Microbiome: At the Interface of Health and Disease," *Nature Reviews: Genetics* 13, no. 4 (April 2012): 260–70.

8. N. Lender et al., "Review Article: Associations between Helicobacter Pylori and Obesity—an Ecological Study," *Alimentary Pharmacology and Therapeutics* 40, no. 1 (July 2014): 24–31.

9. Ilseung Cho et al., "Antibiotics in Early Life Alter the Murine Colonic Microbiome and Adiposity," *Nature* 488, no. 7413 (August 30, 2012): 621–26.

10. E.J. Videlock and F. Cremonini, "Meta-Analysis: Probiotics in Antibiotic-Associated Diarrhoea," *Alimentary Pharmacology and Therapeutics* 35, no. 12 (June 2012): 1355–69.

11. "*Clostridium Difficile* Infection," *Centers for Disease Control and Prevention*, accessed July 26, 2014, http://www.cdc.gov/hai/organisms/cdiff/cdiff_infect.html.

12. J.L. Anderson, R.J. Edney, and K. Whelan, "Systematic Review: Faecal Microbiota Transplantation in the Management of Inflammatory Bowel Disease," *Alimentary Pharmacology and Therapeutics* 36, no. 6 (September 2012): 503–16.

13. David E. Elliott and Joel V. Weinstock, "Helminthic Therapy: Using Worms to Treat Immune-Mediated Disease," *Advances in Experimental Medicine and Biology* 666 (January 2009): 157–66, http://www.ncbi.nlm.nih.gov/pubmed/20054982.

CHAPTER 4

1. Bala Murali Venkatesan and Rashid Bashir, "Nanopore Sensors for Nucleic Acid Analysis," *Nature Nanotechnology* 6, no. 10 (October 2011): 615–24.

2. Scott D. McCulloch and Thomas A. Kunkel, "The Fidelity of DNA Synthesis by Eukaryotic Replicative and Translesion Synthesis Polymerases," *Cell Research* 18, no. 1 (January 2008): 148–61.

3. J.N. Adkins et al., "Toward a Human Blood Serum Proteome: Analysis by Multidimensional Separation Coupled with Mass Spectrometry," *Molecular and Cellular Proteomics* 1, no. 12 (November 15, 2002): 947–55.

4. Andrew J. Percy et al., "Standardized Protocols for Quality Control of MRM-Based Plasma Proteomic Workflows," *Journal of Proteome Research* 12, no. 1 (January 4, 2013): 222–33.

5. "Why Are Larger Sized Hard Drives Consistently Getting Cheaper?," *Record Nations*, accessed July 29, 2014, http://www.recordnations.com/articles/bigger-hard-drives/.

6. Mike Orcutt, "Bases to Bytes," *MIT Technology Review*, 2012, http://www.technologyreview.com/graphiti/427720/bases-to-bytes/.

7. *PatientsLikeMe,* http://www.patientslikeme.com/.

8. *CureTogether,* http://www.curetogether.com.

9. *PXE International,* http://www.pxe.org/.

10. Sarah C.P. Williams, "Mining Consumers' Web Searches Can Reveal Unreported Side Effects of Drugs, Researchers Say," *Stanford Bio-X*, 2013, https://biox.stanford.edu/highlight/mining-consumers'-web-searches-can-reveal-unreported-side-effects-drugs -rescarchers-say.

11. W. Yang et al., "Economic Costs of Diabetes in the U.S. in 2012," *Diabetes Care* 36, no. 4 (April 2013): 1033–46.

12. "Heart Disease Facts," *Centers for Disease Control and Prevention*, 2014, http://www.cdc.gov/heartdisease/facts.htm.

CHAPTER 5

1. Jon Cohen, "Examining His Own Body, Stanford Geneticist Stops Diabetes in Its Tracks," *Science News*, March 2012, http://news.sciencemag.org/biology/2012/03/examining-his-own-body-stanford-geneticist-stops-diabetes-its-tracks.

2. Hangwi Tang and Jennifer Hwee Kwoon Ng, "Googling for a Diagnosis—Use of Google as a Diagnostic Aid: Internet Based Study," *BMJ (Clinical Research Ed.)* 333, no. 7579 (December 2, 2006): 1143–45.

3. Eta S. Berner and Mark L. Graber, "Overconfidence as a Cause of Diagnostic Error in Medicine," *The American Journal of Medicine* 121, no. 5 Suppl (May 2008): S2–23.

4. Maria Fuller, Peter J. Meikle, and John J. Hopwood, "Epidemiology of Lysosomal Storage Diseases: An Overview," in *Fabry Disease: Perspectives from 5 Years of FOS*, ed. Atul Mehta, Michael Beck, and Gere Sunder-Plassmann (Oxford: Oxford PharmaGenesis, 2006), http://www.ncbi .nlm.nih.gov/books/NBK11603/.

5. "Table of Pharmacogenomic Biomarkers in Drug Labeling," *Food and Drug Administration*, http://www.fda.gov/drugs/scienceresearch/ researchareas/pharmacogenetics/ucm083378.htm.

6. "Gene Responsible for Acetaminophen-Induced Liver Injury Identified," *ScienceDaily*, May 11, 2009, http://www.sciencedaily.com/ releases/2009/05/090504171943.htm.

7. Svati H. Shah and Deepak Voora, "Warfarin Dosing and VKORC1/ CYP2C9," *Medscape*, accessed July 28, 2014, http://emedicine.medscape .com/article/1733331-overview.

8. Tom Lynch and Amy Price, "The Effect of Cytochrome P450 Metabolism on Drug Response, Interactions, and Adverse Effects," *American Family Physician* 76, no. 3 (2007): 391–96, http://www.aafp .org/afp/2007/0801/p391.html.

9. Eric Schoch, "Precision Prescribing," *The Art and Science of Medicine*, 2003, http://www.indiana.edu/~rcapub/v26n1/precision.shtml.

10. Martin Dawes, "The Implementation and Evaluation of Genetic Tests to Guide Drug Prescriptions in Primary Care in B.C.," in *What Is Personalized Medicine, and How Does It Affect You?* (Vancouver, BC, 2014). Public talk.

11. Colin J.D. Ross et al., "Genotypic Approaches to Therapy in Children: A National Active Surveillance Network (GATC) to Study the Pharmacogenomics of Severe Adverse Drug Reactions in Children," *Annals of the New York Academy of Sciences* 1110 (September 2007): 177–92.

12. Colin J.D. Ross et al., "Genetic Variants in TPMT and COMT Are Associated with Hearing Loss in Children Receiving Cisplatin Chemotherapy," *Nature Genetics* 45, no. 5 (April 26, 2013): 578.

13. Henk Visscher et al., "Pharmacogenomic Prediction of Anthracycline-Induced Cardiotoxicity in Children," *Journal of Clinical Oncology* 30, no. 13 (May 1, 2012): 1422–28.

14. J. Kirchheiner et al., "Pharmacokinetics of Codeine and Its Metabolite Morphine in Ultra-Rapid Metabolizers due to CYP2D6 Duplication," *The Pharmacogenomics Journal* 7, no. 4 (August 2007): 257–65.

15. G. Köhler and C. Milstein, "Continuous Cultures of Fused Cells Secreting Antibody of Predefined Specificity," *Nature* 256, no. 5517 (August 7, 1975): 495–97.

16. Mark D. Pegram, Gottfried Konecny, and Dennis J. Slamon, "The Molecular and Cellular Biology of HER2/neu Gene Amplification/ Overexpression and the Clinical Development of Herceptin (Trastuzumab) Therapy for Breast Cancer," in *Advances in Breast Cancer Management*, ed. William J. Gradishar and William C. Wood, vol. 103, Cancer Treatment and Research (Boston, MA: Springer, 2000), 57–75.

17. Richard Heimler, "Richard Heimler," *Lung Cancer Alliance*, accessed July 28, 2014, http://www.lungcanceralliance.org/get-help-and-support/ coping-with-lung-cancer/stories-of-hope/richard-heimler.html.

18. "FDA Approval for Crizotinib," *National Cancer Institute*, 2013, http://www.cancer.gov/cancertopics/druginfo/fda-crizotinib.

19. Kent Pinkerton, "Cystic Fibrosis Life Expectancy Statistics," *Disabled World*, 2009, http://www.disabled-world.com/health/respiratory/ cystic-fibrosis/life-expectancy.php.

20. Bonnie W. Ramsey et al., "A CFTR Potentiator in Patients with Cystic Fibrosis and the G551D Mutation," *The New England Journal of Medicine* 365, no. 18 (November 3, 2011): 1663–72.

21. Alex Parker, "A Reflection...," *Kalydeco for Cystic Fibrosis Diary*, accessed July 28, 2014, http://kalydecoforaustralians.blogspot.ca/2012/11/ a-reflection.html.

22. Sining Chen and Giovanni Parmigiani, "Meta-Analysis of BRCA1 and BRCA2 Penetrance," *Journal of Clinical Oncology* 25, no. 11 (April 10, 2007): 1329–33.

23. Angelina Jolie, "My Medical Choice," *The New York Times*, May 14, 2013, http://www.nytimes.com/2013/05/14/opinion/my-medical -choice.html?_r=2&.

24. "SAP and BC Centre for Excellence in HIV/AIDS Pioneer New Technology, Redefine Treatment," *SAP News*, February 25, 2014, http://www.news-sap .com/sap-and-bc-centre-for-excellence-in-hiv-aids-pioneer-new-technology -redefine-treatment/.

25. Allen D. Roses, "On the Discovery of the Genetic Association of Apolipoprotein E Genotypes and Common Late-Onset Alzheimer Disease," *Journal of Alzheimer's Disease* 9, no. 3 Suppl (January 2006): 361–66, http://www.ncbi.nlm.nih.gov/pubmed/16914873.

26. Lindsay S. Nagamatsu et al., "Resistance Training Promotes Cognitive and Functional Brain Plasticity in Seniors with Probable Mild Cognitive Impairment," *Archives of Internal Medicine* 172, no. 8 (April 23, 2012): 666–68.

27. Elaine Westwick, "Huntington's Disease—Genetic Testing, Children and Hope," *The Stuff of Life*, July 2011, http://elainewestwick.blogspot .ca/2011/07/huntingtons -disease-genetic-testing.html.

28. Marilynn Marchione, "Texas Hospital Plans 'Moonshot' against Cancer," *AP: The Big Story*, 2012, http://bigstory.ap.org/article/ texas-hospital-plans-moonshot-against-cancer.

29. Emily Dugan, "Thousands of NHS Patients to Have DNA Sequenced to Help Cancer Research," *The Independent*, July 20, 2014, http://www.independent.co.uk/life-style/health-and-families/ health-news/thousands-of-nhs-patients-to-have-dna-sequenced-to -help-cancer-research-9617513.html.

30. Steven J.M. Jones et al., "Evolution of an Adenocarcinoma in Response to Selection by Targeted Kinase Inhibitors," *Genome Biology* 11, no. 8 (January 2010): R82.

31. Gina Kolata, "In Leukemia Treatment, Glimpses of the Future," *The New York Times*, July 8, 2012, http://www.nytimes.com/2012/07/08/health/ in-gene-sequencing-treatment-for-leukemia-glimpses-of-the-future. html?pagewanted=all.

32. Xiao-jun Li et al., "A Blood-Based Proteomic Classifier for the Molecular Characterization of Pulmonary Nodules," *Science Translational Medicine* 5, no. 207 (October 16, 2013): 207ra142, doi:10.1126/scitranslmed.3007013.

33. Food and Drug Administration, "FDA Approves New Orphan Drug Kynamro to Treat Inherited Cholesterol Disorder," January 29, 2013, http://www.fda.gov/newsevents/newsroom/pressannouncements/ ucm337195.htm.

34. Andrew Pollack, "Experimental Drug Used for Ebola-Related Virus Shows Promise," *The New York Times*, August 20, 2014, http://www. nytimes.com/2014/08/21/business/drug-used-for-ebola-related-virus- shows-promise.html?_r=0.

35. Giorgio Trinchieri, "Inflammation," in *Cancer: Principles and Practice of Oncology*, ed. Vincent T. DeVita Jr., Theodore S. Lawrence, and Steven A. Rosenberg, 9th ed. (Philadelphia: Lippincott Williams and Wilkins, 2011), http://www.lwoncology.com/Textbook/Toc.aspx?id=11000#.

36. Penn Medicine, "Penn Medicine Team Reports Findings from Research Study of First 59 Adult and Pediatric Leukemia Patients Who Received Investigational, Personalized Cellular Therapy CTL019," December 7, 2013, http://www.uphs.upenn.edu/news/news_releases/ 2013/12/ctl019/.

37. Laura Smith-Spark, "UK Takes Step toward 'Three-Parent Babies,'" *CNN.com*, June 28, 2013, http://www.cnn.com/2013/06/28/health/ uk-health-dna-ivf/.

38. Dan Roden, "Engineering a Healthcare System to Deliver Personalized Medicine." Personalized Medicine and Individualized Drug Delivery, joint conference of the Canadian Society for Pharmaceutical Sciences and Canadian Chapter of Controlled Release Society, June 11–14, 2013, Vancouver.

39. *Association for Molecular Pathology et al. v. Myriad Genetics, Inc., et al.* 569 U.S. 12-398 (2013). http://www.supremecourt.gov/opinions/12pdf/ 12-398_1b7d.pdf.

40. Dan Munro, "FDA Slaps Personal Genomics Startup 23andMe with Stiff Warning," *Forbes*, November 25, 2013, http://www.forbes.com/ sites/danmunro/2013/11/25/fda-slaps-personal-genomics-startup -23andme-with-stiff-warning/.

41. Larry Husten, "Can Personalized Medicine and an Adaptive Trial Design Salvage This Hard-Luck Drug?," *Forbes*, December 4, 2013, http://www.forbes.com/sites/larryhusten/2013/12/04/can-personalized -medicine-and-an-adaptive-trial-design-salvage-this-hard-luck-drug/.

42. Elizabeth O Lillie et al., "The N-of-1 Clinical Trial: The Ultimate Strategy for Individualizing Medicine?," *Personalized Medicine* 8, no. 2 (March 2011): 161–73.

43. Jaime L Natoli et al., "Prenatal Diagnosis of Down Syndrome: A Systematic Review of Termination Rates (1995–2011)," *Prenatal Diagnosis* 32, no. 2 (February 2012): 142–53.

44. "Gendercide: The Worldwide War on Baby Girls," *The Economist*, March 4, 2010, http://www.economist.com/node/15636231.

CHAPTER 6

1. Salima Hacein-Bey-Abina et al., "Insertional Oncogenesis in 4 Patients after Retrovirus-Mediated Gene Therapy of SCID-X1," *The Journal of Clinical Investigation* 118, no. 9 (September 2, 2008): 3132–42.

2. Sheryl Gay Stolberg, "The Biotech Death of Jesse Gelsinger," *The New York Times*, November 28, 1999, http://www.nytimes.com/1999/11/28/ magazine/the-biotech-death-of-jesse-gelsinger.html.

3. Bill Clinton, "Remarks on the Completion of the First Survey of the Entire Human Genome Project" (The White House Office of the Press Secretary, 2000), http://clinton5.nara.gov/WH/New/html/ genome-20000626.html.

4. European Medicines Agency, "European Medicines Agency Recommends First Gene Therapy for Approval," July 20, 2012, http://www.ema.europa.eu/ema/index.Jsp?curl=pages/news_and_events/news/2012/07/news_detail_001574.Jsp&mid=wc0b01ac058004d5c1.

5. Food and Drug Administration, "FDA Approves New Orphan Drug Kynamro to Treat Inherited Cholesterol Disorder," January 29, 2013, http://www.fda.gov/newsevents/newsroom/pressannouncements/ucm337195.htm.

6. Alnylam Pharmaceuticals, "Alnylam Reports Positive Phase II Data for Patisiran (ALN-TTR02), an RNAi Therapeutic Targeting Transthyretin (TTR) for the Treatment of TTR-Mediated Amyloidosis (ATTR), and Initiates Phase III Trial," 2013, http://investors.alnylam.com/releasedetail.cfm?ReleaseID=805999.

7. Aaron Krol, "Gene Therapy's Next Generation," *Bio-IT World*, January 29, 2014, http://www.bio-itworld.com/2014/1/29/gene-therapys-next-generation.html.

8. Mark J. Graham et al., "Antisense Inhibition of Proprotein Convertase Subtilisin/kexin Type 9 Reduces Serum LDL in Hyperlipidemic Mice," *Journal of Lipid Research* 48, no. 4 (April 1, 2007): 763–67.

9. María M Corrada et al., "Dementia Incidence Continues to Increase with Age in the Oldest Old: The 90+ Study," *Annals of Neurology* 67, no. 1 (January 2010): 114–21.

10. Michael D. Hurd et al., "Monetary Costs of Dementia in the United States," *New England Journal of Medicine* 368 (2013): 1326–34.

11. National Institute of Mental Health, "The Numbers Count: Mental Disorders in America," *National Institute of Mental Health*, accessed July 28, 2014, http://www.nimh.nih.gov/health/publications/the-numbers-count-mental-disorders-in-america/index.shtml.

12. Rafael Yuste and George M. Church, "The New Century of the Brain," *Scientific American* 310, no. 3 (February 18, 2014): 38–45.

13. Mark W. Stanton, *The High Concentration of U.S. Health Care Expenditures* (Washington, DC: U.S. Department of Health and Human Services, Public Health Services, Agency for Healthcare Research and Quality, 2006).

14. Canadian Institute for Health Information, *Seniors and the Health Care System: What Is the Impact of Multiple Chronic Conditions?*, 2011.

15. "Immortal Worms Defy Aging," *ScienceDaily*, February 27, 2012, http://www.sciencedaily.com/releases/2012/02/120227152612.htm.

16. Kathleen Y. Wolin and Hallie Tuchman, "Physical Activity and Gastrointestinal Cancer Prevention," in *Physical Activity and Cancer*, ed. Kerry S. Courneya and Christine Friedenreich, vol. 26 (Berlin: Springer Science and Business Media, 2010), 400; I.M. Lee and Y. Oguma, "Physical Activity," in *Cancer Epidemiology and Prevention*, ed. David Schottenfeld and Joseph F. Fraumeni, 3rd ed. (New York, NY: Oxford University Press, 2006), 1416; Kathy Matheson, "Exercising May Reduce Lung Cancer Risk," *The Washington Post*, December 12, 2006, http://www.washingtonpost.com/wp-dyn/content/article/2006/12/12/AR2006121200862.html; "Caffeine and Exercise May Be Protective against Skin Cancer Caused by Sun Exposure, Study Suggests," *ScienceDaily*, April 3, 2012, http://www.sciencedaily.com/releases/2012/04/120403142328.htm.

17. Paul D. Thompson et al., "Exercise and Physical Activity in the Prevention and Treatment of Atherosclerotic Cardiovascular Disease: A Statement from the Council on Clinical Cardiology (Subcommittee on Exercise, Rehabilitation, and Prevention) and the Council on Nutrition, Physical," *Circulation* 107, no. 24 (June 24, 2003): 3109–16.

18. Rob Stein, "Exercise Could Slow Aging of Body, Study Suggests," *The Washington Post*, January 29, 2008, http://www.washingtonpost.com/wp-dyn/content/article/2008/01/28/AR2008012801873.html.

19. Steve Horvath, "DNA Methylation Age of Human Tissues and Cell Types," *Genome Biology* 14, no. 10 (January 2013): R115.

20. Elaine Schmidt, "UCLA Scientist Uncovers Biological Clock Able to Measure Age of Most Human Tissues," *UCLA Newsroom*, October 21, 2013, http://newsroom.ucla.edu/releases/ucla-scientist-uncovers-biological-248950.

21. Manisha Sinha et al., "Restoring Systemic GDF11 Levels Reverses Age-Related Dysfunction in Mouse Skeletal Muscle," *Science* 344, no. 6184 (May 9, 2014): 649–52.

22. Robert Langreth, "Venter Starts DNA-Scanning Company to Boost Longevity," *Bloomberg.com*, March 4, 2014, http://www.bloomberg.com/news/2014-03-04/venter-starts-dna-scanning-company-to-boost-longevity.html; Saul A. Villeda et al., "Young Blood Reverses Age-Related Impairments in Cognitive Function and Synaptic Plasticity in Mice," *Nature Medicine* 20, no. 6 (June 2014): 659–63; Lida Katsimpardi et al., "Vascular and Neurogenic Rejuvenation of the Aging Mouse Brain by Young Systemic Factors," *Science* 344, no. 6184 (May 9, 2014): 630–34.

23. Jane Wakefield, "Google Spin-off Calico to Search for Answers to Ageing," *BBC News*, September 19, 2013, http://www.bbc.com/news/technology-24158924.

24. William J. Broad, "Billionaires with Big Ideas Are Privatizing American Science," *The New York Times*, March 16, 2014, http://www.nytimes.com/2014/03/16/science/billionaires-with-big-ideas-are-privatizing-american-science.html?_r=0.

25. L. Bellows, R. Moore, and A. Gross, "Dietary Supplements: Vitamins and Minerals" (University of Colorado Extension, 2013), http://www.ext.colostate.edu/pubs/foodnut/09338.html.

26. Leroy Hood and Nathan D. Price, "Promoting Wellness and Demystifying Disease: The 100K Project," *Genetic Engineering and Biotechnology News*, May 22, 2014.

27. "Biomarkers in Blood Show Potential as Early Detection Method of Pancreatic Cancer," *ScienceDaily*, January 21, 2014, http://www.sciencedaily.com/releases/2014/01/140121164754.htm.

28. "Detecting Dementia through microRNA in Patient Blood Samples," *Biome*, October 2, 2013, http://www.biomedcentral.com/biome/detecting-dementia-through-microrna-in-patient-blood-samples/.

29. John Ericson, "A Breath Test For Lung Cancer: Researchers Develop Biomarker for Pulmonary Tumor Growth," *Medical Daily*, October 18, 2013, http://www.medicaldaily.com/breath-test-lung-cancer-researchers-develop-biomarker-pulmonary-tumor-growth-261201.

30. "Intel Science Winner Develops Cancer Tech," *Wall Street Journal Live*, December 30, 2012, http://live.wsj.com/video/intel-science-winner-develops-cancer-tech/E342B43B-F184-492D-A441-38B28C18D3C1.HTML#!E342B43B-F184-492D-A441-38B28C18D3C1.

31. "Genomic Test Accurately Sorts Viral versus Bacterial Infections," *Duke University Pratt School of Engineering*, September 18, 2013, http://www.pratt.duke.edu/news/genomic-test-accurately-sorts-viral-versus-bacterial-infections.

32. Sarah C.P. Williams, "One Drug to Shrink All Tumors," *Science News*, March 26, 2012, http://news.sciencemag.org/health/2012/03/one-drug-shrink-all-tumors.

33. "Surprising Variation among Genomes of Individual Neurons from Same Brain," *ScienceDaily*, November 1, 2013, http://www.sciencedaily.com/releases/2013/11/131101172313.htm.

34. David J. Hill, "Patient Receives 3D Printed Implant to Replace 75 Percent of Skull," *Singularity Hub*, March 28, 2013, http://singularityhub.com/2013/03/28/patient-receives-3d-printed-implant-to-replace-75-percent-of-skull/.

35. Dan Howarth, "3D-Printed Eye Cells Could 'Cure Blindness,'" *Dezeen*, December 18, 2013, http://www.dezeen.com/2013/12/18/3d-printed-eye-cells-could-cure-blindness/.

36. "Use of Stem Cells in Personalized Medicine," *ScienceDaily*, November 26, 2012, http://www.sciencedaily.com/releases/2012/11/121126151021.htm.

37. Institute of Medicine (U.S.) Forum on Drug Discovery, Development, and Translation, "Introduction," in *Addressing the Barriers to Pediatric Drug Development: Workshop Summary* (Washington, DC: National Academics Press, 2008), http://www.ncbi.nlm.nih.gov/books/NBK3989/.

38. John Sloan, *A Bitter Pill: How The Medical System Is Failing The Elderly* (Vancouver, BC: Greystone Books, 2009), p. 29.

39. Paul Cerrato, "Why Personal Health Records Have Flopped," *InformationWeek*, January 12, 2012, http://www.informationweek.com/healthcare/patient-tools/why-personal-health-records-have-flopped/d/d-id/1102247?.

40. "An Update on Google Health and Google PowerMeter," *Official Google Blog*, June 24, 2011, http://googleblog.blogspot.ca/2011/06/update-on-google-health-and-google.html.

CHAPTER 7

1. Stanislaw Ulam, "Tribute to John von Neumann," *Bulletin of the American Mathematical Society* 64, no. 3 (1958): 5.

2. "Ray Kurzweil Biography," *Kurzweil Accelerating Intelligence*, accessed September 12, 2014, http://www.kurzweilai.net/ray-kurzweil-biography.

3. Ray Kurzweil, *The Singularity Is Near: When Humans Transcend Biology* (New York: Viking, 2005).

INDEX